SURVIVING YOUR YOUR DISSERTATION
2nd Edition

Kjell Erik Rudestam
Rae R. Newton

SURVIVING YOUR DISSERTATION

**A Comprehensive Guide
to Content
and Process**

2nd Edition

Sage Publications, Inc.
International Educational and Professional Publisher
Thousand Oaks ▪ London ▪ New Delhi

For information:

Sage Publications, Inc.
2455 Teller Road
Thousand Oaks, California 91320
E-mail: order@sagepub.com

Sage Publications Ltd.
6 Bonhill Street
London EC2A 4PU
United Kingdom

Sage Publications India Pvt. Ltd.
M-32 Market
Greater Kailash I
New Delhi 110 048 India

Printed in the United States of America

Library of Congress Cataloging-in-Publication Data

Rudestam, Kjell Erik.
  Surviving your dissertation: A comprehensive guide to content and process / Kjell Erik Rudestam and Rae R. Newton—2nd ed.
        p. cm.
  Includes bibliographical references.
  ISBN 0-7619-1961-9 (c) — ISBN 0-7619-1962-7 (p)
  1. Dissertations, Academic—United States. 2. Report writing.
  3. Research—United States. I. Newton, Rae R. II. Title.
  LB2369 .R83 2000
  808'.02—dc21   00-009854

        03   04   05   06   07   7   6   5   4

Acquiring Editor:	C. Deborah Laughton
Editorial Assistant:	Eileen Carr
Production Editor:	Diane S. Foster
Editorial Assistant:	Candice Crosetti
Typesetter/Designer:	Marion Warren
Cover Designer:	Michelle Lee

Contents

PART II Working With Content: The Dissertation Chapters

PART III   Working With Process: What You Need to Know to Make the Dissertation Easier

Preface

The completion of a master's thesis or doctoral dissertation is usually the most difficult academic requirement a student will face during his or her term of graduate education. The process requires discipline, independent initiative, creative thinking, working with others, and the surmounting of self-doubt. It is no wonder that many A.B.D.s never become Ph.D.s. Completion of the dissertation is simply too overwhelming for many.

Surviving Your Dissertation: A Comprehensive Guide to Content and Process represents our combined efforts to facilitate the dissertation process among our students. Our experience comes not only from working with our own students and discovering our own mistakes, but also from listening to others. The positive, self-affirming experiences and the "horror stories" have both served to develop our thinking. Unfortunately, the social organization of the dissertation experience is not one that is well understood by most students or their faculty mentors. The expectations are often vague, the norms unclear, and the social networks among student, chair, and committee members incomplete. Although it is expected that graduate students in the social sciences will have mastered the intricacies of research design and methodology, it is not as likely that they will be systematically exposed to issues of appropriate style and content of the dissertation. We have witnessed the many frustrations that students may experience along the dissertation trail: how to select a suitable topic, how to conduct an appropriate review of the literature, how to build an argument, how to manage data overload, how to work with faculty committees, how to organize time and space, and how to deal with emotional blocks to completing the project.

In response to these challenges, we have developed some useful strategies for managing the process toward a favorable outcome. Success comes from an understanding both of what a dissertation contains and of one's own strengths and weaknesses. We characterize the first as an understanding of *content* and the second as an understanding of *process*. Mastery of the dissertation depends on the ability to negotiate both process and content successfully. This book is organized around these themes. In Part I we discuss how to select a topic and possible methods by which a topic might be approached. In Part II we focus on content. We describe the dissertation chapters, what they might reasonably be expected to include and not include, and how to present that material appropriately. We provide detailed directions for describing the research plan and presenting data and results. In Part III we address issues of process, including common barriers to progress. Separate chapters discuss task and emotional blocks, use of a personal computer and computer software to complete the dissertation, the presentation of numbers, and ethical issues.

Surviving Your Dissertation is not a substitute for courses and texts in research methods or statistics, but a comprehensive "how to" compendium for completing a master's thesis or doctoral dissertation. It should be appropriate for any graduate student about to face this major academic challenge, and it may prove useful for many faculty about to direct such endeavors. Throughout this book we have tried to be broad in scope and to include examples from virtually all the social sciences. Dozens of dissertations are cited as examples of the wide diversity in topics and methods of inquiry. We have included guidelines for both quantitative and qualitative dissertations, and we have solicited and presented suggestions from students who have recently completed their own dissertations.

Throughout we have tried to provide sufficient detail so that the book can serve as a relatively comprehensive reference work for matters of form and content. We appreciate the instructive comments of a number of individuals who reviewed drafts of the manuscript: Lawrence Mohr, University of Michigan; Bruce Thyer, University of Georgia; Bob Greene, Case Western University; Alan Acock, Oregon State

University; and Craig Frisby, University of Florida. We are also indebted to Hilde Keldemans, who produced the figures and graphs, and to Leslie Kunkel, who made valuable suggestions regarding computer-based literature searches.

Special thanks go to C. Deborah Laughton, our continually upbeat editor at Sage, who was an ally from the outset of the project. Our colleagues at The Fielding Institute and California State University, Fullerton have been ongoing sources of wisdom and creativity. In particular, we thank Jody Veroff for her humane approach to scholarly writing, exemplified in her contribution of a chapter to the book. Finally, we cannot envision having completed this project without the help of two groups of individuals: our families, who showed tolerance beyond the bounds of reasonable expectations, and our students, whose own dissertation journeys provided the source material and inspiration for the book. It is they who consistently have demonstrated that the doctoral dissertation can be a transformative professional and personal experience.

Preface to the
Second Edition

Since the publication of *Surviving Your Dissertation* almost 10 years ago, hundreds of students have written us describing its usefulness. Many have offered suggestions, and some critiques, as to how we might make *Surviving Your Dissertation* more user-friendly and comprehensive. We have also witnessed a notable proliferation of methods available to assist students in successfully completing the dissertation. These changes include the significantly increased role of the computer and the dynamic arrival of the Internet as a source of reference material, as a conduit for secondary data, and even as a substitute for traditional data collection methods.

During the past decade the legitimacy of qualitatively based dissertations and the availability of software for accomplishing qualitative analysis have become firmly established. This edition includes a major expansion of the section on the qualitative approach to dissertations in all facets, from method to results to the final write-up. At the same time we have not neglected to update the information on dominant quantitative approach.

A number of chapters have been completely rewritten. **Chapter 6,** which describes the presentation of results, has been greatly expanded, based primarily on requests from doctoral students for more detail, our own increased sensitivity to modifications emerging from recent challenges to null hypothesis significance testing, and our update of the presentation of results of qualitative dissertations. **Chapter 10,** which describes the role of the computer in completing the dissertation, also has been completely rewritten. We now include **tables showing Web addresses (URLs) for quantitative and qualitative software** and numerous other sources of information for the dissertation student. We have completely abandoned the notion that anyone could complete the dissertation without a computer. We also have included additional writing tips and made the entire text congruent with the latest editions of APA publications guidelines and the latest APA ethics guidelines, which are included in **Chapter 12.** Throughout the entire text, we have revised our references to reflect the latest editions of the major reference sources we cite. We hope that you, the student, will experience this book as a valuable guide and companion on your dissertation journey.

In order to shape our own experience in writing this edition, we were fortunate to draw upon and benefit from the wisdom and insight of a great number of individuals, including our students and colleagues at The Fielding Institute and California State University at Fullerton. We especially want to acknowledge the facilitative skill of the staff at Sage Publications, ranging from the enthusiastic support of C. Deborah Laughton, our acquisitions editor, to Diane S. Foster, production editor; A.J. Sobczak, copy editor; Marion Warren, typesetter; Jamie Robinson, proofreader; and Michelle Lee, cover designer.

PART I

Getting Started

CHAPTER 1

The Research Process

There is the story of a Zen Buddhist who took a group of monks into the forest, whereupon the group soon lost their way. Presently one of the monks asked their leader where they were going. The wise man answered, "To the deepest, darkest part of the forest, so that we can all find our way out together." Doctoral research for the graduate student in the social sciences is often experienced in just that manner, trekking into a forest of impenetrable density and false turns. Over the years our students have employed various metaphors to describe the dissertation process, metaphors that support the feeling of being lost in the wilderness. One student compared the process to the Sisyphean struggle of reaching the top of a hill, only to discover the presence of an even higher mountain behind it. Another student experienced the task as learning a Martian language, known to the natives who composed her committee but entirely foreign to her. A third student had perhaps the best description when she suggested that it was like waiting patiently in a seemingly interminable line to gain admission to a desirable event, then finally reaching the front only to be told to return to the rear of the line!

One reason that students become more exasperated than necessary on the dissertation journey is that they fail to understand the procedures and practices that form the foundation for contemporary social science research. Many students who are attracted to their field of interest out of an applied concern are apprehensive about making the leap from application to theory that is an indispensable part of the research enterprise. What may not be so evident is that many of the skills that go into being a consummate practitioner are the same skills that are demanded of a capable researcher. It is well known that curiosity and hypothesis testing are the bedrock of empirical research. In a similar fashion, experienced psychotherapists, to take an example from clinical psychology, are sensitive and keen observers of client behavior. They are persistent hypothesis testers. They are curious about the relationship between family history variables and current functioning. They draw upon theory and experience to help select a particular intervention for a particular client problem or moment in therapy.

Dispassionate logic and clear and organized thinking are as necessary for effectiveness in the field as they are for success in research. In fact, the bridge between research and just plain living is much shorter than most people think. All of us gather data about the world around us, wonder what will happen if we or others behave in particular ways, and test our pet hunches through deliberate action. To a large extent, the formal research enterprise consists of thinking systematically about these same issues.

The procedures outlined in this book are intended to assist the doctoral student in planning and writing a research dissertation. The suggestions are equally applicable to writing a master's thesis. There is considerable overlap between these two challenging activities. For most students, the master's thesis is the first rigorous research project they attempt. This means that, in the absence of strong, supportive faculty consultation, the student often concludes the thesis with considerable relief and an awareness of how not to do the study the next time! With a doctoral dissertation, it is generally expected, sometimes as an act of faith, that the student will be a more seasoned and sophisticated researcher. The consensus opinion is that dissertations are generally longer than theses, that they are more original, and that they make a greater contribution to the field.

In most graduate programs the prelude to conducting a dissertation study is presenting a dissertation proposal. A research proposal is an action plan that justifies and describes the proposed study. We take the completion of a comprehensive proposal as a very important step in the dissertation process. The proposal serves as a contract between the student and his or her dissertation or thesis committee that, when

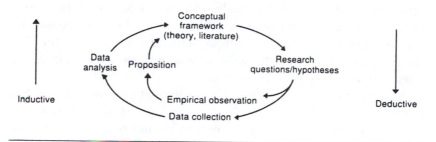

Figure 1.1. The research wheel.

approved by all parties, constitutes an agreement that data may be collected and the study may be completed. As long as the student follows the steps outlined in the proposal, committee members should be discouraged from demanding significant changes to the study after the proposal has been approved. Naturally, it is not uncommon to expect small changes, additions or deletions down the road, because one can never totally envision the unpredictable turns that studies can take.

There is no universally agreed upon format for the research proposal. To our way of thinking, a good proposal contains a review of the relevant literature, a statement of the problem and the associated hypotheses, and a clear delineation of the proposed method and plans for data analysis. In our experience, an approved proposal means that more than half of the work of the dissertation has been completed. This book is intended to help students construct research proposals as well as completed dissertations.

THE RESEARCH WHEEL

One way of thinking about the phases of the research process is with reference to the so-called research wheel (see Figure 1.1). The wheel metaphor suggests that research is not linear but a recursive cycle of steps that are repeated over time. The most common entry point is some form of "empirical observation." In other words, the researcher selects a topic from the infinite array of possible topics. The next step is a process of inductive logic that culminates in a proposition. The inductive process serves to relate the specific topic to a broader context and begins with some hunches of the form, "I wonder if. . . ." These hunches typically are guided by the values, assumptions, and goals of the researcher that need to be explicated.

Stage 2 of the research wheel is a developed proposition, which is expressed as a statement of an established relationship (e.g., "The early bird is more likely to catch the worm than the late bird"). The proposition exists within a conceptual or theoretical framework. It is the role of the researcher to clarify the relationship between a particular proposition and the broader context of theory and previous research. This is probably the most challenging and creative aspect of the dissertation process. A conceptual framework, which is simply a less developed form of a theory, consists of statements that link abstract concepts (e.g., motivation, role) to empirical data. Theories and conceptual frameworks are developed to account for or describe abstract phenomena that occur under similar conditions. A theory is the language that allows us to move from observation to observation and make sense of similarities and differences. Without placing the study within such a context, the proposed study has a "so what?" quality. This is one of the main objections to the research proposals of novice researchers: The research question may be inherently interesting but ultimately meaningless. For instance, the question, "Are there more women than men in graduate school today?" is totally banal as a research question unless the answer to the question has conceptual or theoretical implications that are developed within the study. A study may be worthwhile primarily for its practical implications (e.g., Should we start recruiting more men into graduate schools?), but a purely applied study may not be acceptable as a dissertation. Kerlinger and Lee (1999), authors of a highly respected text on research methodology, have noted that "the basic purpose of scientific research is theory" (p. 5). Generally speaking, a research dissertation is expected to contribute to the scholarly literature in a field and not merely solve an applied problem. Thus, identifying a conceptual framework for a research study typically involves immersing oneself in the research and theoretical literature of the field.

Having stated our position with regard to the role of theory in dissertation research, it becomes necessary for us to take a step back. As a

psychologist and a sociologist, we are most familiar with research conventions within these two disciplines. Other branches of the social sciences have their own standards of what constitutes an acceptable dissertation topic. We have attempted to keep this book as generalizable as
possible and to infuse it with examples from other fields. Ultimately, of
course, you will need to follow the rules and conventions that pertain to your discipline as well as to your university and department.
For example, a few major universities allow a doctoral student to sub-
mit a series of published articles as equivalent to a dissertation. Many
others encourage studies that consist of secondary data analyses
derived from national data bases such as census data or the General
Social Survey, or data obtained from a larger study. Some fields, nota-
bly social work, education, policy evaluation, and professional psychology, may encourage dissertations that solve applied problems
rather than make distinct theoretical contributions. Studies that evaluate the effectiveness of programs or interventions are a case in point
because they sometimes contribute little in the way of validating a theory. Political science and economics are examples of fields that are
diverse enough to accommodate both theoretically based studies and
purely applied studies. Within the subspecialty of international relations, for instance, one could imagine a survey and analysis of security
agreements of European nations after the unraveling of the North
Atlantic Treaty Organization (NATO) that relies on interviews with foreign policy makers and is largely descriptive and applied. In contrast, a
study of the role of a commitment to ideology to the success of political
parties in the United States, based on an analysis of historical documents and voting records, might be grounded in a theory of how ideology attracts or alienates the voting public.

Moving forward along the research wheel, the researcher uses
deductive reasoning to move from the larger context of theory to generate a specific research question. The research question is the precisely
stated form of the researcher's intent and may be accompanied by one
or more specific hypotheses. The first loop is completed as the
researcher seeks to discover or collect the data that will serve to answer
the research question. The data collection process is essentially another
task of empirical observation, which then initiates another round of the
research wheel. Generalizations are made on the basis of the particular
data that have been observed (inductive process), and the generaliza-

tions are tied to a conceptual framework, which then leads to the elucidation of further research questions and implications for additional study.

The kinds of skills called for at the various points of the research wheel are reminiscent of the thoughts about learning presented by Bertrand Russell many years ago. Russell noted that there are two primary kinds of knowledge acquisition: knowledge by description and knowledge by acquaintance. Knowledge by description is learning in a passive mode, such as reading a book on how to change the oil in one's car or hearing a lecture on Adam Smith's theory of economics. It is the type of learning that is especially well suited for mastering abstract information. Knowledge by acquaintance, on the other hand, is learning by doing, the kind of skill training that comes from practicing a tennis serve, driving an automobile, and playing with a computer. This is concrete knowledge acquisition, oriented to solving problems. The research process demands both skills. First, there is the clear, logical thinking that pertains to working with concepts and ideas and building theories. It is our impression that many graduate students, particularly those who have experience as practitioners in their fields, are weakest in abstract conceptualization, and honing this skill may be the major challenge of the dissertation. Second, there is the practical application of ideas, including the need systematically to plan a study, then collect and analyze data. The ability to focus, problem solve, and make decisions will help bring the study to completion.

CHAPTER 2

Selecting a Suitable Topic

The selection of an appropriate topic is the first major challenge in conducting research. In many academic settings, this task is simplified by working with a faculty mentor who is already familiar with an interesting area of study and may even have defined one or more researchable questions. On the other hand, you may not be blessed with a faculty role model who is actively engaged in research in an area of interest to you. There are no simple rules for selecting a topic of interest, but there are some considerations for making a decision as to appropriateness. It is generally unwise to define something as important as a dissertation topic without first obtaining a broad familiarity with the field. This implies a large amount of exploring the literature and talking with the experts. Without this initial exploration you can neither know the range of possibilities of interesting topics nor have a clear idea of what is already known. Most students obtain their research topics from the loose ends they discover in reading within an area, from an interesting observation they have made ("I notice that men shut up when a beautiful woman enters the room; I wonder what the effect of physical attractiveness is on group process?"), or from an applied focus in their lives or professional work ("I have a difficult time treating these alcoholics and want to discover how best to work with them"). Another strategy is to consult with leading scholars in an area of interest and ask them for advice on profitable topics to pursue. Most are happy to talk to and share materials with enthusiastic doctoral students who are obviously familiar with the expert's prior work.

SOME GUIDELINES FOR TOPIC SELECTION

Here are some guidelines for deciding if a topic is appropriate as a dissertation subject.

1. A topic needs to sustain your interest over a long period of time. A suggested study on learning nonsense syllables under two sets of environmental conditions may sound appealing in its simplicity, but remember Finagle's first law of research: If something can go wrong, it will go wrong! Dissertations usually take at least twice as much time as anticipated, and there are few worse fates than slaving hour after hour on a project that you abhor. Remember too that all dissertations are recorded and published with the Library of Congress and you will always be associated with this particular study!

2. At the other extreme, it is wise to avoid a topic that is overly ambitious and overly challenging. Most students want to graduate, preferably within a reasonable period of time. Grandiose dissertations have a way of never being completed, and even the best dissertations end up being compromises among your own ambition, the wishes of your committee, and practical circumstances. It is not realistic for a dissertation to say everything there is to say about a particular topic (e.g., the European Common Market), and you need to temper your enthusiasm with pragmatism. As one student put it, "There are two types of dissertations: the great ones and those that are completed!" Sometimes it makes sense to select a research topic on the basis of convenience or workability and use the luxury of the postgraduate years to pursue more esoteric topics of personal interest.

3. We suggest that you avoid topics that may be linked too closely with emotional issues in your own life. It always makes sense to choose a topic that is interesting and personally meaningful. Some students, however, try to use a dissertation to resolve an emotional issue or solve a personal problem. Even if you think you have successfully

overcome the personal impact of the death of your child, this is a topic to be avoided. It will necessarily stir up emotional issues that may easily get in the way of completing the dissertation.

4. A related issue is selecting a topic in which you have a personal ax to grind. Remember that conducting research demands ruthless honesty and objectivity. If you initiate a study to demonstrate that men are no damned good, you will be able neither to allow yourself the sober reflections of good research nor to acknowledge the possibility that your conclusions may contradict your expectations. It is much better to begin with a hunch ("I've noticed that men don't do very well with housekeeping. I wonder if that has something to do with being pampered as children.") and to regard the research as an adventurous exploration to shed light on this topic rather than as a polemical exercise to substantiate your point of view.

5. Finally, you need to select a topic that has the potential for you to make an original contribution to the field and allow you to demonstrate your independent mastery of subject and method. In other words, the topic must be worth pursuing. At the very least, the study must generate or help validate theoretical understanding in an area, or, in those fields where applied dissertations are permissible, contribute to the development of professional practice. Some students are put off when they discover that a literature review contains contradictory or puzzling results or explanations for a phenomenon. Such contradictions should be taken not as setbacks and reasons to steer away from a topic, but as opportunities to resolve a mystery. When people disagree or when existing explanations seem inadequate, there is often room for a critical study to be conducted.

FROM INTERESTING IDEA TO RESEARCH QUESTION

Let us assume that you have identified a general area of research and that your choice has been based on curiosity and may involve resolving a problem, explaining a phenomenon, uncovering a process by which something occurs, demonstrating the truth of a hidden fact, building on or reevaluating other studies, or testing some theory in your field.

To know whether or not the topic is important (significant) you must also be familiar with the literature in the area. Later on, we will present a number of suggestions for conducting a good review and assessment of the literature. In the meantime, we have noticed that many students have difficulty transforming an interesting idea into a researchable question and have designed a simple exercise to help in that endeavor.

Researchable questions almost invariably involve the relationship between two or more variables, phenomena, concepts, or ideas. The nature of that relationship may vary. Research studies generally consist of methods to explicate the nature of the relationship. Research in the social sciences rarely consists of explicating a single construct (e.g., "I will look at everything there is to know about the 'imposter phenomenon' ") or a single variable (e.g., voting rates in presidential elections).[1] Even the presence of two variables is apt to be limiting, and oftentimes it is only when a third "connecting" variable is invoked that an idea becomes researchable.

An example might help to demonstrate how the introduction of an additional variable can lead to the birth of a promising study. Let us assume that I am interested in how the elderly are perceived by a younger generation. At this level a study would be rather mundane and likely to lead to a "so what?" response. So far it implies asking people what they think of the elderly, perhaps using interviews, or tests, or even behavioral observations. But we really won't learn much about perceptions of the elderly in contemporary society. Introducing a second variable, however, can lead to a set of questions that have promising theoretical (as well as practical) implications: I wonder what the role of the media is in shaping social perceptions of the elderly? I wonder if living with a grandparent makes any difference in how the elderly are viewed? I wonder how specific legislation designed to benefit the elderly has changed our perception of them? I wonder if there is a relationship between how middle-aged adults deal with their aging parents and how they view the elderly? The new variables that were introduced in these potential research questions were, respectively, the slant of the media, presence or absence of a grandparent, type of legislation, and treatment of one's own parents. These variables impart meaning to the research because they offer suggestions as to what accounts for variability in the perception of the elderly.

As an example of generating a research question using three primary variables, let's say that you have inferred that many women lose interest in sexual relations with their husbands after the birth of a child. At this level, the proposed study would consist of checking out this hunch by assessing the sexual interest of women (variable 1) before and after childbirth (variable 2). But what would this finding mean? The introduction of a third variable or construct could lead to a much more sophisticated and conceptually meaningful study. An investigator might ask, "I wonder if the husband's involvement in parenting makes a difference? What's the role of his sexual initiative? How about childbirth complications? Father's involvement in the birthing? The length of time they have been married? Time after delivery? Presence of other children in the home?" There is no end to the number of interesting questions that can be raised simply by introducing a mediating variable into the proposed study. This variable would then help to explain the nature of the relationship between the primary variables. In fact, one could brainstorm a whole list of potential third variables that could contribute to a better understanding of the relationship between childbirth and sexuality.

Note that the precise function of the third, or "connecting," variable will depend upon the logic of the conceptual model underlying the study. In this regard, a distinction can be made between two terms, *mediator* and *moderator*, that have often been used interchangeably (Baron & Kenny, 1986). Strictly speaking, a moderator variable pinpoints the conditions under which an independent variable exerts its effects on a dependent variable; a mediating variable, on the other hand, tries to describe "how" rather than "when" effects will occur by accounting for the relationship between the independent variable (the predictor) and the dependent variable (the criterion). In the health psychology field, social support can be regarded as either a moderating variable or a mediating variable (Quittner, Glueckauf, & Jackson, 1990). Conceptualized as a moderator, social support could be seen to exert beneficial effects on health outcomes only under conditions of high stress (i.e., there is a statistical interaction between stress and social support). Conceptualized as a mediator, social support acts as an intervening variable between stress and health outcomes (i.e., there is an indirect relationship between stress and illness). Arguing from this model, some stressful events might encourage traumatized individuals to shun or exhaust their supportive resources or perceive them as unhelpful, leading, in turn, to increased symptoms of anxiety and depression. The nature of the role of mediating variables in the theoretical model is captured by the path diagram in Table 2.1.

One single research study is not likely to establish and verify all the important elements of a complex conceptual model. As one of our colleagues puts it, you would need a video camera to capture the entire Grand Canyon on film, whereas the dissertation is more like a snapshot, perhaps of a mule and rider descending one small section of the canyon trail. Yet the proposed model can provide a useful context for current and future research studies. Most ambitious research studies rely heavily on just such theoretical models. For example, Gerald Patterson (Patterson, DeBaryshe, & Ramsey, 1989) has for some time been developing and testing a model to explain aggressive and deviant behavior among young males. The model hypothesizes that such antisocial behavior can be causally linked to disrupted parental discipline and poor family management skills. The relationship between these two sets of variables is not direct, but mediated by a network of other variables. The process is thought to begin with parents "training" a child to behave aggressively by relying on aversive behaviors in both punishment and negative reinforcement contingencies. The inability of the parents to control coercive exchanges among family members constitutes "training for fighting," which leads, in turn, to aggressive behavior and poor peer relationships. This lack of social skills generalizes to antisocial behavior in the classroom, which makes it next to impossible for the youth to obtain basic academic skills, thus preparing him poorly to cope with life outside school. Ultimately, this leads to high rates of delinquent behavior. An abbreviated summary of the model is shown in Figure 2.1.

Obviously, a researcher is in no position to test the entire model in a single study. Indeed, Patterson and his colleagues have spent many years testing and elaborating the nature of these relationships. A single study might focus on one particular set of relationships within this complex model. For instance, the investigator might ask whether there is a relationship between physical fighting and poor peer relationships. Each variable would have to be operationalized, probably by obtaining more than one measure of both fighting and peer relationships. In

Table 2.1

Path Diagram

stressful event	$\rightarrow$	social support	$\rightarrow$	health outcomes
independent variable		mediating variable		dependent variable

Patterson's work, for instance, he asks mothers, peers, and teachers to rate levels of physical fighting, because their perspectives may differ. Likewise, peers, teachers, and self-reports are used to obtain measures of peer relations. The objective of the study—that is, attempting to determine the nature and form of the relationship between the primary variables—will determine the research method that is employed.

A second example of using a comprehensive model as a guide to research comes from Rudolf Moos's ongoing studies of work and family environments (Schaefer & Moos, 1998). Basically, Moos has adopted a socioecological view of work. The model describes both environmental variables and personal variables and relates them, via a set of cognitive functions and coping variables, to individual adaptation, including morale, job performance, and overall health and well-being (see Figure 2.2). A single study might focus on a small set of environmental system variables and relate them to something else, such as other environmental system variables, personal system variables, coping responses, or health outcomes. For instance, the researcher might explore the contribution of work pressure and supervisory support on innovation in the workplace.

GENERATING RESEARCHABLE QUESTIONS

The exercise that we use to help students generate researchable questions from their interesting ideas is a brainstorming exercise that begins with labeling one or two variables and generating a second and/or third. Brainstorming consists of openly and noncritically listing all possible ideas in a given period of time. Later on you can return to a more

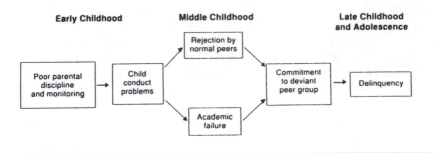

Figure 2.1. A model of antisocial behavior.
Note. See Patterson et al. (1989).

critical analysis of each idea and delete those that are either uninteresting, nonmeaningful, or impractical. Ultimately, of course, it is contact
with the literature that will determine whether or not a research question is viable, because the literature houses the tradition of scholarly
inquiry that goes beyond the limits of your own knowledge.

We suggest that you do the brainstorming exercise in a small group
so that the person receiving the consultation merely serves as a scribe to
record the ideas thrown out by the other group members (see Table 2.2).
After 5 or 10 minutes it is time to move on to the next person's partially
formed research topic. We generally use this exercise in groups of three
or four so that group members can frequently shift groups and draw on
the spontaneous reactions of a larger number of peers uncontaminated
by prior ideas or a particular mind-set. The exercise involves suspend-
ing critical thinking and allowing new ideas to percolate. It should
especially suit divergent thinkers, who will find the demand to be
expansive in their thinking to be exciting and creative. Convergent
thinkers may experience the exercise as a bit overwhelming, but they
will find fulfillment in other stages of the research process that demand
compulsivity, care, and precision. Every chapter of a dissertation contains both divergent and convergent elements.

Note that not all decent research studies focus on three (or more)
primary variables. Many studies look at the relationship between two
variables or concepts, and a few descriptive studies make do with one
variable or construct. This generally occurs in the early stages of

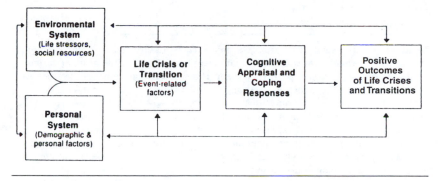

Figure 2.2. A model of work stress and coping.
Note. See Schaefer and Moos (1998).

research in an area when little is known about a topic. Some investigators are pathfinders in terms of opening up new topics of research by trying to understand as much as possible about a phenomenon and generating more informed hypotheses for others to test in the future. Nevertheless, we believe that most students underestimate what is currently known about most topics and that the most interesting, practical, and theoretically meaningful studies are likely to consider the relationships among several variables.

We conclude this chapter with the outline in Table 2.3, which asks you to look at the kinds of issues that need to be considered and responded to during the course of developing the research proposal. By and large, your dissertation committee will need to be convinced of three things in order to be comfortable with your proposal:

1. Is the question clear and researchable, and will the answer to the question extend knowledge in your field of study?

2. Have you located your question within a context of previous study that demonstrates that you have mastered and taken into consideration the relevant background literature?

3. Is the proposed method suitable for exploring your question?

Table 2.2
Brainstorming Exercise

Begin by defining one or two variables (or constructs) of interest. Then generate a list
of additional variables (or constructs) that in some way amplify the original variables
or illuminate the relationship between them. The new variables you list may be either
independent variables, dependent variables, moderating variables, or even mediating variables in the research questions you eventually select. After brainstorming this
list, go back and eliminate those variables that do not interest you or do not seem
promising to pursue. Finally, see if you can now define one or more research questions that speak to the relationship among the two or three variables (or constructs)
you have specified. Ultimately, each of these variables will need to be operationally
defined as you develop your research study.

Here are some examples of the results of this brainstorming exercise applied to topics
taken from different disciplines.

Political Science
Begin with an interest in citizen participation in city council meetings. List variables
or phenomena that might influence, be influenced by, or be related to this variable. A
sample research question is "What is the impact of citizen participation in city council meetings on legislative decision making?"

| citizen participation | $\rightarrow$ | legislative decision making |
| independent variable | | dependent variable |

Education
Begin with an interest in single mothers on welfare who return to school. List variables or phenomena that might influence, be influenced by, or be related to this variable. A sample research question is "What is the effect of the availability of child care
on single mothers on welfare returning to school?"

| child care | $\rightarrow$ | return to school |
| independent variable | | dependent variable |

NOTE

1. A *construct* is a concept used for scientific purposes in building theories.
Constructs (e.g., self-esteem), like concepts, are abstractions formed by generalizing from specific behaviors or manipulations. When constructs are

---

Table 2.2
Continued

Criminal Justice
Begin with an interest in the relationship between neighborhood crime watch programs and robbery rates. List variables that might influence or amplify the relationship between these two variables. A sample research question is "What is the effect of neighborhood crime watch programs, in both urban and rural environments, on the rate of burglaries?"

crime watch programs	→	rate of burglaries
	urban/rural environments ↗	
independent variable	moderator variable	dependent variable

Psychology
Begin with an interest in the relationship between physical attractiveness and self-esteem. List variables that might amplify or influence the relationship between these two variables. A sample research question is "What is the role of body image and physical attractiveness on self-esteem?" Another sample research question is "What is the role of body image in mediating the relationship between physical attractiveness and self-esteem?"

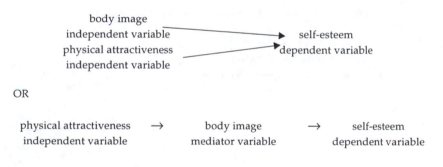

body image
independent variable
physical attractiveness
independent variable

self-esteem
dependent variable

OR

physical attractiveness	→	body image	→	self-esteem
independent variable		mediator variable		dependent variable

---

operationalized in such a way that they can be "scored" to take on different numerical values, they are referred to as *variables*.

Table 2.3
*Outline of Issues for a Student Researcher to Complete in the Development
of the Research Proposal*

Review of the Literature
The classic, definitive, or most influential pieces of research in this area are:

The journals that specialize in the kind of research in which I propose to engage are:

The body(ies) of research to which I wish to add is (are):

The experts in the field of my research are:

Statement of the Problem
The intellectual problem(s) I may help solve through this research is (are):

The moral, political, social, or practical problem(s) I may help alleviate through this
    research is (are):

Method
The method I propose to use to answer my question, prove my point, or gain more
    detailed and substantive knowledge is:

An alternative way to do it would be:

Three important research studies that have been carried out using the method I pro-
    pose are:

The reason(s) this method is a good one for my question, proposition, or subject is
    (are):

Possible weaknesses of this method are:

The skills I will need to use this method are:

Of these skills, I still need to acquire the following:

I propose to acquire these skills by:

BOX 2.1

Student Suggestions

Over the years our students have provided the most useful suggestions for completing the dissertation. Here are some of the suggestions they have offered to one another that pertain to the earliest stages of developing a dissertation. Other suggestions will be noted at the appropriate places in the following chapters.

1. Start an "idea box," a file box to hold 3 × 5 cards or slips of paper where you can store good ideas for future reference. Use the idea box for noting books and articles to get from the library, good quotations, inspirations for future studies, half-baked notions that might be useful in the future, and so on.

2. Think of your topic as a large jigsaw puzzle with a piece missing. That is what you want to research, to fill in the gap in your field. To discover what piece is missing, you must read as much of the literature as possible in your field.

3. Before you begin, read several well-written dissertations recommended by your chairperson.

4. As you progress through the dissertation process and your question shrinks in size due to the necessity of maintaining a manageable project for one person, don't lose heart. Even very small questions can serve much larger purposes. To keep the perspective of "meaningfulness" throughout, keep imagining an audience of individuals who would want to know the results of your work. Even if you can imagine only 25 people in the whole world who would care, keep that group alive in front of your eyes.

CHAPTER 3

Methods of Inquiry:

Quantitative and Qualitative Approaches

The principal characteristic of scholarly and scientific inquiry, as opposed to informal, intuitive kinds of inquiry, is the use of rationally grounded procedures to extend knowledge that a community of scholars regards as reliable and valid (*Inquiry and Research Knowledge Area Study Guide of the Human and Organization Development Program of The Fielding Institute* [HOD], 1998). The dissertation process is a ritual of socialization into that community of scholars, so it is necessary for you, as a student, to master the scholarly procedures within your discipline. The specific methods chosen to attack a problem will depend upon your discipline and the nature of the specific problem. There is no universally accepted approach within the social sciences, although there are rich research traditions that cannot be ignored, as well as a common understanding that chosen methods of inquiry must rest on rational justification. This means that scientific methods differ from more informal methods of inquiry by their reliance on validated public procedures that have been determined to produce reliable knowledge.

Currently there are many disagreements in the social sciences regarding what constitutes knowledge and the procedures for gaining it. One way of thinking about the way in which research generally contributes to the knowledge base of a discipline is by considering the following three-level hierarchy of knowledge, suggested by our colleague Marilyn Freimuth.

Axiologic/Epistemic Level. This is the underlying level of basic world hypotheses that form the foundation for content and method within a field of inquiry. *Epistemology* refers to the study of the nature of knowledge, while *axiology* refers to the study of ethics, values, and aesthetics. Examples of constructs at this level include the explanatory principle of cause and effect and the notion of open systems. In many ways the 20th century represented a new "axial shift" (Mahoney, 1990), or turning point in the history of ideas, away from a rational objectivism, which asserts that scientific knowledge is founded on objective empirical truths, and toward the conception of a more relativistic universe and "poststructuralist" epistemologies.

Theoretical Level. This is the level of models and theories. Theories are premises to account for data, such as the FIRO theory of interpersonal behavior in groups (Schutz, 1966) or the differential association theory in the study of crime (Sutherland, 1924). The term *model* has been used in many, often confusing ways in the social sciences. Here it refers to a higher-order theory, that is, a representational system at a higher level of abstraction that can inform and be informed by alternative theories (close to the framework or worldview that helps guide researchers and has been identified as a "paradigm" by Thomas Kuhn [1962]). Thus, psychoanalysis could be seen as a model, a wide lens with which to view and understand the mysteries of human behavior. Each model carries with it certain sets of assumptions. In the case of psychoanalysis, these assumptions include the unifying importance of causal determinism and unconscious motivation as core constructs.

Empirical Level. In the field of epistemology, *empiricism* refers to a commitment to obtaining knowledge through sense experience (literally, "based on experience" in Greek). Empiricism is frequently contrasted with *rationalism*, which refers to knowledge derived purely through thought and reason, and to more natural philosophical and religious traditions of reaching conclusions. In the present context, the empirical level includes hypotheses and the methods and data of scientific research. Hypotheses are tentative answers to questions, generally based on theory.

The primary role of research within this three-level schema is to link the theoretical and the empirical. Theories need the support of data in order to remain viable, whereas methods themselves carry assumptions that are theoretical in nature. Note that research findings do not contribute directly to the axiologic/epistemic level or even to basic models. Those levels reflect fundamental value commitments and personal preferences that are rarely modified on the basis of additional data, especially the kind of data generated by scholarly research. It is hard to imagine a psychoanalyst becoming a behaviorist or a Republican joining the Democrats without a significant shift in values that goes beyond the accumulated wisdom imparted by a series of research studies. Because most researchers strongly identify with particular values and carry many personal preferences into their work, it becomes especially important to learn to discriminate between beliefs and opinions, on the one hand, and verifiable, data-inspired support for ideas, on the other hand.

A brief look at the history of science is a humbling experience that should put to rest the misguided notion that research discovers truth. Drilling holes in the skull (trephining) used to be an acceptable way of dismissing the demons responsible for mental illness, and it wasn't that long ago that the sun was thought to circle the earth. One wonders what remnants of contemporary scientific truth will be regarded as equally ludicrous tomorrow! Instead, what research does contribute is a series of thoughtful observations that support or question the validity of our theories, which are in turn based on a set of largely untestable beliefs and assumptions. Every once in a while, at opportunistic moments of scholarly upheaval, a new paradigm appears that seems to do a better job of explaining the available data and guiding further inquiry.

Each social science discipline and set of investigators seems to have its own favored approach to generating knowledge. For instance, public opinion studies usually rely on survey research methods, psychoanalytic studies of infants make use of observational techniques, studies of organizational effectiveness may employ action research methods and case studies, historical investigations of political and social events

rely on archival records and content analysis, and laboratory studies of
perceptual processes stress experimental manipulation and hypothesis
testing. Within your chosen field, it is important to ask how a piece of
research acquires legitimacy as reliable knowledge (HOD, 1998). No
doubt part of the answer comes down to underlying epistemological
assumptions and values. Certainly research strategies will differ in
terms of the problems they address and the outcomes they produce. As
we shall see, one important distinction in the choice of method seems to
be the nature of the relationship between the researcher and the topic of
study.

We would argue that researchers in the social sciences have generally been myopic in defining the kinds of studies that might legiti-
mately lend themselves to research dissertations. Most students in the
social sciences are taught early on about the difference between independent and dependent variables and how experimental research
implies active manipulation of independent variables to observe a subsequent impact on dependent variables. This basic and time-honored
strategy has an earthy history in the systematic evaluation of fertilizers
for agricultural productivity. It remains a cornerstone in conducting
social science research with human subjects. Yet it is certainly not the
only way to conduct research.

The only universal in scientific knowledge is a general commitment
to using logical argument and evidence to arrive at conclusions that are
recognized as tentative and subject to further amendment (HOD, 1998).
Good scientists in action often deviate from an "official" philosophy of
science and a prescribed methodology. As William Bevan (1991), former president of the American Psychological Association, has noted:

> If you want to understand what effective science making is about, don't
> listen to what creative scientists say about their formal belief systems.
> Watch what they do. When they engage in good, effective science mak-
> ing they don't, as a rule, reflect on their presuppositions; they engage in
> a practical art form in which their decisions are motivated by the
> requirements of particular problem solving. (p. 478)

The key to evaluating a completed study is whether or not the
selected method is sufficiently rigorous and appropriate to the research
question, and whether or not the study is conceptually and theoreti-

cally grounded. The more familiar you are with the full range of alternative research strategies, the more enlightened and appropriate your choice of a particular method is apt to be. Too often students become so enamored with an approach to research that they will choose the method prior to determining the question. Unless the dissertation is designed to illustrate the use of a promising and innovative methodology, this is putting the cart before the horse. In general, the method needs to evolve out of the research question and be determined by it.

QUANTITATIVE METHODS

The epistemological foundation of most social science inquiry throughout the 20th century was logical positivism, a school of thought that maintains that all knowledge is derived from direct observation and logical inferences based on direct observation. To a great extent, the notion of objectively studying human beings is derived from a love affair social scientists have had with the natural sciences, which sought to understand nature by isolating phenomena, observing them, and formulating mathematical laws to describe patterns in nature. Current research in the social sciences is very steeped in the empirical and quantitative traditions.

Statistical methods are especially useful for looking at relationships and patterns and expressing these patterns with numbers. Descriptive statistics describe these patterns of behavior, whereas inferential statistics use probabilistic arguments to generalize findings from samples to populations of interest. Kerlinger (1977) focuses on the inferential process when he defines *statistics* as "the theory and method of analyzing quantitative data obtained from samples of observations in order to study and compare sources of variance of phenomena, to help make decisions to accept or reject hypothesized relations between the phenomena, and to aid in making reliable inferences from empirical observations" (p. 185). Note that the focus in the natural science model of research is the study of average or group effects as opposed to the study of individual differences. The kinds of inferential statements that derive from this model of research refer to groups of people or groups of events; that is, they are probabilistic (e.g., "Surveys find that most people believe that police officers use excessive force in dealing with criminals" or "Emotional expressiveness is related to coping effectively with natural disasters").

In experimental research, quantitative research designs are used to determine aggregate differences between groups or classes of subjects. Emphasis is placed on precise measurement and controlling for extraneous sources of error. The purpose, therefore, is to isolate a variable of interest (the independent variable) and manipulate it to observe the impact of the manipulation on a second, or dependent, variable. This procedure is facilitated by the "control" of extraneous variables, thus allowing the researcher to infer a causal relationship between the two (or more) variables of interest.

Methodological control is generally accomplished by two procedures that rely on the principle of randomness. One is *random sampling*, which uses subjects that have "randomly" been drawn from the potential pool of subjects so that each member of the population has an equal chance or known probability of being selected. Random selection of subjects permits the researcher to generalize the results of the study from the sample to the population in question. The second procedure is *randomization*, which assigns subjects to groups or experimental conditions in such a way that each subject has an equal chance of being selected for each condition. Subject characteristics are thus randomly distributed in every respect other than the experimental manipulation or treatment, allowing the researcher to infer that resultant differences between the groups must be the result of the isolated variable in question.

Unfortunately, these efforts at experimental control are often impractical in social science research with human subjects. Psychology, for instance, has an honorable tradition of laboratory research using tight experimental designs, but research in the clinical or social arena may not permit the kind of control stipulated by the experimental method. This dilemma is equally prominent in field studies in the disciplines of sociology, education, and political science. One cannot practically conspire to rear children using two distinct parenting styles, nor ethically proceed to instill child abuse to study its immediate impact in a controlled fashion. Researchers can, however, study analogues of these variables using pure experimental designs (for example, one can ask parents to use specific interventions at the onset of particular child behaviors). *Change studies,* in which a treatment or program is being evaluated for its effectiveness, may also lend themselves well to experimental designs. Even so, it may not be possible to randomize subjects into groups that receive a treatment or intervention and those that do not. A number of ingenious solutions have been proposed to deal with the ethics of denying treatment to the needy, including the use of placebos and waiting-list controls (Kazdin, 1977).

More typically, the research method of choice in the social sciences seems to be a "quasi-experimental" design that compromises some of the rigor of the controlled experiment but maintains the argument and logic of experimental research (Cook & Campbell, 1979). This kind of research has also been called "ex post facto research," a systematic empirical approach in which the investigator does not employ experimental manipulation or random assignment of subjects to conditions because events have already occurred or they are inherently not manipulable (Kerlinger & Lee, 1999). So-called causal statements become correlational statements in quasi-experimental research, although it is often possible to infer a sequence of events in causal form. That is one reason why it is crucial to have a theoretical model as a foundation for an empirical study. The model itself will help to inform you in meaningfully interpreting the results of the study.

There is also a need to exercise caution in interpreting the meaning of results whenever subjects assign themselves to groups. A colorful example is the apparent negative correlation that exists between the numbers of mules found in the various states and the number of Ph.D.s living there. The fact that states that have a lot of mules don't have so many Ph.D.s, and vice versa, is an empirical observation that can be statistically expressed in the form of a correlation coefficient. A researcher would be hard pressed to argue a causal relationship between these two variables unless she drew upon an underlying theoretical model that links the two variables through a third (mediating) variable such as the degree of urbanization. Note that this simple correlational study could, at least theoretically, be transformed into an experimental study by, for example, flooding some states with mules to see if the Ph.D.s leave or wooing the Ph.D.s across state lines to see if the number of mules increases!

This is not a book on research design, but the adoption of a particular research strategy will affect the final form of the dissertation.

Whether or not a study employs a true experimental design or a quasi-experimental design, the most common strategy in the social sciences is a comparison between groups. That is, independent groups of subjects are used for each experimental or control condition. The best known variant of this strategy is to use two equivalent groups of subjects, which both receive pretests and posttests and differ only in the experimental treatment that is given to one group (see Table 3.1).

It becomes possible to evaluate the impact of an intervention because the control group offers a baseline for comparison. One could use this design to evaluate, for example, whether the inclusion of spouses in an aftercare program for heart bypass surgery patients will encourage greater compliance with medical regimens. Or one could design a study to evaluate the effect of introducing air bags in automobiles on the rate of physical injury to passengers. Some automobiles of a given make would receive air bags, some would not, and the change in types and rates of injuries would be the dependent measure.

The straightforward pretest, posttest, control group design makes it possible to attribute the impact of experimental interventions to the interventions themselves rather than to some extraneous variable. The interpretation of results of studies using this design may be compromised, however, if the subjects have not been assigned to conditions in a truly random manner. In the proposed "air bag" study, for example, if automobiles and drivers are not randomly assigned to conditions, it may well be that inherently safer drivers will choose automobiles with better safety features. Because randomization is not always possible, it becomes crucial to argue for the "equivalence" of the two groups even if they do not derive from the identical population of subjects. One way in which researchers attempt to make this argument is by matching the groups on key variables that are critical to the understanding of the study, such as age, sex, symptomatology, or, in the current example, the previous driving records of the participants.

The basic pretest, posttest, control group design, shown in Table 3.1, also does not adequately control for any effect that the pretest evaluations might themselves have on the subjects. Some assessments can sensitize subjects by making them aware that they are now participating in a study or providing a practice experience that contaminates the validity of posttest results. A simple posttest-only design may get around this difficulty and is probably underutilized in the literature

Table 3.1
Pretest, Posttest, Control Group Design

	Pretest	Treatment	Posttest
Experimental	yes	yes	yes
Control	yes	no	yes

(Campbell & Stanley, 1966). In any case, the choice of a basic research design does not eliminate the need for you to think carefully and creatively about potential sources of error and alternative explanations to account for findings.

Most experimental designs are variants of the treatment and control group format described above.[1] Such designs permit the researcher to make causal inferences regarding the relationships among the variables. In contrast, correlational (or "observational") studies do not generally enable the researcher to demonstrate causal relationships among variables. Any conclusions regarding causality must be inferred from the underlying theory rather than from the results of the study itself.

Studies built around experimental or correlational designs generate data that are subsequently analyzed using appropriate inferential statistics. Statistical techniques that are used to evaluate the effectiveness of an intervention or a difference between groups, such as an analysis of variance (ANOVA) or *t* test, compare the size of "between-group" differences with the size of "within-group" differences due to individual variability. They represent the experimental tradition. The logic of the correlational paradigm is quite different (Cronbach, 1975). Correlations depend upon comparing two distributions of scores, that is, scores that are broadly dispersed along two dimensions, such as longevity and alcohol use. Statistical techniques that emerged from this tradition, such as multiple regression, are especially popular in social science research that relies on questionnaires, surveys, or scales, and the relationship between continuous variables. Be aware, however, that it is the design of the study and not the choice of statistical method that principally governs the types of statements that can be made about the relationships among the variables.

Both experimental and correlational traditions have a rightful place in the evaluation of quantitative data, and a detailed comparison of them goes beyond the scope of this book. It is important to remember that although statistics is an indispensable tool for scientific inference, the appropriate application of statistics cannot make up for a faulty research design. In many instances statistical methods drawn from both the experimental and correlational paradigms are equally legitimate choices (see Gigerenzer, 1991). As a matter of fact, the same data usually can be analyzed in multiple ways. If you are looking at the relationship between locus of control and frequency of medical visits for preventive health, for example, you could express it using a correlation coefficient or by dividing your sample into two or more subgroups on the basis of the personality construct of locus of control and comparing the resulting groups on medical visits. Generally speaking, it is not a good idea to throw away data (you are throwing away data if you have a continuum of locus of control scores but arbitrarily reduce the continuum to two or more discrete values, such as internal or external categories), but these kinds of decisions require statistical expertise and theoretical grounding.

There are two additional points we wish to make regarding the use of quantitative research. One is that there is a tendency in the social sciences to overemphasize the importance of "statistically significant" findings and to underemphasize the importance of clinically or socially significant findings. In other words, simply because a difference is significant at a certain probability level (typically .05 or .01) does not mean that the difference will be meaningful in practical terms. For instance, a difference of five points on a depression scale might be statistically meaningful but may not be meaningful clinically. Too often students will assume that the object of research is to achieve statistical significance rather than to make meaningful inferences about behavior. The primary reason that Jacob Cohen (1990), the father of power analysis, was drawn to correlational analyses is that they yield an r, a measure of effect size. That is, unlike probability (p) values, correlation coefficients can straightforwardly indicate the magnitude of the relationship between variables, which may be far more informative than the presence or absence of statistical significance. Cohen (1990) goes on to note that we sometimes learn more from what we see than from what we compute, and he argues for an increased use of the graphic display of data, using simple scatter plots and so-called "stem and leaf" diagrams (see Table 3.2) prior to or instead of performing complicated statistical analyses.

Second, as you consider the kinds of designs and controls that are available to the social science researcher, we urge you to be aware of a fundamental dilemma. Good research is a constant balancing act between control and meaningfulness. At one extreme is an emphasis on controlling the observation and measurement of a variable by eliminating the influence of as many confounding variables as possible. What results might be a tight laboratory study in which the findings inspire confidence but are not particularly interesting. At the other extreme is the observation of complex human behavior in the field, without invoking any controls at all, so that the results seem fascinating but are highly unreliable and difficult to replicate. The fashion in social science research has moved back and forth between these poles of emphasizing precision of measurement versus emphasizing meaningfulness. Today the pendulum seems to be swinging in the direction of meaningfulness, hastened by the availability of a greater number of permissible research strategies together with a reevaluation of research epistemology.

QUALITATIVE METHODS

The researcher who employs experimental and quasi-experimental designs attempts to control the playing field of the study as much as possible, restrict the focus of attention to a relatively narrow band of behavior (often manipulating experimental conditions in order to further narrow the object of study to a single variable), and get out of harm's way as a detached and objective observer of the action. A countervailing trend in social science research calls for sidestepping the artificiality and narrowness of experimental studies by promoting studies that allow researchers to be more spontaneous and flexible in exploring phenomena in their natural environment. Some of these methods of inquiry are challenging the epistemological and philosophical foundations of traditional social science research (see Denzin & Lincoln, 1998; Patton, 1990; Spradley, 1979).

Table 3.2
Stem and Leaf Displays

A new graphic display for presenting the distribution of continuously scaled data is the stem and leaf display. A stem and leaf display presents the data in a manner that highlights characteristics of the distribution that might not be obvious from an examination of the frequency distribution. For example, the table below presents the frequencies of age at first marriage for a sample of 91 U.S. residents selected from the National Opinion Research Center General Social Survey of 1990.

Age at First Marriage	f	Age at First Marriage	f
15	1	26	4
16	2	27	4
17	5	28	2
18	8	29	1
19	10	30	2
20	10	31	1
21	12	32	1
22	8	33	1
23	6	34	0
24	6	35	1
25	5	36	1
		Total	91

In a stem and leaf display the first digit of the variable is broken away from the second digit. The first digit forms a "stem" and the second a "leaf." The stem is placed to the left of a vertical line and the leaf is placed to the right. In the age at first marriage data the stems are "10s" and the leaves are "1s." Thus, a person married at 21 would be represented by a 2 stem and a 1 leaf. A person married at 25 would also be represented by the 2 stem but would have a 5 leaf.

The steps in constructing a stem and leaf display from the above data would be first to select the stems from the above frequency distribution, as follows:

At one extreme, proponents of alternative approaches question the validity of a logical positivistic science applied to human behavior and social systems and take issue with the ideal or even the possibility of having a neutral, disengaged investigator (see Feyerabend, 1981a, 1981b; Popper, 1965; Toulmin, 1972). Taking their hint from modern physics, they suggest that the presence of an observer inevitably alters that which is being observed, that, in fact, one cannot separate the

---

TABLE 3.2
Continued

Stems
1
2
3

Then add leaves for each case by observing its second digit and adding that digit to the stem to form the leaf. Thus, in this display, each case is represented by one leaf:

Stems	Leaves
1	5667777788888888999999999
2	000000000011111111111122222222233333334444445555566667777889
3	0012356

When working with data that are not ordered, the leaves can be added and then ordered in a final step. The above figure indicates that most persons in this sample were married in their early twenties or late teens. Though there is nothing particularly surprising about this, more complex displays can present a large amount of data in an efficient and descriptive figure that allows the reader to view the distribution in a manner that a simple frequency table does not. Chapter 2 of Hamilton's (1990) *Modern Data Analysis* presents detailed instructions on the construction of complex stem and leaf displays.

---

investigator from the object of inquiry. Feminist theorists have other reasons for criticizing the traditional experimental method, claiming that it creates a hierarchy of power in which the omnipotent researcher, often a male, instructs, observes, records, and sometimes deceives the subjects (Peplau & Conrad, 1989). It should be noted, however, that whether a study uses experimental or nonexperimental methods does not necessarily imply anything about the researcher's commitment to nonsexist research.

The impact of these developments in the philosophy of science upon method is far from clear. We are probably experiencing just the initial foray into the application of alternate research paradigms to the pursuit of research itself. Because a thrust of this book is to advise the use of the most appropriate method for the study of a particular research question, it might be useful to describe briefly some of the distinctions among the various alternative methods. The labels given to these approaches include "phenomenological," "hermeneutic," "naturalistic," "experiential," "dialectical," and so on. The label most commonly used to incorporate these research strategies is "qualitative research." *Qualitative* implies that the data are in the form of words as opposed to numbers. Whereas quantitative data are generally evaluated using descriptive and inferential statistics, qualitative data are usually reduced to themes or categories and evaluated subjectively. There is more emphasis on description and discovery and less emphasis on hypothesis testing and verification. According to Polkinghorne (1991), qualitative methods are especially useful in the "generation of categories for understanding human phenomena and the investigation of the interpretation and meaning that people give to events they experience" (p. 112). Piaget's theory of cognitive development, for instance, was developed using qualitative methods. Whereas the quantitative researcher is apt to record a small set of previously identified variables, the qualitative researcher seeks a psychologically rich, in-depth understanding of the individual, and would argue that experimental and quasi-experimental methods cannot do justice to describing phenomena such as the therapeutic relationship or the experience of the homeless (Searight, 1990).

The distinction between quantitative and qualitative research can be misleading. Qualitative researchers do not possess a distinct set of methods that are all their own (Denzin & Lincoln, 1998). They can make use of interviews, hermeneutic inquiry, survey research, participant observation, even statistics. Over time, different research traditions have evolved that bring to bear particular value-laden perspectives by which to investigate particular topics, such as psychoanalytic studies of children and ethnographic studies of cultures. Within these domains the researcher may draw upon many specific methods, such as the ethnographer who employs both interviews and observational descriptions. In general, qualitative research implies an emphasis on processes and meanings over measures of quantity, intensity, and frequency (Denzin & Lincoln, 1998). The newer generation of qualitative researchers emphasizes the socially constructed nature of reality, a close relationship between the researcher and the object of study, and the context that influences the inquiry. Although there exists great heterogeneity within the literature on qualitative methodologies, it is probably fair to say that such methods generally share three fundamental assumptions

(Patton, 1990): a holistic view, an inductive approach, and naturalistic inquiry.

A Holistic View. The holistic approach stresses that the whole is different than the sum of its parts. Consequently, qualitative methods seek to understand phenomena in their entirety in order to develop a complete understanding of a person, program, or situation. This is in contrast to the experimental paradigm, which aims to isolate and measure narrowly defined variables, and where understanding is tantamount to prediction and control.

An Inductive Approach. Qualitative research begins with specific observations and moves toward the development of general patterns that emerge from the cases under study. The researcher does not impose much of an organizing structure or make assumptions about the interrelationships among the data prior to making the observations. This is, of course, quite different from the hypothetico-deductive approach to experimental designs that prescribes specification of variables and hypotheses prior to data collection.

Naturalistic Inquiry. Qualitative research is intended to understand phenomena in their naturally occurring states. It is a discovery-oriented approach in the natural environment. Experimental research, by comparison, uses controlled conditions and a limited set of outcome variables.

The appropriate selection of methods of inquiry is contextual and depends to a large extent upon learning the standards used in your own discipline. Qualitative methods have an especially comfortable home in the ethnographic and field study traditions of anthropology and sociology that emerged in the 19th century. Psychologists and psychiatrists also developed detailed case histories of their patients at about that time. Any classification of qualitative methods today is apt to be a simplification. Three dimensions that seem important in contrasting the various qualitative research traditions are (a) the problems and concerns of the researcher, (b) the nature of knowledge, and (c) the relationship between the researcher and the subject matter. These dimensions are summarized in relation to the research traditions of phenomenology, hermeneutics, and ethnographic inquiry in Table 3.3.

PHENOMENOLOGY

When phenomenology is applied to research, the focus is on what the person experiences and its expression in language that is as loyal to the lived experience as possible (Polkinghorne, 1989). Thus phenomenological inquiry attempts to describe and elucidate the meanings of human experience. More than other forms of inquiry, phenomenology attempts to get beneath how people describe their experience to the structures that underlie consciousness, that is, to the essential nature of ideas. Phenomenologically oriented researchers typically use interviews or extended conversations as the source of their data. Important skills for the researcher include listening, observing, and forming an empathic alliance with the subject. The investigator remains watchful of themes that are presented but resists any temptation to structure or analyze the meanings of an observation prematurely. Once the basic observations are recorded the data may be reduced, reconstructed, and analyzed as a public document.

Moustakas (1994) distinguishes between two main trends in phenomenological research. One has been called "empirical" phenomenological research and is represented by a tradition of studies from Duquesne University starting with van Kaam's (1966) study of "feeling understood." Giorgi's (1985) ongoing work is illustrative: The researcher collects naïve descriptions of a phenomenon from open-ended questions and dialogue with a participant and then uses reflective analysis and interpretation of the participant's story to describe the structure of the experience. Moustakas's (1994) own version of phenomenological inquiry is called "heuristic research," meaning "to discover" or "to find." The process begins with a question or a problem which the researcher seeks to illuminate or answer which is personally meaningful in terms of understanding the relationship between oneself and world and has social significance. Moustakas's (1994) early study of loneliness serves as an example. According to Moustakas, heuristic research has a somewhat different flavor from the Duquesne approach:

Table 3.3

Qualitative Research Traditions

Phenomenology

Problems and concerns of the researcher: Concerned with describing the lived experience of the person as free as possible from theoretical or social constructs. Concerned with accessing the meaning of human phenomena as expressed through the individual.

Nature of knowledge: Interested not in "What causes X?" but in "What *is* X?" Interested in the essential features of experience or consciousness.

Relationship between researcher and subject matter: Researcher is co-creator of the narrative, generated typically through interviewing.

Hermeneutics

Problems and concerns: Concerned with deriving a rich understanding of the context for data, the setting out of which it arises and that gives it meaning.

Nature of knowledge: An openly dialogic process of returning again and again to the object of the inquiry (the text), each time with an increased understanding and a more complete interpretation.

Relationship between researcher and subject matter: Researchers are very involved in the explanatory process, which intrudes into the context of the data.

Ethnographic Inquiry

Problems and concerns: Concerned with capturing, interpreting, and explaining the way in which people in a group, organization, community, or society live, experience, and make sense out of their lives, their world, and their society or group.

Nature of knowledge: May use description, interpretation, and explanation and be inductive (descriptive and interpretive) or deductive (working from theory).

Relationship between researcher and subject matter: The researcher must have maximal detachment while also being immersed in the subject matter and living it. Takes nothing for granted.

Note. This table is adapted from the *Inquiry and Research Knowledge Area Study Guide of the Human and Organization Development Program of The Fielding Institute* (HOD, 1998).

The process maintains closer contact with the individual stories of the participants than does structural analysis. At the same time, it is broader in scope than a single situation in the life of a participant and may go beyond narrative description to include stories, self-dialogues, journals, diaries, and artwork as sources of data (Moustakas, 1994).

Several of our doctoral students have developed dissertations based on phenomenologically oriented qualitative interviews. In one study, a student interviewed families shortly after a reunion with an adult member who had been released from prison (Wardell, 1985). The object of the interviews was to get as close as possible to the experience of the transition between prison and family life. In another study a doctoral student interviewed married couples to understand how they attempt to negotiate intimacy and autonomy in their relationships (Sherman, 1998). A third student sought to learn about identity formation in gay and lesbian adolescents by interviewing young women who self-identified as homosexual (Nicholas, 1995).

HERMENEUTICS

Hermeneutics has been described as the interpretation of texts or transcribed meanings (Polkinghorne, 1983). One engages in a hermeneutic approach to data in order to derive a better understanding of the context that gives it meaning. Hermeneutics, as a specialized field of study, was pioneered by biblical scholars who used textual analysis and interpretation to elicit the meaning of religious text. More recently, researchers in the social sciences have extended the application of hermeneutics to the interpretation of secular texts.

Apparently there is ongoing debate within the field of hermeneutics between the "objectivists," who consider the text to contain meaning independent of the interpreter, and others who view active interpretation as primary to all understanding, a position quite similar to modern constructivist thinking in the philosophy of science (Winograd & Flores, 1986). From this latter orientation, understanding is the fusion of the perspective of the phenomenon and the perspective of the interpreter. All of us bring life experiences and expectations to the task of interpretation, but because even our understanding of ourselves is limited and only partially expressible, interaction with the meaning of the text can help produce a deeper understanding of both the observer and the observed. As Mahoney (1990) puts it, "New or changed meanings arise from the active encounter of the text and its reader" (p. 93).

Texts from ancient cultures, for instance, may be analyzed in their historical context with the notion of applying their meanings to current issues. This understanding, which must show the meaning of a phenomenon in a way that is both comprehensible to the research consumer and loyal to the frame of reference of the subject, may then lead to more formal research questions. This is a bit different from the task of phenomenological inquiry. In hermeneutics, the data are given to the researcher, whereas in a standard phenomenological study the researcher helps to create the transcribed narrative that has usually been obtained by interviewing the participant-subject(s) (Hoshmand, 1989).

The hermeneutic approach to research is quite complex. It demands frequent return to the source of data, setting up a dialogue with it, so to speak, asking what it means to its creator and trying to integrate that with its meaning to the researcher (HOD, 1998). Consequently, although we are all hermeneutically inclined whenever we seek to learn the contexts of things, ideas, and feelings, hermeneutic inquiry is relatively rare as a formal approach to research in the social sciences. Ambitious, well-known examples of the hermeneutic method are psychodynamically guided biographies, such as Erik Erikson's *Young Man Luther*, and the work of Carl Jung, who used an archetypal, mythic perspective to describe contemporary problems.

A different kind of hermeneutic inquiry is represented by Martin Packer's (1985) interpretive study, using video recordings, of moral conflicts between young adults. From Packer's perspective, the hermeneutic approach is applicable to the study of all human action, where the action is treated as though it has a "textual" structure. The investigator studies what people do when they are engaged in everyday, practical activities. What sets hermeneutics apart from more empirical or rational orientations is the belief that a particular activity can be understood only in conjunction with understanding the context in which it occurs rather than as an abstraction or a set of causal relationships. As Packer puts it, "The difference between a rationalist or empiricist explanation and a hermeneutic interpretation is a little like the difference between a map of a city and an account of that city by someone who lives in it and walks its streets" (1985, p. 1091). The mapmaker's product is formal and abstract; the inhabitant's map is personal and biased. At the dissertation level, the hermeneutic approach is exemplified by Elliott's (1997) study of five Renewal of Canada conferences, in which the materials that were studied included videotapes, formal and informal papers and reports, press releases, and media coverage of the conference workshops and meetings. The outcome is an understanding of the conditions that contribute to or hinder the quality of the communicative interaction in a discursive attempt to bridge differences.

ETHNOGRAPHIC INQUIRY

The naturalistic-ethnographic paradigm includes anthropological descriptions, naturalistic research, field research, and participant observations (Hoshmand, 1989). Ethnographers attempt to capture and understand specific aspects of the life of a particular group by observing patterns of behavior, customs, and lifestyles. The focus is on obtaining full and detailed descriptions from informants.

Ethnographic inquiry can be found on a continuum ranging from relatively pure description to more theoretically guided explanations of cultural, social, and organizational life (HOD, 1998). On the more inductive end of the continuum, the researcher develops theory out of the descriptive and interpretive process; on the deductive end of the continuum, the researcher builds a study out of an established theoretical framework.

Typically, the ethnographer initiates prolonged contact and immersion in a setting of interest, while at the same time maintaining as much detachment as possible from the subject matter. The naturalistic setting could be the mental hospital explored in the work of Erving Goffman (1961) or the street corner populated by unemployed Black men (Liebow, 1967). A more traditional anthropological example would be a study of health practices among Native Americans living on a reservation or the early immersion in non-Western cultures by Mead, Malinowski, or Boas. The investigator might obtain some preliminary understanding of the history of the culture by referring to archival records and artifacts in preparation for living among the informants for several months. During that time the researcher would keep field notes of all observations and interactions and perhaps follow up the observations with intensive, qualitative interviews. The data are recorded verbatim, if possible, using the language of the participant.

Obviously, the data that emerge from this research strategy must be reduced in some way to be meaningfully communicated in a dissertation. One method for analyzing such data is called the *constant comparative method*. Data are systematically coded into as many themes and meaning categories as possible. As the categories emerge and are refined, the researcher begins to consider how they relate to one another and what the theoretical implications are. Gradually the theoretical properties of the meaning categories crystallize and form a pattern. The pattern that emerges is sometimes called "grounded theory" (Glaser & Strauss, 1967; Strauss & Corbin, 1998). The constant comparative method can be seen in many qualitative studies in the social sciences, including research on the client experience of psychotherapy (Rennie, Phillips, & Quartaro, 1988) and in a study by one of our students on the yearning of older women to have a child (Rasche, 1991).

DISSERTATION IMPLICATIONS OF QUALITATIVE RESEARCH

The distinctiveness of qualitative research has implications for the write-up of the research proposal and dissertation. Qualitative research designs typically are not intended to prove or test a theory, and it is more likely that the theory will emerge once the data are collected (an inductive approach rather than a traditional deductive approach). This does not mean, however, that the researcher can ignore the theoretical perspectives of previous work cited in the literature review. We are in general agreement with Miles and Huberman (1994), who take a moderate position on the role of theory in naturalistic studies. They view a conceptual framework as the "current version of the researcher's map of the territory being investigated" (1994, p. 20). This means that the framework may change as the study evolves. The amount of prestructuring will depend upon what is known from the literature about the phenomenon being studied, the measures or instruments that are available, and the time allotted for the study. Very loose designs imply the collection of great amounts of data that may initially look important but turn out to be tangential or irrelevant, along with great amounts of time to sift through these data. At the very least, a conceptual framework allows different investigators who are exploring a sim-

ilar phenomenon to communicate with one another and compare experiences and results.

Adopting a tentative conceptual framework allows the researcher
to focus and bound the study with regard to who and what will and
will not be studied. Miles and Huberman (1994) choose to express their
conceptual frameworks in terms of graphic "bins" that consist of labels
for (a) events, (b) settings, (c) processes, and (d) theoretical constructs.
They reason that the researcher will come to the study with some ideas
about the content of these bins. For instance, a qualitative study on
prison behavior could reflect working decisions focusing on current
behavior rather than prior history (events), high-security prisons (settings), interactions among prisoners and between prisoners and guards
(processes), and authority relations and organizational norms (theoretical constructs). These choices and distinctions are, of course, informed
by the theoretical and empirical literature.

Research questions can then be formulated as a way of explicating
any theoretical assumptions and orienting the investigator (and the
student's committee) to the primary goals and tasks of the study. One
cannot study every aspect of prison life—the issues adopted by the
researcher and expressed as research questions have direct implications for the choice of methodology. A focus such as "how prisoners
and guards negotiate conflict and express power in relationships" has
implications for the behavioral events that will be sampled and the
research tools that will be used to obtain information (e.g., field notes,
interview transcripts, diaries, prison documents, etc.). Research questions in qualitative research can be revised or reformulated as the study
proceeds.

Students selecting a qualitative design need to convince their committees that they understand the role of the qualitative researcher. This
includes experience with the sensitive kind of interviewing found in
naturalistic studies, whereby the investigator enters the world of the
participant subject without a fixed agenda and maintains sufficient scientific rigor in the process. Because the researcher is regarded as a person who comes to the scene with his or her own operative reality, rather
than as a totally detached scientific observer, it becomes vital to understand, acknowledge, and share one's own underlying values, assumptions, and expectations. This perspective should become clear in the
Review of the Literature and Method chapters of the dissertation.
Moreover, researcher subjectivity can be reduced by a variety of data-

handling procedures. Will there be audio- or videotaping to augment written field notes? How will these materials be reduced in scope? Will process notes be included that describe the researcher's reactions at various points of the study? Will pilot studies be used to test the suitability of procedures? Specification of these ingredients can be convincing documentation of the rigor of the proposed study without compromising the necessary "open contract" of the proposal.

Because qualitative data may consist of detailed descriptions of events, situations, and behaviors, as well as direct quotations from people about their experiences and beliefs, the "Results" chapter of the dissertation will be directly influenced as well. We have found that students often have the mistaken belief that a qualitative study might be easier to conduct because there are no specific hypotheses and no statistical tests to perform. However, the sifting and resifting of huge amounts of transcripts or open-ended responses into a coherent pattern generally takes as much effort and leads to as much frustration as the statistics that were being avoided. Good research is always taxing in some way.

OTHER POSSIBLE APPROACHES TO DISSERTATIONS

MIXED MODEL: QUANTITATIVE AND QUALITATIVE STUDY

In our experience, a combination of quantitative and qualitative methodologies is often a good choice of method. This approach combines the rigor and precision of experimental (or quasi-experimental) designs and quantitative data with the depth understanding of qualitative methods and data. There are many ways of mixing models. One is to use both quantitative and qualitative methods and data to study the same phenomenon within the same study or complementary studies. Creswell (1995) notes four mixed-method designs: (a) sequential studies, in which the researcher begins with generating quantitative data and then gathers qualitative data (or vice versa) in two distinct phases; (b) parallel/simultaneous studies, where the quantitative and qualitative phases occur simultaneously; (c) equivalent status designs, where both quantitative and qualitative approaches are used with more or less equal emphasis in order to understand the phenomenon being studied; and (d) dominant less dominant studies, where either the quantitative or qualitative approach provides the dominant paradigm and the other approach is a small, supplementary component of the study. A recent text by Tashakkori and Teddlie (1998) enumerates several possible designs, including "mixed methodology studies," that combine aspects of both paradigms throughout the study. Theirs is a pragmatic approach in which questions of method are secondary to the adoption of an overriding paradigm or worldview guiding the investigation. Thus, it might be possible to mix research hypotheses of a confirmatory nature with general questions of an exploratory nature, structured interviews and scales that are quantitative with open-ended interviews and observations that are qualitative, and methods of analysis that draw upon both traditions to expand the meaningfulness of the findings. An example of an innovative mixed methodology was employed by Mary Gergen (1988) to study the way in which women think about menopause. Gergen held a "research event" at her home and invited several women there to complete questionnaires that addressed attitudes toward menopause, followed by a group discussion on the topic. The research report combines a quantitative analysis of the responses to the questionnaire with a qualitative analysis of themes generated by the discussion. An example from another field would be an analysis of the effect of timber dislocation on a logging community by quantitatively assessing the economic impact and qualitatively assessing the emotional impact on families in the community.

Perhaps the most common application of the mixed methodology is to assess a large number of participants using standardized scales and measures in a field study or an experimental study and then conduct open-ended interviews with a subset of the original sample to derive a richer understanding of the phenomenon in question. We find that an increasing number of students are electing this approach to dissertation projects in spite of the increased task demands of such studies. A good example is a study by one of our doctoral students who sought to understand what makes extreme, high-risk athletes engage in what laypersons view as self-destructive behavior (Slanger, 1991). The resulting dissertation combined the objectivity of validated measures of sensation-seeking and perceived competence with open-ended interviews conducted with a random subsample of the total group.

A major reluctance to adopt the mixed model approach comes from scholars with strong epistemological commitments to either quantitative or qualitative research because they view the underlying assumptions of the approaches as fundamentally incompatible. At the risk of oversimplification, quantitative studies generally rest upon an "objectivist" epistemological tradition that seeks to validate knowledge by matching the knowledge claims of the researcher with phenomena in the real world (the "correspondence theory of truth"). In this tradition, theories are proposed as universal hypotheses to be tested empirically. Qualitative studies, on the other hand, may derive from the "constructivist" tradition associated with the postmodern movement. Here knowledge is not discovered but invented, situated within a specific context heavily determined by local practices, and validated through internal consistency and social consensus (the "coherence theory of truth") (Neimeyer, 1993). In practice this means that the researcher maintains an open curiosity about a phenomenon and the theory emerges from the data; there is no one true reality on which to validate our theories deductively.

Our own position is that both quantitative and qualitative studies can be approached from a myriad of philosophical perspectives. In the purest sense, statistics is merely a shorthand for communicating information about complex phenomena elegantly and precisely. We encourage students to think clearly about a research topic and then apply the methods that make the most sense in answering the questions of interest and that are consistent with the values of the researcher.

THEORETICAL DISSERTATIONS

Another possible approach to writing a dissertation is to write a *theoretical dissertation* and bypass the need for data collection entirely. This is by no means an easy alternative. Original theoretical contributions are a profound intellectual challenge. One way of describing the difference between a knowledge of the literature required for a standard quantitative or qualitative study and that required for a theoretical study is by referring to the difference between being a native of a foreign country and a tourist in that country. As a tourist in a foreign environment, it might be necessary to learn as much as possible about the country by studying maps, reviewing the customs, and learning the language, but chances are you will never master the country as well as the native speaker. It's the same with research. If you know an area of inquiry inside out and are intimately familiar with the issues and controversies in the field, you have the chance to contribute a new theory; if you are beginning to review an area of interest to formulate a study, you are probably better off with an empirical study. Of course, most doctoral dissertations have theoretical implications, and the data you gather and analyze may create the opening for a brand new way of thinking in the field. That, however, is quite different from starting with the expectation of creating a new theory of consciousness or, a bit more modestly, a revised theory of short-term memory.

If you do choose to pursue a theoretical dissertation, you will be expected to argue from the literature that there is a different way of understanding a phenomenon than has heretofore been presented. Some of the more viable theoretical dissertations in the social sciences are those that bring together or integrate two previously distinct areas. For instance, one of our graduate students was of the opinion that there is a significant breach between the theory of psychotherapy and the practice of psychotherapy, which led to an ambitious, high-quality theoretical dissertation on the relevance of personal theory in psychotherapy (Glover, 1994). Another student created an eloquent theory of "belonging" out of the constructs of self, home, and homelessness (Volkman, 1991). Finally, Demoville (1999) used computer simulation software to create a systems dynamics model of organizational performance. The data that served as the input for the model came from organizational case studies and the social science literature. The model showed the interrelationships among key organizational components under both stable and chaotic environmental conditions. A panel of expert organizational leaders and consultants then helped validate the model by providing feedback on its performance.

META-ANALYSIS

Meta-analysis is a form of secondary analysis of preexisting data that aims to summarize and compare results from different studies on the same topic. Meta-analyses have become increasingly common in the social science literature because they pool the individual studies of an entire research community, thus providing the reader with a much richer understanding of the status of a phenomenon than any single study can offer.

The term "meta-analysis" has been attributed to Glass (1976) as an "analysis of analyses." A more complete description of the various meta-analytic methods is available in Newton and Rudestam (1999). Basically, existent studies are screened for their methodological rigor and those that measure up, so to speak, are included in the analysis. Then statistical techniques are used to convert the findings of all the studies to a common metric. Finally, the summary analysis yields information about the strength of relationships among variables (the "effect size") across studies, using the newly expanded large sample.

All dissertations, of course, involve a critical review of the literature on the topic in question. In a meta-analysis it is this review of the literature, including a finally tuned statistical analysis, that constitutes the study. In our opinion there is no reason why a carefully conducted meta-analysis could not serve as a suitable dissertation.

ACTION RESEARCH

Action research provides another possible approach to completing a doctoral dissertation, although it may be too prodigious a challenge for most graduate students. *Action research* has been defined as "a form of research that generates knowledge claims for the express purpose of taking action to promote social change and social analysis (Greenwood & Levin, 1998, p. 6). The authors go on to say that action research is quite distinct from theoretical research carried out as a purely academic exercise. It is research that (a) involves broad participation in the research process and (b) generates action leading to significant social change for the stakeholders.

Most action researchers acknowledge the seminal contributions of Kurt Lewin (1948) and his commitment to social change. Action research can be either quantitative or qualitative in nature, drawing upon such diverse techniques as surveys, interviews, focus groups, ethnographies, life histories, and statistics. In the early days of action research the researcher tried to initiate change in a particular direction; more recently the goals and targets of change are determined by the group members themselves through participatory problem solving. Members of an organization or community that constitutes the focus of the research become co-researchers in the process. Thus, the researcher is a facilitator who needs to possess good group process skills in order to effectively mobilize a group of participants to study their own behavior, including their defensive reactions to change. A good action research project seeks to understand the context or frame into which a problem situation can be placed. This is the theory-building aspect of action research. It is particularly evident in "action science," which is a significant avenue of development in action research promulgated by Chris Argyris and his colleagues (Argyris, Putnam, & Smith, 1985), wherein the focus is to solve an immediate problem and to contribute to scientific knowledge and a theory of action.

The typical steps in action research can be listed as follows (HOD, 1998):

1. Identify a problem area.

2. Form hypotheses or predictions that imply a goal and a procedure for achieving it.

3. Carefully record the actions taken and desired goal.

4. Form inferences based on the data relating the actions taken to the extent of achieving the desired goal.

5. Continue retesting the generalizations in the situation in an ongoing iterative process.

These steps can be configured into an action research cycle (Susman & Evered, 1978) consisting of five phases: analysis, action planning, implementation, evaluation, and learning. New questions emerge from the learning phase, which leads to a new cycle of research as part of a continuous learning process. This action research cycle was used by a student in her dissertation to explore a community college's use of collaborative organizational learning in its planning and decision-making processes (Witt, 1997). The student worked as a co-researcher with members of the college administration, faculty, and staff. Each member of the team brought specific skills to the project. The dissertation student, of course, provided her expertise in action research. The team analyzed archival data, as well as data from meetings, journals, interviews, and participant observation field notes, to evaluate the effectiveness of the institution's learning processes.

In summary, positivism maintained that there was a single method, that of the natural sciences, that was valid everywhere. Today postmodern critics are circling like vultures to pick over the spoils of positivism (Smith, 1991). Yet the natural sciences are still very much alive, and their commitment to empirical observation and scientific rigor continues to be dominant in social science research. Whereas some critics maintain that the humanities, with their focus on the interpretation of meaning and values, will ultimately serve to provide a superior ideological alternative, that is far from clear. What is clear is the need to begin the research enterprise by asking an essential question and then asking what you must do to convince yourself and others of the validity of the ideas supporting it (Bevan, 1991). Along the journey, be wary of rigid methodological rules and draw on any method with a clear understanding of its advantages, its limitations, and whether it compromises assumptions about the phenomena you are researching.

NOTE

1. An exception is the use of single-subject or $N = 1$ research designs. This is different from the case study approach favored by many qualitative researchers. It is an empirical, quantitative approach associated with specific statistical procedures (see Hersen & Barber, 1992; Kratochwill & Levin, 1992). Single-subject quantitative studies can be used to assess changes in a phenomenon over time through the use of repeated measures or to assess the impact of a particular treatment by removing or "reversing" the intervention and evaluating differences in the dependent variable. Single-subject research strategies are especially appropriate in developing or refining novel interventions and in closely examining the behavior of individual subjects.

PART II

Working With Content: The Dissertation Chapters

CHAPTER 4

Review of the Literature and Statement of the Problem

The previous chapters provided an orientation to research in the social sciences and offered suggestions on how to develop an appropriate topic. In this chapter, the research question begins to take shape using the vehicle of the review of the literature. A subsequent chapter (Chapter 10) can also be consulted for suggestions on using a personal computer to compile a literature review.

THE INTRODUCTION

The Review of the Literature is generally preceded by a brief introductory chapter. The Introduction consists of an overview of the research problem and some indication of why the problem is worth exploring or what contribution the proposed study is apt to make to theory and/or practice. The Introduction is usually a few pages in length. Although it may begin by offering a broad context for the study, it quickly comes to the point with a narrowly focused definition of the problem. The form of the Introduction is the same for both the research proposal and the dissertation itself, although there are likely to be some changes made to the understanding of the research problem after the study has been completed. Ironically, it is usually impossible to write a final Introduction chapter prior to completing the Review of the Literature and Method chapters, because those chapters will inform the problem and its operationalization.

The wording of the research problem should be sufficiently explicit to orient the most inattentive reader. There is nothing wrong with beginning the chapter with a sentence such as "In this study I attempted to evaluate the impact of environmental protection legislation on atmospheric pollutants in the chemical industry." The chapter would proceed to stipulate the assumptions and hypotheses of the study, identify the key variables, and explain the procedures used to explore the questions. It should include a synopsis of the arguments that explain the rationale for the research question and the study. It is perfectly acceptable to cite one or more studies that are directly relevant to the proposed investigation and may have inspired it or lent it empirical or theoretical justification. But this is not the place to conduct a literature review. Avoid technical details and keep the Introduction short.

REVIEW OF THE LITERATURE

Often the lengthiest section of the research proposal, the Review of the Literature is placed just after the introductory overview of the study. This chapter of the dissertation provides a context for the proposed study and demonstrates why it is important and timely. Thus, this chapter needs to clarify the relationship between the proposed study and previous work conducted on the topic. The reader will need to be convinced not only that the proposed study is distinctive and different from previous research but also that it is worthwhile doing. This is also the place where the student's critical abilities as a scholar become evident. Many students erroneously believe that the purpose of the literature review is to convince the reader that the writer is knowledgeable about the work of others. Based on this misunderstanding, the literature review may read like a laundry list of previous studies, with sentences or paragraphs beginning with the words "Smith found. . . . ,"

"Jones concluded. . . ," "Anderson stated. . . . ," and so on. This not only is poor writing but also misses the whole point of an effective review of the literature.

A colleague of ours, Jeremy Shapiro, has noted that much of the labor that goes into writing is often wasted effort because it is not based on a clear understanding of the purpose of an essay or thesis (Shapiro & Nicholsen, 1986). As a general rule, if you have difficulties in your basic writing skills—that is, in constructing grammatical sentences, using appropriate transitions, and staying focused and concise—a research dissertation will glaringly reveal these weaknesses, and the logic and persuasiveness of your arguments will be diminished. One suggestion is to obtain remedial help in strengthening basic writing skills. Furthermore, the style of writing that is appropriate to research papers is somewhat different from the style of writing associated with literary prose. Scientific writing tends to be more direct and to the point, and less flowery and evocative. Effective writing is an acquired skill that is taken up as a separate topic in Chapter 9.

A good way to formulate a question that is appropriate to a research study is to determine what bothers you (Shapiro & Nicholsen, 1986). As you consider one or more possible questions and draw upon the observations and ideas of others who are interested in the same and related questions, you are in fact formulating the argument. The forum for the argument is the literature review, which is played out in the form of a dialogue between you and the reader. In order to dialogue effectively, the writer must anticipate the kinds of questions and apprehensions that the reader might have in critically examining your argument. It is common for critical evaluations of academic papers to be peppered with comments such as "What is your point here?" "What makes you think so?" "What is your evidence?" and "So what?" The more you can anticipate a reader's questions, the easier it will be to formulate your arguments in a way that produces mutual understanding. Dissertations go through many drafts, and the revision process consists of asking and responding to these questions from the point of view of a circumspect and knowledgeable reader.

The literature review is not a compilation of facts and feelings but a coherent argument that leads to the description of a proposed study. There should be no mystery about the direction in which you are going. ("Where are you going with this?" is a good question to ask yourself repeatedly in a review of the literature.) You always need to state explicitly, at the outset, the goal of the paper and the structure of the evolving argument. By the end of the literature review, the reader should be able to conclude that "Yes, of course, this is the exact study that needs to be done at this time to move knowledge in this field a little further along." The review attempts to convince the reader of the legitimacy of your assertions by providing sufficient logical and empirical support along the way. You will continually need to decide what assertions it is reasonable to assume the reader accepts as common understanding and what assertions require data as support. For instance, if you were to assert that survivors of suicide need professional help, a peer reader probably would want to know on what basis you are making that assertion and request some evidence about the needs of survivors of suicide and why professionals (as opposed to nonprofessionals, for instance) are necessary. On the other hand, the claim that "Freud was the father of psychoanalysis" is likely to be well established as a fact within the professional psychological community and thus not require further backing.

Becker (1986) reminds us that there is no need to reinvent the wheel and that it is perfectly permissible to draw upon the thoughtful arguments of others and incorporate them into your own research project. This is very much in keeping with our understanding of the incremental, cumulative process that characterizes the development of normal science (Kuhn, 1962).[1] On the other hand, a skillful researcher draws upon original source material rather than relying upon review articles and secondary sources. Becker uses the image of a jigsaw puzzle, in which some of the pieces have been designed by you while others are borrowed in their prefabricated form from the contributions of other scholars. In addition, it is worth noting that becoming overly preoccupied with the literature can deform your argument so that you lose your privileged place at the center of the study. In any case, do not neglect to give proper credit to the source of ideas by citing complete references in your writing.

COMMON PROBLEMS

A principal failing of novice researchers at every stage of a project, and especially evident in the Review of the Literature, is giving away their own power and authority. As a researcher, you need to accept that you are in charge of this study and that, in the case of dissertations, it is likely that ultimately you will be the world's leading expert on the narrow topic you have selected to address. One way of giving away authority is to defer to the authority of others in the review, assuming, for instance, that because Émile Durkheim or John Dewey said something, it is necessarily valid. You need to adopt a critical perspective in reading and relating the work of others. The main reason why sentences beginning with "Jones found . . ." are best kept to a minimum is that they shift the focus of the review from your own argument to the work of others. A preferable strategy is to develop a theme and then cite the work of relevant authors to buttress the argument you are making or to provide noteworthy examples of your point or counterexamples that need to be considered.

Another way of limiting your own authority is by using quotations in excess. The overuse of quotations tends to deflect the argument away from the control of the author. Restrict the use of quotations to those with particular impact or those that are stated in a unique way that is difficult to recapture. Besides, using your own words to present difficult concepts will help convince you (and others) that you really understand the material.

Once you have read the literature in an area, it may be tempting to report everything you now know. Avoid this temptation! A good literature review needs to be selective, and it is taken for granted that the majority of source material you have read will not make it directly into the literature review. That does not mean that it wasn't necessary to read all those books and articles; they provide the expertise required to make your contribution. But remember, in the dissertation itself your task is to build an argument, not a library. One of our colleagues likens the process to a courtroom trial, where all admissible testimony by the witnesses must be relevant to the case and question at hand. Consistently ask yourself, "Why am I including this study or reference?" Similarly, each sentence in the dissertation needs to be there for a purpose, sometimes to provide relevant content and sometimes to facilitate communication to the reader, but never as filler.

The relevant studies need to be critiqued rather than reported. The critique serves to inform the reader about the status of reliable knowledge in the field and to identify errors to avoid in future research. Although the primary task is to build an argument and you are expected to present your own point of view, it is not fair to exclude references that contradict or question your case. You must be objective enough to present both sides of an argument and acknowledge where the weight of the evidence falls. Throughout the review, leave enough signposts along the way to help orient the reader. One way to do this is to inform the reader of what you have done and what conclusions you have drawn on the basis of the available evidence. You also need to convince the reader that your knowledge of the existing literature is extensive and intensive enough to justify your proposed study.

CRITIQUING A RESEARCH ARTICLE

As you read the available research in an area, you need to maintain a critical perspective, evaluating the study on its own merits and in comparison with other studies on the same or a similar problem. A critique does not imply that you must discover and identify a major flaw or weakness in every study you read. You are evaluating the content for its application to your research. The following outline consists of a rather comprehensive set of recommendations for critiquing a research article. Not all these items will be included in any given citation within the literature review. The amount of attention a study receives will depend on its direct relevance to the proposed research question and should not detract from the flow of the argument. Nevertheless, this list can act as a reminder for how to read and evaluate critically a research article's contribution to a proposed study:

1. Conceptualization
   a. What is the major problem or issue being investigated?
   b. How clearly are the major concepts defined/explained?

2. Theoretical Framework and Hypotheses
   a. Is there a clearly stated research question?
   b. Are there hypotheses? Are they clearly stated?
   c. Are the relationships among the main variables explicit and reasonable?
   d. Are the hypotheses stated in a way that makes them testable and the results, no matter what, interpretable?

3. Research Design
   a. What is the type of research design?

b.   Does the research design adequately control for extraneous variables?

c.   Could the design be improved? How?

d.   Are the variables clearly and reasonably operationalized? Is the choice of categories or cutting points defensible?

e.   Are the reliability and validity of the measures discussed? Is the choice of measures appropriate?

f.   Is the population appropriate for the research question being studied? Is the sample specified and appropriate? Can the results reasonably be generalized on the basis of this sample, and to what population?

4.   Results and Discussion
   a.   Are the data appropriate for the study?
   b.   Are the statistical techniques appropriate and adequately described?
   c.   Are the control variables adequately handled in the data analysis? Are there other control variables that were not considered but should have been?
   d.   Are the conclusions of the study consistent with the results of the statistical analyses?
   e.   Are alternative conclusions that are consistent with the data discussed and accounted for?
   f.   Are the theoretical and practical implications of the results adequately discussed?
   g.   Are the limitations of the study noted?

5.   Summary
   a.   What is your overall assessment of the adequacy of the study for exploring the research problem?
   b.   What is your overall assessment of the contribution of the study to this area of research?

LONG SHOTS AND CLOSE-UPS

Our colleague Joseph Handlon has drawn an analogy between doing a literature review and making a movie. In filmmaking there are "long shots," "medium shots," and "close-ups," which refer to the relative distance between the camera and the subject matter. As a metaphor, a long shot suggests that the material is background for a particular topic. Background material needs to be acknowledged but not treated with the same detail as foreground material; it is not figural. A study on the stressful impact of relocation, for instance, might begin with the following observation:

> There have been three basic ways of approaching the topic of stress empirically. One is by regarding stress as an independent variable and focusing on the nature and strength of the stressor, exemplified in the empirical contributions of Holmes and Rahe (1967). A second approach is to view stress as a dependent variable, focusing on the physiological and psychological impact of stressful events, illustrated by the seminal work of Hans Selye (1956). An alternative approach is to view stress as a transaction between a stimulus and a response, which is moderated by a set of cognitive variables. This approach, elaborated in the work of Lazarus and his colleagues (Lazarus & Folkman, 1984), forms the conceptual foundation for this study.

In this way, considerable literature can be referenced without attending to details or critical evaluations of each study.

The medium shot is somewhere between the long and the short focus and requires a bit more descriptive material. As an example, let us assume that a researcher wishes to explore the effect of social protest and threats of violence on the well-being of workers in abortion clinics. It would be appropriate to obtain a good overview of the impact of potentially violent social protest in other contexts as well as a good understanding of the emotional demands of working in a clinic serving women with unwanted pregnancies. Studies that bear on these relevant issues may not need to be presented in critical detail, but they certainly need to be summarized sufficiently to give the reader a clear indication of the status of the research as it pertains to the orientation of the proposed study.

Finally, the close-up requires a careful examination of the research and is reserved for those studies that have the most direct relevance to the proposed research question. In some cases, this might refer to one or two studies that are being modified or amended in some critical way to form the basis for the current study. More frequently, it refers to a collection of work on a relatively narrow topic that is clearly central to the proposal. These studies are not merely referenced but critically examined, so that the reader obtains a clear sense of what is already known about the phenomenon, how reliable and valid the conclusions based on that work are apt to be, and how the proposed study will deal with previous limitations and move the field ahead. The researcher who is interested in exploring the impact of infertility treatments on communication between husbands and wives might present the following close-up statement after having carefully described the samples, measures, and procedures of the two most relevant (fictitious) studies in that literature.

> Of the two studies that bear directly on the proposed question, Sterile (1998) found that couples reported improved communication after experiencing prolonged infertility treatment, while Ripe and Fertile (1999) concluded that behavioral exchanges between infertile couples more frequently escalated into arguments the longer that medical interventions continued. Of particular concern in Sterile's study is the fact that because men and women were interviewed together, the couples may not have been totally honest and responses by one member of a couple may have been prejudiced by those of the other member. Beyond this threat to validity, the conflicting findings of the two studies suggests the need for a more definitive investigation of the impact of infertility treatment on communication patterns within couples.

A good strategy for reviewing the literature can be found by referring to a Venn diagram (see Figure 4.1) of three intersecting circles, which is derived from the previously discussed exercise on formulating research questions. The long shots, or those through wide-angle lenses, are represented by the portions of the three primary variables that are independent of the other two variables. The medium shot is illustrated by the intersections of any two variables. The close-up, or shot through a narrow-angle lens, refers to the joint intersection of all three variables. As a general rule, any studies in the existing literature that incorporate all the major variables or constructs that are present in the proposed study will require very careful scrutiny because they are particularly relevant. Studies that relate some of the variables (e.g., two) also deserve a short description. Studies that deal with only one of the selected variables, perhaps in conjunction with other, less relevant variables, are merely background. They are generally too numerous to

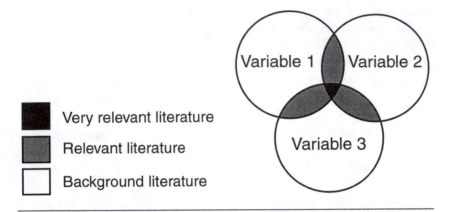

Figure 4.1.   Venn diagram guide to the literature review.

examine in detail and include a great deal of content that does not pertain to the current study. Certainly, one need not review all studies dealing with sexual dysfunctions, for instance, in order to focus on male impotence in midlife. Nor will one need to consider all previous work on men or midlife. Yet gender issues and midlife development issues may provide important background material and a theoretical foundation for the proposed study. Moreover, the researcher will not have to introduce every study on impotence but will probably need to be familiar with a broad range of previous work in the area.

STATEMENT OF THE PROBLEM

At the conclusion of the literature review, the reader should have obtained a fairly clear idea of the study. By this time you will have carefully crafted your argument and moved the reader along as you build your case. You will have convinced your reader of your mastery of the subject matter by having reviewed and critiqued the existent literature that pertains to your study and gives it a suitable context. The next immediate challenge is to form a transition between the literature review and the next section of the dissertation, the Statement of the Problem. One way to build this transition, so that the literature review chapter appears connected to the proposed study, is to write a summary of the review you have conducted. This summary would highlight your main conclusions, including reference to the most relevant literature (which you have previously reviewed), and leave the reader anticipating the next steps.

The Statement of the Problem is sometimes written as a separate chapter and sometimes located at the very end of the Review of the Literature. Although you probably have offered a general statement of the problem early in the introductory chapter of the dissertation, this is the place for a more specific statement. The specificity of the problem statement is very important. A research problem consists of much more (and less) than a misunderstood collection of unidentified relationships. The statement is usually framed in the form of one or more research questions and research hypotheses. Although we recommend the inclusion of formal hypotheses as a general standard, whether or not to include them may depend on the type of study, what is known about the question, and the conventions of your discipline and department. Similarly, the statement of the problem may contain conceptual definitions of major concepts. This is particularly true when competing definitions of the concepts exist within the field of inquiry (e.g., it might be important to point out that the study will focus on trait anxiety as opposed to state anxiety or other conceptualizations of the construct of anxiety).

It is critical that a research question have an explanatory basis. This means that the statement of the problem contains a brief summary of the conceptual underpinnings for the proposed research. *Dust bowl empiricism* is the derogatory term used to refer to a shotgun approach to research, in which the investigator levels his or her sights to see what is out there without developing a convincing chain of presuppositions and arguments that lead to a prediction. There is no research problem in "wondering" how the variables of gender, voice quality, and persuasion intercorrelate, so this will not pass for a suitable problem statement. Hypotheses have the virtue of being explanatory expressions of research questions because they imply a commitment to a particular understanding of how variables relate.

An example of a research question without a specific hypothesis is "What is the role of male significant others on the criminal activities of female criminals?" This research question implies a study that obtains information from or about women who have been convicted of crimes regarding the influence of boyfriends and male acquaintances in their criminal activities. A study that poses this question without predictive hypotheses (perhaps because of a lack of available information about this topic) might be termed "exploratory."

In most instances it is possible to project hypotheses, even in those instances where there is a relative lack of research in an area; it is likely that studies and theories exist on related topics that can inform the proposed study. In the above example, the investigator may have developed some reasonable hunches about the research question from her knowledge of women's developmental theory and the role of the peer group in criminal behavior. These hunches would be reflected in one or more hypotheses. An example of a research hypothesis is "There is a negative relationship between positive body image and motivation for augmentation mammoplasty." A second example is "Couples in stable, unhappy marriages use more conflict avoidance methods than couples in stable, happy marriages." The first hypothesis suggests a study in which the variables of body image and motivation for breast augmentation will be statistically correlated, whereas the second hypothesis suggests a study using two groups of couples who will be compared on how they manage conflict. In either case, the variables specified in the hypotheses will need to be *operationalized*, or clarified with regard to how they are to be measured. Such specification usually takes place in the Method chapter. In the first example, the researcher might predict, as did one of our students, a negative relationship between scores on the Jourard-Secord Body Cathexis Scale and a 10-item Likert-type scale of motivation to seek augmentation mammoplasty (Ewing, 1992). It is obviously important to specify each and every variable. In the second example, the terms *stable/unstable marriage* and *conflict avoidance methods* would need to be conceptually defined and operationalized, and the two groups of couples would need to be identified.

It usually takes several rewritings to come up with research questions and hypotheses that are optimally clear, concise, and meaningful. Note that hypotheses typically are written in the present tense and they are written as positive assertions. They are not written as "null" hypotheses. The reader may be aware that inferential statistics work on the assumption of rejecting null hypotheses, that is, hypotheses that assume there are no significant differences between or among groups or no significant relationships among variables. Research hypotheses, on the other hand, should be stated not as null hypotheses but as directional hypotheses (or hypotheses that specify a relationship between variables) that follow from the argument that has been established in the preceding chapter. As research hypotheses, null hypotheses are confusing because they reflect the opposite of the argument you have been proposing. If the logic behind the stated hypotheses is not totally evident, it is always a good idea to follow or precede each hypothesis with a short rationale that reminds the reader how it emerged out of theoretical propositions established in the Review of the Literature.

One recommended statement of the criteria for a good hypothesis is that it (a) be free of ambiguity, (b) express the relationship(s) between two or more variables, and (c) imply an empirical test (Locke, Spirduso, & Silverman, 1997). A common pitfall is to have more than one hypothesis embedded in a single, complex statement (e.g., "Women who earn more than their husbands have more self-confidence, have more friends, and receive more help on household tasks than women who earn less than their husbands").

Some dissertations contain both research questions with hypotheses and research questions that stand alone. The hypotheses might cover those relationships that directly challenge previous work or test a theory, whereas research questions without hypotheses are more open-ended opportunities to satisfy your curiosity. For instance, a student studying self-disclosure patterns among psychotherapists might have specific hypotheses about the relationship between self-disclosure and friendship (e.g., "Therapists who are high in self-disclosure with their patients have fewer personal friends") but no clear expectations about the relationship between self-disclosure and stages of therapy (e.g., "What is the relationship between therapist self-disclosure with patients and the stage of psychotherapy?").

Another way of combining research questions and hypotheses is to use research questions as more general investigatory themes, which are then followed by specific hypotheses that make predictions in a testable form. This example is very loosely based on a dissertation by one of our students (Davenport, 1991):

Research question: How do dyslexic adolescents cope with the effects of their learning disabilities?

Hypothesis 1: Dyslexic adolescents who accept the diagnosis of having a learning disability use more problem-focused coping strategies than dyslexic individuals who reject or deny the diagnosis.

Hypothesis 2: Dyslexic adolescents who accept the diagnosis of having a learning disability rely more on social support than dyslexic adolescents who reject or deny the diagnosis.

Hypothesis 3: Dyslexic adolescents who reject or deny the diagnosis of having a learning disability use more avoidant coping strategies than dyslexic adolescents who accept the diagnosis.

Hypothesis 4: Dyslexic adolescents who reject or deny the diagnosis of having a learning disability deny negative affect more than dyslexic adolescents who accept the diagnosis.

Goodman (1998), in a recent dissertation on the relationship between coping skills and adolescent violence, chose to present two sets of five hypotheses, one set framed in theoretical language and the second set expressed operationally. Here are a couple of examples taken from her study:

Theoretical Hypotheses

Hypothesis 1: The higher the adolescents' facility for affect discrimination (the ability to differentiate between feelings), the less likely they will be to engage in interpersonal violence.

Hypothesis 2: The greater the adolescents' abilities in desomatization (the ability to name feelings), the less likely they will be to engage in interpersonal violence.

Operational Hypotheses

Hypothesis 1: The higher the adolescents' scores on the "Clarity of Feeling" subscale of the TMMS, the lower their scores will be on the physical assault scale of the Conflict Tactic Scale-Revised (CTS2).

Hypothesis 2: The lower the adolescents' scores on Factor 2 of the TAS-20, the lower their scores will be on the physical assault scale of the Conflict Tactic Scale-Revised (CTS2).

Problem Statements in Qualitative Research

The precise form of a good problem statement will vary according to the discipline of the study and the research tradition it represents. Qualitative studies are more likely to support more open-ended questions. Within the phenomenological tradition, a dissertation on the exploration of childbirth might have as an overview question "What is the experience of giving birth to a child?" Taking the lead of Moustakis (1994), one chooses a topic rich with personal significance and social meaning, a topic that reflects an experience that the researcher has had and about which there is a passionate interest in understanding its nature. The characteristics of the question, according to Moustakis (1994, p. 105), are that it

1. Seeks to reveal more fully the essences and meanings of human experience

2. Seeks to uncover the qualitative rather than the quantitative factors in behavior and experience

3. Engages the total self of the research participant and sustains personal and passionate involvement

4. Does not seek to predict or to determine causal relationships

5. Is illuminated through careful, comprehensive descriptions and vivid and accurate renderings of the experience rather than measurements, ratings, or scores

One of our graduate students, Sara Katz (1995), completed a phenomenological study on the experience of coping with chronic, recurrent vulvar pain, a relatively unusual medical condition that can be quite debilitating and extremely resistant to treatment. The primary research questions in her study were as follows:

1. How do women live with chronic vulvar pain?

2. In what ways do women with chronic vulvar pain construct definitions of their illness, self, and situation?

3. How do a woman's somatic perceptions of her vulvar pain develop, change, and give rise to consequences?

4. How do a woman's emotional responses to her vulvar pain develop, change, and give rise to consequences?

5. How is shaping of the self related to the meanings the woman with chronic vulvar pain makes of the somatic sensations of the conditions and her emotional reactions to them?

Note that all these questions follow up on the themes and contexts that define the experience of the phenomenon of chronic vulvar pain and help to provide a structure for holding the feelings and thoughts about the experience.

The overarching research question within the phenomenological tradition usually asks about the "meaning" of an experience or phenomenon. The wording of the primary research question in a grounded theory study is more likely to be a "process" question (Morse, 1994), although, as the example above suggests, there is often some overlap in practice between these two research traditions. Adopting the previous childbirth theme, a typical research question using the grounded theory approach might be "How do women prepare for childbirth in a managed care health system?" This question is certainly not appropriate for a quantitative study in that it is much too broad and open ended. Recall, however, that the primary purpose of a grounded theory study is to generate a theory that relates to this phenomenon.

The primary question is usually followed by a series of further questions that have direct implications for data analysis. For instance:

➤   How does the process develop over time?

➤   What are the noteworthy events in the process?

➤   What facilitates the process?

➤   What hinders the process?

➤   Who are the key participants in the process and what are their roles?

➤   What are the outcomes?

The dissertation of another Fielding student, Nancy La Pelle (1997), was conducted to "discover what contextual, personal, and process variables support both motivating and demotivating performance evaluation experiences for intrinsically motivated supervisees in orga-nizations, using a grounded theory design and resulting in a theory that fits the experiential participant data that were systematically obtained and analyzed" (pp. 2-3). The primary research question was:

> What are employees' significant experiences of performance evalua-tions in organizations and what are the factors that affect motivation and subsequent performance? More specifically, which features of the evaluation and of the surrounding management context will lead per-formance evaluations to have a positive effect and which will lead to their having a negative effect? (p. 6)

A number of subquestions were subsequently generated. Among them were:

1. Do organizations intend performance evaluations to have an impact on motivation and performance either positively or negatively? What is their purpose and impact in different organizations or as imple-mented by different supervisors?

2. What is the process and experience of those who are motivated or demotivated by performance evaluations? Under what conditions is performance appraisal harmful to employees' motivation?

3. Does performance feedback work to improve performance and moti-vation, and under what conditions? Are providing feedback and eval-uating performance the same thing?

4. What hypotheses might experiential data reveal? What existing bod-ies of theory might be related to the outcomes of this study that could help explain the revealed relationship between performance apprais-als and motivation? How might they be integrated to form a unifying theory?

In an ethnographic study, the wording of the research question is apt to focus on a "description" of aspects of a culture (Morse, 1994). Fol-lowing through with our childbirth example, an overarching question might be "How can the culture of a delivery room in a major urban hos-pital be described and interpreted?" Such a question would imply describing the context where childbirth occurs, analyzing the main themes, and interpreting the behavior of patients and medical staff. The interested reader is referred to Spradley's (1979) 12-step "decision research sequence," which can serve as subquestions that the participant observer researcher aims to address in his or her study.

Other research traditions have their own chosen formats for presenting the research question. In action research, for example, Stringer (1999) does not specify a research question following a review of the literature. Rather, the statement of the problem is embedded in the introductory chapter, which describes:

➤   The issue or problem to which the study responds

➤   The location of the study and its stakeholders

➤   Organizations, policies, programs, and services that affect the problem

➤   The purposes of the research

➤   The significance of the study

➤   An overview of the content of each chapter of the report that follows

The literature review includes both the academic literature and official and unofficial documents (governmental policies, organizational procedural manuals, reports, news articles, etc.) that have interpreted the issue that is being studied. According to Stringer (1999), these materials are deconstructed to expose the underlying assumptions, concepts, and theories that buttress their claims and set the stage for the methodology of the research that is then described. The write-up of these sections, as well as the entire document, may be more narrative in style than, say, an experimental research study.

The statement of the research problem, together with the precise exposition of the research questions and/or hypotheses, serves as a transition between the review of the literature and the description of the methods of the study. The following chapter offers guidelines and suggestions for presenting the methods.

NOTE

1. Kuhn has also identified "paradigm shifts" as discontinuous, more disruptive changes in the evolution of scientific thinking.

BOX 4.1 Student Suggestions	1. Use the APA style manual at the outset. It is much easier to get into the habit of referencing articles and books correctly than to go back and revise the format at a later time. This is especially true for direct quotes, where it is critical to keep page numbers! A software program such as Manuscript Manager will make it much easier to use APA format conventions automatically within the text and for references. 2. You'll know when to stop your literature review when the articles you read become redundant and when the authors and articles that are cited become familiar to you. 3. Develop a system for organizing and cataloging what you read. I began to note, in the margins of the books and articles I read, numbers representing the topic being covered. I just started numbering as I discovered topics and I ended up with 38 topics that included everything I wanted to be able to retrieve. Later on I organized the references according to the numbers in a computerized filing program.

(Continued)

4. Read the original writings of the theorists you are studying, not just what someone else says about their theories. I have found that other people tend to misinterpret original writings. Piaget, for instance, is terribly misunderstood in America. Plus, the original source is so much richer. Trust yourself before you trust others. Take your time to pinpoint those parts that aren't completely clear to you, since those are usually higher level thoughts that you need to struggle to understand.

5. One of the problems that students will likely encounter is tracking a given subject matter through different disciplines, for example, social psychology, sociology, anthropology, communications, cross-cultural studies, and so on. Often research in one discipline is isolated from another not by differences in philosophical orientation but rather by the sociological barriers of a fragmented academia. The subject matter may even have a different name for the same basic phenomenon. Scanning basic textbooks in these different fields can give you clues to follow-up in the library directory. Journals are extremely valuable in following academic debates between members of a research tradition or identifying battles between research traditions. Bibliographies can be very useful in tracking down new sources.

6. It is much easier to record complete references for source materials when you initially read them than later on. It is very frustrating and time- consuming to retrieve a publication date or page number after an entire paper has been written!

7. Use an ample number of subheadings in your Review chapter in order to maintain organization and flow. Make sure that your headings convey enough information to assist and orient the reader to the material that follows.

CHAPTER 5

The Method Chapter:

Describing Your Research Plan

The Method chapter of a dissertation, article, or proposal describes the exact steps that will be undertaken to address your hypotheses and/or research questions. For this reason the Method section follows logically from the statement of the problem in much the same way as research questions follow from the review of the literature. The goal of this chapter is to provide a clear and complete description of the specific steps to be followed. It is necessary to describe these steps in sufficient detail to permit a naïve reader to replicate your study.

In Chapter 3 we suggested that students select a suitable problem before selecting the appropriate method with which to study that problem. In some dissertations, however, the "method" may in fact be the topic of study. A student may become excited about the possibilities of a particular data collection technique or method prior to generating a suitable problem. In most cases, though, the appropriate method of study is generated by careful consideration of the research questions and the applicable method by which those questions may be studied. The following material is divided into two major sections, one that focuses primarily on the quantitative dissertation and one on the qualitative dissertation; we strongly recommend, however, that the student read both sections. The issues to be considered are not independent of each other, and there is considerable overlap in the content of this chapter regardless of the method being employed.

THE METHOD CHAPTER
IN A QUANTITATIVE DISSERTATION

The Method chapter is the place in which the exact steps you will be following to test your question(s) are enumerated. The Method chapter typically contains the following three subsections: Subjects or Participants, Instrumentation or Measures, and Procedures. In addition, the Method chapter of a dissertation proposal often contains a "Statistical Analysis" or "Data Analysis" section in which procedures for approaching the data are outlined. Research that utilizes special equipment frequently contains an "Apparatus" section in which the nature and type of equipment used is described.

A frequent mistake contained in first drafts of Method chapters involves overuse of the opportunity to rehash the material contained in the review of the literature or statement of the problem already presented in another chapter. This chapter should be viewed primarily as a set of directions for conducting a specific piece of research. We follow this perspective in describing each of the subsections of a Method chapter below.

HOW TO BEGIN A METHOD CHAPTER

A reasonable way to begin a Method chapter is to develop an introductory paragraph that describes both the design of the study and the organization of the chapter. This prepares the reader for what is to follow and provides a framework within which to incorporate the materials. This paragraph says to the reader, "This is the Method chapter, this is how it is organized, and this is the type of design I used." The most difficult component of the introductory paragraph may appear to be the design statement. There are dozens of books that take "research design" as their sole topic. Our purpose here is not to review this extensive material. In this context we are suggesting only a short sentence or two that informs the reader of the general type of design and any suitable label that may be applied to it.

For example, imagine a study in which you plan to mail 700 surveys to retired male executives in an attempt to assess their adjustment to retirement. It is probably sufficient simply to state something like the following: "This study utilized a cross-sectional survey design to assess adjustment to retirement of a sample of retired male executives." Similarly, imagine an experimental design in which two dichotomous variables will be used as independent variables. It may be sufficient to describe the design as "an experimental study utilizing a 2 × 2 factorial design." An example of such a design is described in a dissertation by Sangster (1991):

> An experimental, 2 × 2 factorial, pretest-posttest design was used to test the hypothesis. The independent variables were (a) training type and (b) management experience. Respective levels of independent variables were descriptive and prescriptive training, and high and low management experience.

Determining exactly what type of design description best fits your study can be accomplished by reference to one of the many texts that describe designs (e.g., Campbell & Stanley, 1966; Kerlinger & Lee, 1999), but a specific label may not be as important as a clear explanation of the structure of your study. For example, a study by Macdonald (1990) examined the relationships among empathy, personal maturity, and emotional articulation. She described her design as follows:

> The research design was a correlational design utilizing cross-sectional survey methodology and includes a number of survey instruments. The purpose of the design was to correlate the scores of the personality tests listed below with the scores on responses to the short stories, as well as measure the interrelationship of the responses to the short stories.

DESCRIBING YOUR SAMPLE

The Subjects section of the Method chapter describes the source and number of subjects you will be using (in a proposal) or the source and number of subjects actually obtained (in a completed project). Note that we use the term *subjects* in a very broad context. The subjects may be informants or participants in the research, organizations or events, documents or segments of commercials edited from television programs, or even an entire society, as in the case of anthropological research. In studies of human beings, the term "participants" is generally preferable to the term "subjects." The concern in this section of the Method chapter is to describe why and how the particular unit of analysis was selected.

A frequent problem we have observed is that students often confound a description of the sampling of subjects with the procedures used to collect data from these subjects. The former belongs in the Subjects section, whereas the latter belongs in the Procedures section. Of particular importance in the Subjects section are the specific sampling procedures used, the rationale for selecting a given number of subjects, and the source of the subjects. What type of sample will you draw: random, stratified, purposive? Where will your subjects be located? How many subjects are necessary for your particular design? Each of these questions is important and should be dealt with in the Subjects section. We discuss each in turn below.

The Sampling Design. As is the case with research design in general, the issue of sampling is a complex one. Our purpose, however, and your purpose as researcher, is not to discuss the knotty problems of sampling. Your job is to describe how you will accomplish this task in your study, taking all the theoretical and practical issues into account. A knowledge of the various types of sampling design is a prerequisite to developing an appropriate description of your particular sampling problem.

Two examples may be of assistance in developing your approach. In a dissertation examining gender differences in professional identity among practicing psychotherapists, New (1989) obtained a mailing list of all licensed psychologists in the state of California. Beginning at a randomly selected start point, she then sampled every *n*th name until she had exhausted the list. Her dissertation describes this process as follows:

> A systematic random sample was drawn from a list of all psychologists who have been licensed in the state of California for five or more years. The sample was obtained from a research center specializing in the distribution of selected sampling lists. A table of random numbers was used to locate the initial sampling point. Every 20th person was selected such that an initial group of 400 was obtained. These persons were mailed the study materials.

In a second instance, illustrating a nonrandom procedure, Caddell (1989) selected students from classes at three universities to examine moral education in the college environment. He describes his sampling procedure as follows:

> The questionnaire was administered to selected undergraduate and graduate level classes at California State University–Fullerton, California Baptist College and Pacific Christian College. The sample was divided into a subset from the morally nondirective institution (Cal State–Fullerton, $N = 178$) and a subset from morally directive institutions (Cal Baptist College, $N = 104$ and Pacific Christian College, $N = 71$).

Locating Subjects. Of the two examples presented above only one describes both *where* and *how* the subjects were obtained as well as the sampling design used. In the study using university students, Caddell (1989) fails to describe how the "selected undergraduate and graduate level classes" were obtained. In fact, the procedure was one of asking professors at each institution for permission. This decidedly nonrandom procedure could probably best be described as a "convenience" sample.

The Appropriate Number of Subjects. Determining the appropriate number of subjects for a given design is one of the most difficult sampling problems. Generally, given considerations of cost and time, students wish to obtain as few as their committee will allow; however, this decision is not arbitrary. Most students tend to underestimate the number of subjects necessary to draw meaningful conclusions from the data.

For example, imagine a study from the field of education in which the researcher wishes to compare the level of creativity of students who are sent to public schools to those who receive home schooling. If in fact there is a difference, the student-researcher must collect enough data for this difference to appear in the results. The smaller the difference is, the more data must be collected to find it.

The best method to approximate the number of subjects is to conduct a power analysis. A *power analysis* lets the researcher know how many subjects are necessary to detect any effects that result from the independent variables, given (a) the size of the effect of these variables in the population, (b) the type of statistical tests to be utilized, and (c) the level of significance (or alpha level) of the study. The level of power, expressed as a probability, lets the researcher know how likely he or she is to avoid a Type II error. A *Type II error* occurs when one fails to reject the null hypothesis even though it is false. Failing to reject a false null hypothesis means that an effect existed but was not detected by the study. As the probability of a Type II error increases, the power of the study decreases. In fact, power is equal to 1 minus the probability of a Type II error. Thus, if a probability of a Type II error is .15, power is .85 (1 − .15 = .85). Historically, power calculations have been difficult to conduct, and students and their committees frequently rely on general rules of thumb to determine the appropriate number of subjects. Computer programs now simplify these calculations, and we strongly recommend that they be used in dissertation planning (see page 245).

In the example of the student interested in comparing home-schooled with traditionally schooled youngsters, a *t* test might be used to compare levels of creativity between these two groups. Table 5.1 gives an example of a power analysis designed to answer the question "How many subjects will I need to test the difference between the means of two groups, if I use a level of significance of .05 and desire a power of .80?" The table shows the number of subjects necessary to obtain the specified power level of .80 (a standard level, generally considered acceptable) using an alpha level of .05 (also a generally acceptable criterion) if the size of the effects (i.e., the mean differences) are small, medium, or large.

Table 5.1 shows that if medium effects were predicted, it would require 64 subjects per group to achieve a power of .80 when using an alpha level of .05. Even if the effects are large, it would require at least 26 subjects per group to achieve the same power level (.80). Another

Table 5.1
Power Analysis for a t *Test*

To achieve a power level of .80, while setting the level of significance (alpha) at .05.

Effect Size	N Per Group	Total N
Small	393	786
Medium	64	128
Large	26	52

way to say this is that even if the research hypothesis is true, the researcher may fail to support this hypothesis because of insufficient sample size. As the sample size increases, it becomes more likely that the statistical tests will detect any effects that exist in the data.

Finally, it is important to make two critical points about the use of power analysis. First, in many dissertations the use of power analysis may be unrealistic. Enough subjects to meet the requirements of a purely mathematical procedure may not exist in some cases, and qualitative dissertations, case studies, oral histories, and intensive interviews may rely more on what the student and committee deem reasonable to develop a convincing argument, independent of statistical testing. Second, in cases where quantitative analysis is essential, students often use a multivariate framework with many variables. The number of subjects necessary in these contexts is likely to be much higher than that suggested above for a simple two-group *t* test.

INSTRUMENTATION: DESCRIBING YOUR RESEARCH TOOLS

The Instrumentation section of a Method chapter describes the particular measures you will employ and how they will measure the variables specified in your research questions and hypotheses. This section "makes your case" for the use of particular measures as the best and most appropriate to your specific research environment.

If you are using instruments that have been used previously, particularly standardized and widely recognized scales, then you should consider the following three areas as particularly relevant to your description: (a) information about the appropriateness of the use of the instrument with the population and setting described in the proposal, (b) information about the measurement characteristics of the instrument, and (c) information about the administration and scoring of the scales. Each of these three areas will be discussed separately below.

Is the Measure Appropriate? A number of scales may exist that measure the same phenomenon. How is the researcher to select which is the "best"? (Or how does one guard against the claim that he or she should have used something else?)

The first step is to support the use of a given instrument with the population selected for your study. Measures that work well with adults may not be particularly effective with adolescents or children. Measures designed for use in one culture may work very poorly in another. The writer's goal is to locate empirical studies that demonstrate the utility of an instrument with a population as closely representative as possible of the population to be used in his or her study.

The second step is to demonstrate that the authors of the measure you select conceive of the phenomenon in terms similar to the manner in which you have conceptualized the same phenomenon. For example, all measures that assess depression are not the same because those who originally designed the measures have viewed depression from different theoretical positions. The contents of the measures reflect these different positions. Thus, it may be important to indicate that you have chosen a particular instrument because it reflects the conceptualization of the phenomenon in a manner that is consistent with your position.

What Are the Measurement Characteristics of the Instrument? By *measurement characteristics* we mean the reliability, validity, and structure of the measure. *Reliability* refers to the ability of a measure to produce consistent results. *Validity* indicates that a measure in fact measures what it purports to measure. *Structure* refers to the number and meaning of subscales contained in a given instrument. For example, the Bell Object Relations Reality Testing Inventory (Bell, 1988) contains 90 items, 45 of which assess object relations and 45 of which assess reality testing. Within each of these broad divisions there are additional subscales, four for object relations and three for reality testing. This breakdown describes the structure of the measure. A complete description of the measurement characteristics of this instrument would also contain information about the reliability and validity of the total scale, scores for object relations and reality testing, and information about the seven subscales.

It is important to realize that in a *proposal* the only information likely to be available regarding an instrument's reliability and validity is that which is contained in the existing literature. After the student has collected his or her data, it is important to add to this body of literature by reporting on the reliability and validity of the instrument as evidenced in the new sample. The reliability of an instrument is a characteristic of the population in which that instrument is used. Thus, an instrument that achieves high reliability in one sample will not necessarily receive that same level of reliability in another sample representing a different population.

How Does One Administer and Score the Measures? It is important for the reader to understand how an instrument is administered and scored. Some measures are self-administered and may simply be mailed or passed out with instructions to "check the box that most represents your feelings at the present time." Others, such as the Rorschach, require extensive training to administer and score. For others, the scoring methods are a well-guarded secret, and completed protocols must be sent to a central location for computerized scoring (for a fee, of course). Sometimes it may be sufficient to include a copy of the instrument, with its instructions to the respondent, in an appendix to the Method chapter; however, this usually is not appropriate with copyrighted instruments.

The example below, drawn from a doctoral dissertation (Hardwick, 1990), provides what we consider to be a clearly written description of a rather complex instrument. The section we quote contains information about the structure, scoring, and administration of the instrument. Information about the reliability and validity of the instrument is contained in materials we have not chosen to quote here.

The Bell Object Relations Reality Testing Inventory (BORRTI) is a 90-item "true-false" self-report inventory which was used to operationalize the dependent variables, object relations and reality testing. The BORRTI was administered to each participant. . . . It yields four object relations (OR) subscales and three reality testing (RT) subscales. Each dimension, OR and RT, is measured by 45 items which are worded to reflect various levels of object relations and reality testing. The four OR subscales are: Alienation, Insecure Attachment, Egocentricity, and Social Incompetence. The three RT subscales are Reality Distortion, Uncertainty of Perception, and Hallucinations and Delusions. The test also yields a quasi-summary score for each overall OR and RT construct. This score is the sum of all items to which the participant responded in a pathological direction. Thus, a participant could conceivably have normal subscale scores while still responding to any number of pathological OR and/or RT items.

The author then goes on to describe examples of test items and the meaning of each subscale, including the interpretation of high and low scores as well as the measurement characteristics of each subscale, including the reliability and validity demonstrated in recent research.

THE USE OF COPYRIGHTED SCALES

Copyrighted scales typically are not reproduced in a dissertation or research publication. In order to use copyrighted scales in a study, permission should be obtained in writing from the holder of the copyright.

WHAT IF I DESIGN MY OWN INSTRUMENTS?

In rare instances, a student may not be able to locate any existing measures that tap the construct he or she desires to measure. Our first recommendation is to send the student back to the library with the instruction "keep looking." This advice reflects our strong belief that developing your own instrument is generally not a good idea. Research based on hastily thrown together instruments, which lack sufficient pretesting and are questionable in terms of reliability and validity, is of little scientific value. If the student is unable to locate a satisfactory instrument, he or she may wish to consider changing the focus of the research from one that attempts to relate the construct in question to other constructs, to one that attempts to design and assess a new instrument, a valid dissertation topic in and of itself. In this case, building the instrument becomes the central topic, and examining its relationships to other variables becomes part of the process of establishing the validity of the new instrument.

It is not uncommon for a student to modify questions or add questions to validated instruments to facilitate those instruments' use. For example, when using some instruments with younger populations it may be necessary to reword or eliminate questions regarding relations with the opposite sex. Phrases such as "My sex life is satisfactory" may not be appropriate for 7-year-old children.

Our position is that the modification of an existing instrument is perfectly acceptable but that such changes may make the norms invalid and may affect both the reliability and the validity of the instrument. A close examination of many instruments currently in use reveals that there has been considerable borrowing among various authors over a lengthy time period. When borrowing and/or modification occurs, it becomes the responsibility of the student to justify such changes and make his or her case for the reliability and validity of the instrument in its revised form.

It is often advisable to use an existing instrument in conjunction with a new instrument of the student's design. Even if the student feels that his or her instrument is "better," the use of multiple measures of a single concept can be very useful when establishing the reliability and validity of a new instrument. Of course, when a new instrument fails, as they often do, the old standard can be used in its place.

Most dissertations contain some form of "demographic data sheet." These sheets contain questions that assess gender, ethnicity, years of employment, marital status, education, and the like. Although such questions need to be thought through carefully, we do not consider adding such questions to a battery of existing instruments in the same context as "scale development." We suggest examining surveys from the National Opinion Research Center General Social Survey (National Opinion Research Center, 1990) for examples of how to solicit "demographic information." For GSS data see the following websites:

http://www.icpsr.umich.edu/GSS99/index.html

http://www.norc.uchicago.edu/gss/homepage.htm

Research that concentrates on instrument development is a valuable enterprise and often makes greater contributions than research that attempts to relate existing measures to each other in some new and as yet untried fashion. Nevertheless, such research requires large numbers of subjects, frequent retesting, and sophisticated statistical models. Both the student and his or her committee must carefully weigh the pros and cons of undertaking such an enterprise.

WHAT IF I AM NOT USING A QUESTIONNAIRE TO COLLECT DATA?

Questionnaires are not the only type of data collection instrument. Behavioral observations, extended interviews, and archival data all constitute valid sources of data for dissertation research. The sources of this information, as well as checks for reliability and validity of the information, will need to be considered. For example, Newton's (1991) dissertation examined the incidence of depression, substance abuse, and eating disorders in the families of anorexics. Data were obtained from existing medical records. Newton supports his data collection procedures as follows:

> A number of authors have studied the validity of data found in medical records (Harlow & Linet, 1989; Horwitz, 1986; Paganini-Hill & Ross, 1982; and Hewson & Bennett, 1987). Horwitz (1986) compared epidemiological data collected from medical records and by interview for 462 subjects who were part of a case-control study of chronic disease. Results showed that agreements between medical record and interview data are variable, and depend on the type of data examined and the strategy for handling incomplete or ambiguous responses. Horwitz did find a 93% agreement between medical records and interviews for family history of breast cancer. (p. 45)

In the above quotation, the author lets the readers know that (a) he is aware of potential problems with his method, (b) he has read the literature, and (c) the literature supports the validity of this technique in some instances.

PROCEDURES: DESCRIBING HOW YOU DID (OR WILL DO) IT

The Procedures section provides a detailed description of the exact steps taken to contact your research participants, obtain their cooperation, and administer your instruments. After reading this section one should know when, where, and how the data were collected. For example, in a mailed survey, one might describe the following steps: (a) mail precontact letter, (b) 1 week later mail survey packet, (c) 2 weeks later mail follow-up survey for nonrespondents. Exact copies of the precontact letter and cover letters accompanying the survey measures should be provided in appendices. Note that the sampling procedures have been described in the Subjects section and the measures described in the Instrumentation section. There is no need to repeat this information in the Procedures section. When procedures are complex and require the administration of multiple instruments over multiple time periods, a flowchart or table presenting the procedures visually becomes very helpful.

It is important that any information that might potentially affect the number of participants or their characteristics be included in this section. For example, much social research is conducted with college students. Were the students asked to volunteer? Were they given extra credit? Was participation mandatory as part of a course requirement? Similarly, when administering mailed surveys such simple information as whether the addresses were handwritten or mailing labels were used can affect response rates. Such information is critical to replicating the experiment and understanding the exact nature of the population sampled. It is also important to describe the procedures undertaken to gain access to the population. For example, if working with high school students, was it necessary to obtain permission of the school board or the principal, or did one simply sample all sixth-period classes? Finally, the procedures for obtaining informed consent should be described in detail and a copy of the informed consent statement, if any, provided in an appendix. This is particularly important when working with minors, who are legally not permitted to provide their own consent to participate in research. (Chapter 12 contains a more detailed discussion of informed consent and other ethical issues.)

Typically, instructions to subjects, as well as ethical release forms, are included in the appendices. The ethical release forms are crucial because they inform subjects about the potential hazards of participating in the study (e.g., emotional upset), limits to confidentiality, and use of the data, and make it clear that participation is voluntary. (In some rare instances participation may not be voluntary.) The purpose of the release forms is protection both for you and for those who participate in your research. Release forms also force you to think about the implications of your study on the physical and emotional well-being of humans or animals employed as subjects. Most universities have stringent procedures for conducting ethical research, which generally include passing proposals through a Human Subjects Committee. A sample copy of a typical human subjects release form can be found in Chapter 12. These forms should include a description of the study, the right of refusal, an explanation of risks and potential discomfort, an opportunity to withdraw without penalty, and the potential for feedback.

DATA ANALYSIS: HOW TO JUSTIFY AND DESCRIBE AN ANALYSIS

A research proposal often includes a statement that describes the statistical tests that will be used to address the hypotheses and research questions. This section is usually the one that scares students the most (because students learn statistics in the abstract, not as applied to specific research questions). The great benefit of including this statement is that it forces you to think through how you will treat the data from your dissertation at the time the proposal is generated, rather than after the data are collected. Time spent thinking about these issues at the proposal stage saves considerable time and pain later. In this way, one can avoid spending countless hours collecting data that ultimately are not analyzable because they are not in the correct format in the first place. In the next chapter, we describe in detail how to present the results of a study once the data have been analyzed. In this section, we discuss how to "propose" a particular sort of analysis prior to having actually undertaken it.

This section is particularly difficult for a number of reasons, beyond the fact that students may not be prepared to apply statistics to their own research. First, statistical analysis is virtually never a one-shot affair. Data may be analyzed and reanalyzed many times before the researchers are satisfied that the data have been given the correct treatment. A technique that initially seemed perfectly reasonable will later seem inappropriate because of the number of cases or distributions presented by the completed sample. Second, interesting questions often arise after initial analyses are completed. If a hypothesis is not supported, one may search for control variables that might help explain the lack of support. For example, a hypothesis may be supported only among the highly educated. Research with a large number of non–college graduates in the sample may obscure the relationship until the college graduates are analyzed separately from the non–college graduates (i.e., education becomes a motivator variable).

What, then, is the student to do? First, we strongly recommend that, in consultation with your advisers, and experts if necessary, you describe which technique seems most appropriate given (a) the nature of your hypothesis, (b) the number of independent and dependent variables, and (c) the level of measurement of each of the variables. The following chapters contain recommendations regarding the use of statistical techniques. Computer programs also can assist with the selection of statistical techniques, and many statistics texts present flowcharts directing students to appropriate statistical methods. Do not turn your data analysis section into a treatise on a particular technique paraphrased from a statistics text; instead, present a short, reasoned statement that a particular technique seems most appropriate. An example of a straightforward data analysis proposal is provided by Connell's (1992) study of stress in psychotherapists.

> The primary hypothesis, that there will be a significant difference between Group 1 and Group 2 on level of stress, will be tested using a one-tailed *t* test. . . . The expectation that Group 2 will score differently than Group 1 in 12 of the subscales of the Essi System StressMap will be tested using a multivariate analysis of variance (MANOVA).

SHOULD YOU DISCUSS THE LIMITATIONS
OF YOUR RESEARCH?

A final section of the Method chapter that we encourage students to include in a dissertation proposal is a statement on "Limitations and Delimitations" of the study. *Delimitations* imply limitations on the research design that you have imposed deliberately. These delimitations usually restrict the populations to which the results of the study can be generalized. For example, you may decide to study only males, either because the theory upon which your hypotheses are based has not been studied in females or because you have a readily accessible population of males but not females. *Limitations,* on the other hand, refer to restrictions in the study over which you have no control. For example, you may be limited to only a narrow segment of the total population you wish to study, or you may be limited by the method you elect to use.

THE METHOD CHAPTER IN A
QUALITATIVE DISSERTATION

Too often students view the relatively unstructured nature of qualitative research designs as license to omit clarity and specificity in the method chapters of their dissertations. Qualitative studies should not be considered as opportunities to ignore the planning process in research. Issues of identifying and soliciting participants, selecting and preparing research materials and data collection tools, and formulating procedures pertain here as in all studies. The reader needs to understand what you did and how you thought about it in order to appreciate the links among the research problem, the method, and the results.

Qualitative research adopts views of sampling, instrumentation, and data analysis that are often directly contrary to views held by those conducting more traditional "rationalistic" inquiry. Lincoln and Guba (1985) call this "The Paradox of Designing a Naturalistic Inquiry" and argue that "The design specifications of the conventional paradigm form a procrustean bed of such a nature as to make it impossible for the naturalist to lie in it—not only uncomfortably, *but at all*" (Lincoln & Guba, 1985, p. 225). Nevertheless, Lincoln and Guba outline a broad series of design considerations that, in some respects, go beyond those required by conventional methodologies. These considerations describe what must be considered, in advance, in preparing a naturalistic study. These 10 design considerations are reproduced below.

1. Determining the focus for the inquiry

2. Determining fit of paradigm to focus

3. Determining the fit of the inquiry paradigm to the substantive theory selected to guide the inquiry

4. Determining where and from whom data will be collected

5. Determining successive phases of the inquiry

6. Determining instrumentation

7. Planning data collection and recording modes

8. Planning data analysis procedure

9. Planning the logistics

10. Planning for trustworthiness

The above 10 "elements of a naturalistic design" cover what we would identify as the Statement of the Problem and Method chapters of a proposal. The first three (focus, fit of paradigm to focus, and fit of paradigm to theory) pay explicit attention to the assumptions that underlie a study as well as to the fit of these assumptions to the methods being used. Thus, Lincoln and Guba (1985) seek to make distinct the fit between the purpose of the study, the basic guiding principles underlying the approach, and the substantive theoretical framework. Often this "fit" is assumed in much research when in fact it should not be. The lack of fit between purpose, approach, and theory in research may become apparent when findings and conclusions seem to make no sense in the light of the original questions.

SAMPLING AND SAMPLE SIZE
IN QUALITATIVE STUDIES

The fourth element mentioned above, determining where and from whom data will be collected, is directly analogous to our consideration of "sampling." The naturalist's approach to sampling, however, is quite different from that of the rationalist. According to Lincoln and Guba (1985):

> The naturalist is likely to eschew random or representative sampling in favor of purposive or theoretical sampling because he or she thereby increases the scope or range of data exposed (random or representative sampling is likely to suppress more deviant cases) as well as the likelihood that the full array of multiple realities will be uncovered. (p. 40)

A phenomenological study usually involves identifying and locating participants who have experienced or are experiencing the phenomenon that is being explored. As described by Bailey (1992):

> Phenomenological research uses sampling which is idiographic, focusing on the individual or case study in order to understand the full complexity of the individual's experience. From this perspective, there is no attempt to claim an ability to generalize to a specific population, but instead, the findings are relevant from the perspective of the user of the findings. (p. 30)

The participants, if you will, are the experiential experts on the phenomenon being studied. This means that the sample probably would not be randomly drawn from a group of college sophomores. Rather, the researcher uses "criterion sampling," selecting participants who closely match the criteria of the study. Katz's (1995) participants, for instance, had to meet both inclusionary and exclusionary criteria: a deliberately diverse and representational sample of women who had experienced "ongoing, intractable symptoms of discomfort in the skin of the vulva and/or the vaginal vestibule, which may be diffuse or in specific loci, and either persistent or episodic" (p. 91) for a period of 1 year or more. Referral of participants came directly from medical providers. Moreover, most phenomenological studies engage a relatively small number of participants (10 might be appropriate) for a relatively long period of time (at least 2 hours). These factors should be carefully noted in the Method chapter.

Because the grounded theory study is inductive and theory evolves as the data are collected and explored, it may be neither possible nor advisable to establish the precise sample size beforehand. In our experience, 20 to 30 participants may constitute a reasonable sample. Strauss and Corbin (1998) stress that several forms of sampling are appropriate at various stages of the study. The trick is to choose participants who can contribute to an "evolving theory," participants whose main credential is experiential relevance. Thus, at the outset, "open sampling" might be most appropriate. This means selecting participants or observations without prejudice because no concepts have yet proven to be theoretically meaningful. In practice that might mean systematically choosing every *n*th name on a list, staying maximally flexible and open to discovery.

As the study proceeds, the chief criterion for sampling moves toward theoretical relevance. At this point, the researcher has begun to assimilate some early theoretical hunches and wishes to identify examples that demonstrate the range or variation of a concept in different situations and in relation to other concepts. The sampling is done to "saturate" a concept, to comprehensively explore it and its relationship to other concepts so that it becomes theoretically meaningful. Because the theory emerges from the data, there is no viable way of determining these sampling dimensions beforehand. This does not mean selecting a specific category of clearly defined people; it does mean becoming increasingly selective in collecting a sample by adding to it based on the core variables that emerge as important to the theoretical understanding of the phenomenon under study. The coding becomes increasingly selective as the researcher engages in "discriminate sampling," choosing persons, sites, and documents that enhance the possibility of comparative analysis to saturate categories and complete the study. This might mean returning to previous interviews or sources of data as well as drawing upon new ones. The study proceeds until there is "theoretical saturation," gathering data until no new relevant data are discovered regarding a category and until the categories are well developed and validated.

Strauss and Corbin (1998) go into great detail in describing the varieties of sampling relevant to grounded theory research. Miles and Huberman (1994) also provide a comprehensive account of the types of sampling associated with qualitative inquiry.

The ethnographer has different challenges to anticipate. The researcher's relationship with the group to be studied must be fully acknowledged and described. In some ethnographic studies the researcher may already have membership status. More frequently, there is a "gatekeeper" or conduit for accessing the group. Once contact has been established, will everyone be approached to participate? Will sampling take place according to some thoughtful criteria? Will participants be selected opportunistically, according to convenience or eagerness to participate? The same rules apply in describing the use of artifacts and other sources of data that the ethnographer observes and records.

Elizabeth Moore's (1995) ethnographic study of organizational culture includes her list of 11 criteria for choosing an appropriate company to study, including issues of size, age and tenure of employees, and opportunities for observation and access to company documents and employees. She received entry into a chemical company that met her criteria and gave her unlimited access to the organization. She offered all 29 employees the opportunity to participate in confidential interviews and ended up interviewing a majority of the employees as well as the founders and their wives. The interviews were of four types:

1. Critical event interviews, which focused on critical periods in the evolution of the organization

2. Ethnographic interviews, which dealt with the artifacts and values within the organization

3. Spouse interviews

4. A customer interview

She also relied upon a month of participant observation activities and analysis of organizational documents. The sampling procedures, interviews, observation activities, and documents were described in the Method chapter, and the interview protocols were placed in appendices to the dissertation.

INSTRUMENTATION IN QUALITATIVE STUDIES

The sixth element above, determining instrumentation, is analogous to the Instrumentation section of a proposal described earlier; however, the instrument of choice for the naturalist is the human observer. Thus, qualitative researchers place particular emphasis on improving the human observer and make no claims for the "reliability and validity" of the instrument in the rationalistic sense. (A discussion of reliability and validity in qualitative studies follows later in this chapter.) The task for the student proposing an observational study would be to place considerable emphasis on the training and practice of the observer(s).

Qualitative researchers also recognize the utility of other, more traditional sorts of instrumentation, provided that these are grounded in the central focus of the research and axioms underlying the method. Typically our students have used interviews to generate discussion surrounding the major research questions. For example, Dong (2000) designed an interview schedule to examine the experience of ethnic identity formation for Southeast Asian young offenders, and Jonas (1996) designed a schedule to discover how individuals journey from trauma to resilience. In both instances, the task of the instrumentation section was to describe the interview and demonstrate how the interview served as a sufficient device to focus discussion on the research questions of the study. Questions of reliability and validity are posed differently in this setting because these interviews serve to focus discussion between the researcher and research participant, producing data that are textual rather than numerical.

Although the interview itself may be quite loosely structured and flexible, phenomenological researchers generally prepare some questions in advance, preferring to alter them if it seems appropriate as the interview progresses. Although the precise wording of questions may vary from time to time, certain types of questions are pro forma. Think of the questions as tools to draw out the participant to reflect on the experience itself and its implications in his or her life. Thus, one might request that a participant relax and focus on the incident or the phenomenon and "describe the experience, how you felt, what you did, what you said, what thoughts you have about it." Further questions serve as probes to encourage the interviewee to dig deeper and reflect on the meaning of the experience. These might include the following:

➤   What aspects of the experience stand out for you?

➤   How has the experience affected you?

➤   What changes have you made in your life since the experience?

Some of this can be anticipated and should be meticulously described in the procedure section of the Method chapter.

Several excellent texts are available for guidance in preparing and conducting qualitative research interviews. Among the more popular ones are Mishler (1991), Kvale (1996), Weiss (1994), and Rubin and Rubin (1995). Because these authors take somewhat different perspectives, it is a good idea to become familiar with more than one approach, then determine what best suits your own style and orientation.

Grounded theory studies generally make primary use of interview techniques as well, although journals and other written records, as well as participant observation methods, may also be employed. Interviews may be either individual or group based, including what are popularly known as "focus group." La Pelle's (1997) dissertation provides a good example of a prepared opening statement to the interviewees:

> I would like you to think about performance review experiences that significantly affected your interest, motivation, or performance in your job or subsequent career decision. Please describe, in as much detail as you can remember, the circumstances surrounding these experiences. (p. 37)

Subsequent probes included possible circumstances, such as work responsibilities, interaction with supervisor, inclusion of rewards or recognition of work, skill development as a function of the review, and personal meaning of the review, among others. More objective questions were included to obtain clarification of work history and work environment after the narrative portion of the interview was completed.

DATA COLLECTION IN QUALITATIVE STUDIES

Issues of determining the successive phases of a study (Item 5 in the list of design considerations provided earlier), planning data collection and recording modes (Item 7), and planning the logistics (Item 9) are subsumed under what we have described as Procedures. Regardless of the sort of study one is conducting, attention always must be paid to how the data are to be collected, independent of the form that the data might take. Data recording may be described along two dimensions, fidelity and structure. An open-ended interview, when properly recorded, has high fidelity and little structure, whereas a standardized paper-and-pencil test has both high fidelity and high structure. We recommend the use of tape recorders to record interviews and place little reliance on the use of field notes (i.e., low fidelity and low structure). A diary or journal to record impressions, reactions, and other significant events that may occur during the data collection phase of research, however, can be a useful source of information, and we encourage use of such a diary or journal.

The issue of data analysis (Item 9) may be more problematic for those considering qualitative research than it is for those undertaking conventional quantitative research. One perspective comes from Lincoln and Guba (1985), who state, "Not very much can be said about data analysis in advance of the study" (p. 241). This leaves the student in a difficult position, particularly if a committee is clamoring for a data analysis section.

The fact of the matter seems to be that quite a bit can be said about data analysis within the context of qualitative studies. Chapter 12 of Lincoln and Guba's *Naturalistic Inquiry* (1985) considers the issue of "processing naturalistically obtained data" in considerable detail. Marshall and Rossman (1999) describe five steps in the analysis of qualitative data, and Miles and Huberman (1994) devote an entire text to the issue of qualitative data analysis. We consider some of these works in more detail in the following chapter. The main point is that even though a student may not be able to refer to specific statistical procedures, we believe that the general framework of an analysis can be specified in advance. Students should expect that both qualitative and quantitative dissertations are likely to involve multiple phases of data analysis.

VALIDITY AND RELIABILITY IN
QUALITATIVE DISSERTATIONS

Trustworthiness (Item 10) is a general term representing what conventional researchers think of as internal and external validity, reliability, and objectivity. Qualitative researchers have developed their own language to describe these terms. In naturalistic research the "trustworthiness" of the design becomes the standard upon which it is likely to be judged, and the Method chapter becomes a major component upon which this judgment is based.

In traditional empirical research, we are mindful of the importance of reliability, internal validity, and external validity of measures and procedures. The corresponding terms in naturalistic inquiry are auditability, credibility, and fittingness (Guba & Lincoln, 1981).

1. *Reliability* concerns the replication of the study under similar circumstances. The naturalistic investigator derives consistency through coding the raw data in ways so that another person could understand the themes and arrive at similar conclusions. The researcher's coding scheme needs to be introduced in the Method chapter, with the understanding that the analysis is likely to be modified both during and after data collection.

2. *Internal validity* refers to the validity of a causal inference. In naturalistic inquiry, credibility or truth value is ascertained through structural corroboration. Such corroboration might be accomplished by spending sufficient time with subjects to check for distortions (prolonged engagement), exploring the participant's experience in sufficient detail (persistent observation), and checking multiple sources of data such as other investigators, written records, diaries, field notes, and so on (triangulation). Peer debriefing, revising working hypotheses as more data become available, clarifying tentative findings with the participants, and videotaping interviews for comparisons with the recorded data are typical procedures for adding to the credibility of the study. These activities would need to be noted in the Method chapter.

3. *External validity* refers to the generalizability of the findings of the study. The qualitative study emphasizes the "thick description" of a relatively small number of participants within the context of a specific set-

ting. The descriptions of the participants or setting under study are sufficiently detailed to allow for transferability to other settings. Samples
can change as the study proceeds, but generalizations to other participants and situations are always modest and mindful of the context of
individual lives.

Part of the challenge of completing a dissertation proposal using
qualitative methods is to master the language of the qualitative paradigm of inquiry. The following are some specific procedures that can be
employed to enhance the trustworthiness of qualitative research project. If adopted, they should be described in the procedure section of the
Method chapter.

Criteria of Adequacy and Appropriateness of Data (Morse, 1998). "Adequacy" pertains to the amount of data collected in a qualitative study,
analogous to ensuring sufficient power by insisting on an adequate
number of participants in a quantitative study. Adequacy is achieved
when you have obtained enough data so that the previously collected
data are confirmed ("saturation") and understood. "Appropriateness" means that information has been sampled and chosen purpose-
fully rather than randomly, to meet the theoretical needs of the study.
Multiple sources of data are obtained to provide saturation and confir-
mation of the emerging model.

The Audit Trail. An audit trail refers to keeping a meticulous record of
the process of the study so that others can recapture steps and reach the
same conclusions. An audit trail includes not only the raw data but
also evidence of how the data were reduced, analyzed, and synthe-
sized, as well as process notes that reflect the ongoing inner thoughts,
hunches, and reactions of the researcher. A further possible step, called
an "external audit," involves asking an external consultant who has no
relationship to the study to review the materials and assess the findings and interpretations for consistency (Creswell, 1998).

Member Checks. It is common in the qualitative literature for researchers to return to informants and present the entire written narrative, as
well as the interpretations derived from the information, with the in-
tention of confirming the accuracy and credibility of the findings. For

some researchers, this is consistent with elevating the informant from the role of a participant in the study to the role of "co-researcher."

Triangulation. Triangulation refers to soliciting data from multiple and different sources as a means of corroborating evidence and illuminating a theme or a theory. The different sources may include additional participants, other methodologies, or previously conducted studies.

Peer Review or Debriefing (Creswell, 1998). Many qualitative researchers make use of peers or colleagues to play the role of "devil's advocate," asking tough questions about data collection, data analysis, and data interpretation in order to keep the researcher honest. The other role of the peer reviewer is to provide professional and emotional support by being an empathic listener to the researcher along the way. Both the researcher and the debriefer typically keep written accounts of their sessions together.

This concludes the presentation of the basic elements of a Method chapter for a thesis or dissertation. When the study is completed and the Results and Discussion chapters have been added to the document, it is necessary to go back to the Method chapter and change the verb tense from future to past. We also recommend removing any detailed sections on data analysis from the Method chapter and incorporating that material into the Results chapter.

BOX 5.1

Student Suggestions

1. Pilot test any instruments you use, whether you make them up yourself or they are standard research tools. Every person can misread or misunderstand something different. It also helps to ask your pilot subjects specific questions, such as inquiring if a section was interesting or difficult.

2. I was amazed how well-known instruments can contain vague or ambiguous items. You can't trust that other researchers have constructed scales that will be appropriate for your use. If you want to compare your results to scores reported in the literature, however, you can't tamper with the instrument.

3. If you decide to construct your own instrument, never start with demographic items. Most researchers put them at the end. They are boring. Be sure your questionnaire looks nice and aesthetic. Questionnaires done on dot matrix printers go in the trash. It must be clear and easy to understand. Put your response alternatives in columns rather than rows. It is easier for the eye to follow.

4. It helps a lot to give an incentive to subjects. Include a stamped, self-addressed envelope. Most important is personal contact. My committee thought I would get a 10% return rate from a mailing to APA members, so I made sure to contact people who had access to subjects directly.

5. One relatively inexpensive way to encourage subjects to participate is to offer a lottery or drawing for money, a gift certificate, or some item of value. That way it will not cost an arm and a leg to pay every subject but create a really worthwhile reward for one or a few subjects.

CHAPTER 6

Presenting the Results of Empirical Studies

The purpose of a Results section is to present the findings as clearly as possible. To do this it is necessary to plan the presentation before one writes it. One major difficulty students have is that they do not begin with a plan for the order in which to present the results. A second problem is the simple fact that students are most likely inexperienced, and the insecurity generated by this inexperience tends to result in the inclusion of too much information in the Results chapter. In most dissertations the Results chapter contains JUST THE FACTS: tables, figures, transcript summaries, and the author's description of what is important and noteworthy about these. Extended discussion of the results, though very important, belongs in the Discussion chapter. Additional literature summaries and a rehash of the conceptual framework or methods are unnecessary and detract from the purpose of the Results chapter.

Of course, there are counterexamples to these general organizing principles, particularly in the case of qualitative dissertations that may combine Results and Discussion chapters, and some departments may encourage students to present the results and discussion as a single interconnected chapter. We are aware of this alternative format and agree that in some cases it may improve the readability and flow of the dissertation. Nevertheless, we base the organization of this chapter on the assumption that the student's dissertation will contain separate Results and Discussion chapters.

How should the results be organized? There is no one standard answer that applies to every case, and it may not matter, but only if (a) there is an organizational logic that can be described to the readers and (b) one does a good job of leading the reader through the results. A few suggestions might be of benefit.

1. Begin with a simple statement that describes the structure of the results chapter. Usually this will be a short paragraph that essentially states, "This is the Results chapter and this is how it is organized." When this is clearly done the reader begins with an understanding of the logic behind your organization of the Results chapter and a sense of what the chapter contains.

2. Second, the results should be organized in such a way that the reader is not confronted with a large mass of data. Although it is true that computer printouts provide extensive information, not all of this should appear in your dissertation.

3. Third, forgo engaging in an extended discussion of the meaning of the findings; these discussions belong in the Discussion chapter. Also, avoid rehashing all the information in the tables. The task is to give a simple, clear, and complete account of the results. LEAD THE READER CAREFULLY THROUGH THE FINDINGS, MAKING SURE THAT THE READER KNOWS WHAT YOU CONSIDER TO BE THE IMPORTANT OBSERVATIONS.

WHERE TO BEGIN?

Most Results chapters can be divided into three basic sections: a description of the sample, the examination of research questions and/ or testing of hypotheses, and the examination of additional questions generated by earlier analyses or further exploratory investigation.

Most Results chapters begin with a description of the sample. Simple demographics (sex, marital status, age, etc.) can be presented in written or tabular form. If the unit of analysis is not a person, then variables that describe the characteristics of the unit being studied should be presented. For example, if the unit of analysis was the city, then it might be appropriate to describe population density, ethnic composition, median house price, and so on. This gives the reader a picture of the basic unit or units in the study. Such information may be presented in a table or a figure, or simply discussed in the text. It depends on what provides the reader with the best overall picture of the results. It is not necessary to supply the raw data, but one must make sense of the data for the reader. (If you are not sure which way to present the data, try presenting it in different ways and ask a friend to read the different presentations, and always consult with your committee.)

ADDRESSING RESEARCH QUESTIONS AND HYPOTHESES

After describing the sample, the next step probably will be to address research questions and/or hypotheses. Sometimes it may be appropriate to address one at a time under separate subheadings, but subheadings such as "Hypothesis 1" tend not to work. This is because more than one hypothesis is often addressed by a single analysis, and use of a hypothesis number as a section heading provides little information. It seems much more effective to create subheadings that describe the content of the hypothesis being addressed. For example, "The Relationship Between Anxiety and Employee Performance" seems to make a better heading than "Hypothesis 2." It also may be awkward to use subheadings that isolate a single statistical procedure, such as "Results of Analysis of Variance." This is because a number of different statistical procedures may be needed to address a single question, such as the relationship between performance and anxiety suggested above. One method that appears to work is to address one research question at a time. This may involve discussing the results of several different statistical analyses and the testing of several different hypotheses. Every situation is different, so remember the main goal, a clear and simple presentation.

For example, suppose you are interested in susceptibility to group influence. One *research question* (there probably would be more than one) might ask about the specific relationship between gender and conformity. (Conformity is one indicator of group influence.) One *research hypothesis* (there may be more than one) might be that females are more conforming than males. The specific *statistical hypotheses* might be that (a) the mean conformity rate for females will be equal to or less than the mean conformity rate for males (the null hypothesis) and (b) the mean conformity rate for females will be higher than that of males (the alternative hypothesis, suggesting a specific direction of influence to be examined by a one-tailed statistical test). In the above design a one-tailed t test probably would be used, given that conformity rate was a continuously distributed dependent variable. If the null hypothesis was rejected, the alternative hypothesis would be supported, thus providing support for the research hypothesis.

It is typically best to organize the results around answering the *research question(s)*. For example, the above question concerning the relationship between gender and conformity would compose one section of the Results chapter. Remember that there may be a number of statistical analyses that bear on a specific research question or hypothesis. For example, given the question of gender differences in conformity behavior, there may be two indicators of conformity. Thus, one would examine gender differences for each measure, resulting in two statistical tests. One or more paragraphs within this section would present these analyses. Each analysis would specifically address one (or in some cases more than one) null and alternative hypothesis (i.e., the *statistical hypotheses*). When all the analyses relating to this research question have been presented and explained, the analyses relating to the next *research question* would begin, typically starting a new section.

One should try to avoid presenting tremendous amounts of data, but this is not always possible. Complex studies, with many measures, may leave the author no choice but to present a large amount of information. The more data that must be presented, the greater the burden on both the author and the consumer. Later in this chapter we present some hints for reducing large amounts of data. Sometimes it is appropriate to note that certain findings were not significant, without actually presenting the findings, but this is usually *not* appropriate if the findings confront major hypotheses. Accept the fact that, as an author, you are in a better position to judge the importance of specific findings than anyone else, and organize the results to emphasize what is important. It is reasonable to ignore or give passing reference to what is unimportant, but remember that there is a difference between what is unimportant and what fails to support your hypotheses.

The material that follows is directed primarily to quantitative analysis. We address the issue of qualitative analysis at the end of this chapter. We suggest that the reader read both sections.

THE NUTS AND BOLTS OF DESCRIBING QUANTITATIVE RESULTS

The Results section usually presents the outcome of multiple analyses of data. Each analysis can be broken down into a series of different statements. These statements present the major findings, some of which may also be presented in tabular or graphic form (i.e., in tables and figures). The major focus, however, remains the text and the presentation of important findings, together with test statistics, within the text. An explanation of four different types of statement is given below.[1]

Statement Type I. Refers the reader to a table or a figure and describes what is being measured or presented.

> Example 1—Describing a table of correlations.
> The correlations between student ratings and final examination marks are given in Table 1.

> Example 2—Describing a table of percentages.
> Table 1 presents the percentage of responses for each of the five possible categories.

> Example 3—Describing a table of means.
> Table 1 presents the means and standard deviations by drug category.

Statement Type II. Describes the major findings shown in a table or figure. Comparisons of means, standard deviations, frequencies, and correlations between the various measures or conditions represent examples. Frequently these sentences are combined with the third type of statement discussed below.

Example 1—Description of correlational table or figure.
Of the 10 correlations, it can be seen that 9 are positive and 8 are above $r = .32$.

Example 2—Description of an experiment.
Males rated applicants who wore cologne as lower in intelligence and friendliness. In contrast, females rated the applicants who wore cologne higher in intelligence and friendliness.

Example 3—Description of figure.
As shown in Figure 2, the rate of typing increased from a baseline of about .7 words per minute to about 1.5 words per minute during the treatment period.

Statement Type III. Presents the results of a statistical (inferential) test, such as F or t. These statements typically are combined with statement type II. We recommend that you make a habit of citing the exact probability levels observed in your analyses, except when summarizing a number of analyses simultaneously. When findings are not statistically significant we recommend that you also report the probability level. For example, you would report $p = .024$ rather than $p < .05$ for a statistically significant finding, and you would report $p = .324$, rather than NS for a nonstatistically significant finding. This is inconsistent with long-standing practices of many researchers and the fourth edition of the *Publication Manual of the American Psychological Association* (1994). We believe, however, that the next edition of the APA manual will make recommendations more similar to our own, and there are numerous reasons for following our suggestions, which are by no means unique. First, reporting the exact probability level provides more information than simply reporting that a value is or is not statistically significant at some predetermined level. For example, a probability level of .051 and .859 could both be reported as NS (not significant), but clearly these values are quite different. This helps avoid unsatisfactory language, such as "marginally significant" or "almost significant," that is recommended against by all authors discussing good practice in this area. Second, the information contained in probability (i.e., *p*) values is valuable to those who wish to conduct a "meta-analysis" of your dissertation findings. The difference between a *p* value of .051 and one of .859 would be extremely valuable for such an analysis, but with a report of NS it would be difficult, if not impossible, to reconstruct these values, particularly in the absence of an effect size indicator. The practice of reporting *p* values as not significant (e.g., NS) or as less than some predetermined level (e.g., $p < .05$) is based on conventions developed prior to the ready availability of exact probability levels from computer printouts. Using these earlier conventions one would hand calculate a test statistic and look up a "critical value" in a table. These two values (the calculated and the critical) would be compared, and the comparison would provide the basis for the decision to reject or fail to reject the null hypothesis. Our argument is simply that these procedures are no longer necessary and exclude valuable information from your presentation of findings.

Example 1—Describing correlations (summary statement).

Six of the correlations between amount of homework and GPA were found to be positive and significant at $p < .05$.

Example 2—Describing an experiment.

The retention of communication content was found to vary significantly as a function of the time and method of measurement, $F(2, 80) = 34.45$, $p = .003$.

The image instructed groups were significantly faster, $F(1, 60) = 7.34$, $p = .007$, and made fewer errors, $F(1, 60) = 9.94$, $p = .004$, than the no image groups.

Combining Statement Types II and III.

Example 1—Describing correlations.

The correlation between mean parent IQ and child IQ was statistically significant, $r(190) = .87$, $p = .041$.

Example 2—Describing an experiment.

> The mean score for females (75.5) was significantly greater than the mean score for males (70.7), $F(1, 28) = 23.1$, $p = .022$.

Statement Type IV. Summary statements of the major findings or conclusions.

> Example 1—The results suggest that students who reported very heavy drug use had significantly higher maladjustment scores than other students.
>
> Example 2—In sum, these analyses suggest that educational achievement among those raised in single-parent families is consistently lower than among those raised in two-parent families, even when controlling for parents' education and income.

The statements above provide examples of the variety of comments that might be used to describe the results of an empirical study. When describing results, try to avoid editorializing with such statements as "Unfortunately, the findings were not significant" or "This result was quite surprising." Such statements do little to enhance the reader's understanding of the results and may make your writing appear sophomoric.

SPEAKING OF SIGNIFICANCE

Students often have difficulty summarizing the results of statistical tests, or tests of statistical significance. Below we present a few examples of poorly written statements that describe the results of statistical tests and explain why the writing is poor. These examples are all taken from an exercise in which students were asked to write a Results section explaining an analysis of variance of the differences in recorded number of behavior problems for foster children. The three independent variables were ethnicity (African American, Hispanic, or Caucasian), gender (male or female), and placement type (placement with a relative or nonrelative). We try to cite examples of typical errors in an attempt to help you avoid such pitfalls in writing about quantitative results.

Statement 1

The African American males show a slightly higher number of problems when placed in foster care, but not of enough significance.

Comment: The author is trying to indicate that the results were not statistically significant, but as written the statement makes little sense and the comparison group is unclear.

Better: The African American males show a slightly higher number of problems than Hispanic or Anglo males when placed in foster care, but these differences were not statistically significant.

Statement 2

The main effects are only statistically significant for type of placement, which has a higher effect than any other factor with $p < .01$.

Comment: The author misinterprets significance level as size of effect by assuming that, because the p value for type of placement was smaller than the p value for the other factors in an analysis of variance, the effect of placement was larger or stronger. This is not generally true.

Better: Of the main effects for type of placement, race/ethnicity, and gender, only the main effect of type of placement was statistically significant, $F(1, 60) = 7.34$, $p = .003$.

Statement 3

Hispanic females and African American males also show a slight effect of the type of placement, the mean scores of behavioral problems being significantly lower for the relative placement.

Comment: When there are multiple independent variables, it is important to make clear which categories of which variables are being compared. In the above statement it is not clear if the comparison is being made across gender, ethnicity, or placement type. It is also not clear what a "slight effect" is.

Better: Within the relative placement group, the mean number of behavioral problems for Hispanic males is slightly larger than that for
Hispanic females (Hispanic males, 36.3; Hispanic females, 33.5).

Statement 4

The effect of ethnicity by itself is slightly significant, as shown in Table 1.

Comment: Avoid statements such as "slightly significant," "highly significant," and "marginally significant." These are statistically incorrect. An effect is either significant at some preset level of significance or it is not.

Better: The main effect of ethnicity was statistically significant, $F(2, 80) = 3.45$, $p = .026$.

Statement 5

Apparently, the analysis of variance sheet listed the significance of F
ratio to be .003. Therefore, one can say that the probability of ran-
dom error that may have produced this effect will be at the $p < .003$ significance level.

Comment: Often writers think that they need to "explain" the meaning
of a statistical test; however, it is generally acceptable to assume
that this is within the realm of "common knowledge." Thus, unless
your statistical analysis is novel or unique, avoid language like that
above. If you sound like your statistics text, you probably are on the
wrong track. Note also that the specific effect being evaluated is
not stated.

Better: The analysis of variance in Table 1 shows the main effect of type
of placement to be statistically significant, $F(1, 66) = 34.45$, $p = .003$.

Following the guidelines above, one would most likely address the
issue of mean differences in behavior problems using a combination of
statement Types I, II, and III, as follows:

Table 1 presents the mean differences in behavior problems by gender, ethnicity, and type of placement. As can be seen in Table 1, for every gender by race/ethnicity comparison, children placed in relative foster care evidence fewer behavior problems than children placed in nonrelative foster care. An analysis of variance of these results is presented in Table 2. The results reveal that of the three main effects, only placement setting (the home of a relative vs. the home of a nonrelative) had a significant effect on children's behavior problems, $F(1, 609) = 9.089, p = .007$.

PRESENTING TABLES AND GRAPHS

GENERAL CONSIDERATIONS

Nearly all dissertations contain one or more tables or figures (i.e., graphs) designed to organize the results of statistical analyses. This section, and the sections that follow, presents the basic principles and logic of describing statistical analyses. The first question an author should ask him- or herself is "Should these results be presented in a table, in a figure, or simply as part of the text?" Generally, a table containing only a few numbers is unnecessary. For example, a table showing the sex distribution in a sample is unnecessary because this information could be covered adequately in the text by simply stating the percentage of males or females in the sample. In a study with many groups, however, where the sex distribution within each group is important, it probably would be more efficient to present this information in tabular form.

Similarly, many dissertations contain graphic presentations of data. These usually are called "figures." A figure may be a chart, graph, photograph, line drawing, or just about anything else that is not a table. The decision to use a figure is an important one and should be thought through carefully. Figures take considerable space and may clutter a dissertation rather than make it easier to follow. For example, there is little value in using bar charts to present information that can be displayed easily and economically in a table, unless the presentation dramatically illustrates a comparison that is not readily apparent from a table. Students may become enthusiastic about their ability to produce bar and pie charts with existing computer programs; however, the tendency to fill a dissertation with such charts should be avoided.

Considerable planning should precede the construction of tables and figures. You need to think carefully about the optimal number of tables and their content, as well as how to design the specific organization of each table to most effectively illustrate the important aspects of the analyses you wish to emphasize. In addition, you may be required to meet the formatting demands of your university or style requirements of an organization such as the American Psychological Association (APA). In this chapter we follow many of the guidelines and recommendations of the American Psychological Association for constructing tables, and in Chapter 12 we discuss how to describe results in text in accordance with APA guidelines. Note that we have also deviated somewhat from the APA recommendations for the presentation of significance levels (see Statement Type III, above). You should check both your department's and your library's requirements before assuming that the exact format presented in this chapter, or by the APA, is appropriate for your needs.

Below we provide a few simple guidelines that can greatly improve the look and readability of tables regardless of the specific requirements of your university.

1. Even though computer analyses produce values with many decimal places, a rounded value often conveys information more clearly than a value with many decimal places. Is there really any logic to reporting that 36.92273% of the sample was single, when you can simply report that 37% was single? (It is generally important to report correlations or covariances only to three decimal places to facilitate the reproduction of analyses based on these values. Otherwise, keep it simple and round to a reasonable number of decimal places.)

2. Values can be compared both down columns and across rows. There is some debate over which is best and easiest to visualize for the purpose of comparisons. The following two sections suggest that percentages in univariate (one-variable) and bivariate (two-variable) tables be calculated within columns, to facilitate comparisons across rows; however, it may be necessary to do just the opposite when attempting

to include many comparisons within one table. Try to be consistent in this regard.

3. Column and row averages and totals can provide much additional information, without cluttering the table. When excluding these values, make certain that the base number and direction for calculating percentages (i.e., within rows or columns) are clear.

4. It is unnecessary, and undesirable, to cram every number on a computer printout into a table. Select the information to be included carefully, organize it to make the information visually appealing, and use plenty of white space to improve visual organization.

5. The tables and figures in a Results section should relate to one another and to the text. This relationship should be represented in both the structure of the tables and the use of language. Tables and figures should use similar formats, and results should be organized similarly. If a table refers to a measure or scale using a particular designation, the same designation should be used in all tables and figures as well as in the text. The author's familiarity with the scales and measures used in a dissertation will not be shared by most readers. If something is referred to as an "inventory," it should be referred to as an inventory throughout, not as a scale, battery, or subscale. If one refers to "reaction time" in the text, this should not become "response latency" in a table.

6. Finally, avoid the use of computer-based variable names when possible. Tables that contain labels such as CHTOT or ABANY are obtuse. Sometimes it is necessary to use "shortened" labels in a table to save space in columns, but try to create labels that describe the variable. For example, CHTOT stands for "Child's Health Total Score." Although this is a long label, it could be represented in a table with a label such as "Child's Health."

THE PARTS OF A TABLE

Tables typically contain five major parts: number, title, headings, body, and notes. Each of these is described briefly below. More detailed discussion directed toward specific types of tables, such as frequency distributions, cross-tabulations, and analysis of variance, is presented in the following sections.

Numbering Tables

Every table must be numbered. The American Psychological Association suggests that all tables be numbered with Arabic numerals in the order in which they are first mentioned in the text. Begin with Table 1, and continue throughout. Do not use Table A, Table B, and so forth, and do not use Roman numerals (Table I, Table II, etc.). Do not number tables within chapters (Table 3.1, Table 3.2, etc.), and do not number tables containing related or similar information with letters (Table 5a, Table 5b, etc.). Instead, consider combining the tables. The only exception to these rules concerns the numbering of tables within appendices. The third table in Appendix B is Table B-3, and the first table in Appendix A is Table A-1.

Table Titles

Every table must have a title. Generally, a good title presents the name of the major variable or variables and type of analysis but does not contain information that unnecessarily lengthens the title. Information that can be presented in table headings does not have to be in the title. Good table titles often take considerable trial and error to construct. The following sections, which highlight specific types of analysis, give many examples of clear table titles, as well as completed tables to use as guidelines or templates. The APA suggests that all table titles be italicized and that major words be capitalized.

Table Headings

Headings tell the reader what variables and statistics are being presented and establish the organization of the table. It is considered legitimate to use abbreviations for headings, including "f" for frequency and % for percent, but the meaning of the abbreviation should be obvious. *Do not* use computer mnemonics or variable names, and do not use scale acronyms without including a note as to their meaning. For example, a mnemonic used with the National Opinion Research Center General Social Survey is XMARSEX. Most people would not realize that this refers to the respondent's attitude regarding extramarital sex, and it is not advisable to use such mnemonics as labels in tables. Similarly, many persons might assume that BDI refers to the Beck Depression Inventory, but a note to this effect must be included in a table that uses BDI as a heading.

Table Body

The table body contains the numbers, or data. As indicated above, do not clutter the table with unnecessary numbers, and round numbers to improve readability. When cells of the table are empty, it is customary to enter a dash (—) to indicate that no data are contained within the cell. This prevents the reader from thinking that a number was excluded inadvertently.

Table Notes

There are three kinds of table notes: general notes, specific notes, and notes indicating the statistical significance of findings, called "probability notes." A general note is indicated by the word *Note*. APA format requires that this be italic and followed by a period. General notes are used to provide information referring to the table as a whole, including the meaning of symbols or abbreviations. For example, one would use a general note to indicate that BDI referred to the Beck Depression Inventory. Specific notes are used to refer to the content of a specific cell and are given superscript lowercase letters, beginning with the letter "a." Specific notes should begin in the upper left of a table and be lettered from left to right across table rows. Probability notes indicate the outcome of significance tests. Asterisks are used to indicate the probability levels, one asterisk being used for the lowest level, two for next lowest, and so on. Probability notes usually appear at the bottom of tables as follows:

$*p < .05. **p < .01. ***p < .001.$

A one-tailed test may be distinguished from a two-tailed test by using an alternative symbol in the probability notes. For example:

$*p < .05$, two tailed. $+p < .05$, one tailed.

Note that we have recommended *against* the use of probability notes in favor of providing the exact probability level (i.e., level of significance or p value) available from a computer printout; however, your institution may require that you include these in accordance with APA format. Thus, it seems reasonable to inquire of your committee regarding the use of probability notes as opposed to the presentation of exact probability values as a separate row or column of a table. If you do choose to use probability notes, you should remember two very important points about them. First, notes are relevant to only one table. Thus, just because you used a note to define BDI in one table, it is not appropriate to assume that it need not be defined in future tables. Second, these notes should be consistent across all tables. Thus, if one asterisk indicates $p < .05$ in one table, it should also indicate $p < .05$ in the next, not $p < .01$ or some other level.

Many of the major critics of the "null hypothesis significance test" approach to data analysis also call for the inclusion of confidence intervals and/or measures of effect size in all tables presenting the results of statistical tests. This issue is too complex to be fully addressed here, but you should know that null hypothesis significance testing has come under attack during the past few years. Critics range from those who wish to condemn the entire tradition to those who recommend relatively modest changes in the way that results of hypothesis-testing research studies are presented. The arguments behind these positions are summarized in Newton and Rudestam (1999) and fortified by a set of papers published in Harlow, Mulaik, and Steiger (1997). The primary implication for students who continue to draw upon the hypothesis-testing tradition of quantitative research—and that includes most graduate students in the social sciences—is to be aware of the limited information conveyed by *only* reporting whether or not group differences or relationships between variables are statistically significant at some predetermined level of significance (p value).

Statistical significance is merely a statement about the likelihood of the observed result, that is, the probability of making an error in generalizing findings from a sample to a population. In research terms, this refers to maintaining reasonable control over Type I error. What statistical significance does not deal with is the size or strength of a relationship between variables (called the "effect size"). The clearest demonstration of this distinction is to note that many findings that are not statistically significant at the .05 level, let's say, would be statistically significant at the .05 level if a greater number of subjects had been included in the study. For instance, a simple product-moment correlation of .179 is statistically significant at the .05 level with a sample size of 120. To achieve the same level of significance with a sample size of 15 would necessitate a corresponding correlation of .512! One implication of this phenomenon is the wisdom of including a sufficient number of participants in a quantitative study to give yourself a fair chance of obtaining statistically significant results. (This is what Cohen [1988] refers to as "power" and is directly related to reducing Type II error. Power is discussed in Chapter 5.) Another implication, particularly relevant to this book, is that you should augment your presentation of data to include enough useful information so that the reader (as well as the researcher) can learn more about your empirical findings than merely whether or not they are statistically significant. The types of information to be considered include precise p values, effect sizes, and confidence intervals.

In the following exposition of tabular presentation, we offer some alternatives for the presentation of findings from the most common statistical tests.

PREPARING THE DATA FOR ANALYSIS

The first type of "results" information likely to be presented in a dissertation is a description of the sample. The researcher is likely to present a number of one-variable (or univariate) tables called "frequency distributions." Some standard guidelines for the presentation of frequency distributions will be discussed below. The first consideration, however, is to guarantee that the data have been tabulated correctly. Whether working by hand or with a computer, correct tabulation of the results is a necessity. The following steps outline the process leading to the production of both meaningful tables and reasonable statistical analysis.

STEP 1: IS THE VARIABLE
IN THE CORRECT FORM?

Mutually Exclusive Categories. The variable must be constructed so that each observation may be placed in one and only one category. For example, demographic descriptions often include a "Marital Status" item that includes the categories single, married, divorced, and widowed. It is possible that a person could check both the single and divorced categories. This pattern may be reduced or eliminated by wording the question to read, "Are you *currently* never married, divorced," and so on.

When questions assume the "Check all that apply" character, each response must become a separate variable. For example, when assessing a respondent's feelings, behavior, and experience related to a parent's alcohol use, a checklist of items is presented and instructions are to "Check all that occurred in your family." Responses include "Lost sleep because of a parent drinking," "Ever heard parents fight when one was drunk," and "Wish parent would stop drinking." Items in the checklist each become a separate variable, with a "Yes" and "No" value. When the Yes values are assigned or coded a "1" and the No values are coded a "0," the sum of the Yes codes becomes a new variable that can be used to assess the extent of the damage from alcoholism within the family.

Exhaustive Categories. Every item in a questionnaire, scale, or instrument must have a response for every case, even if the response is "Not Applicable." Thus frequency distributions and their tables must include the percentage of "Valid Responses," those for which meaningful answers were obtained, and the number of invalid responses, often called "Missing Values," for which irrelevant or meaningless answers occurred. When working with frequency distributions, check to make sure that you can account for (i.e., exhaust) the entire sample for every distribution. (This prevents having to figure out after the fact where some of your data went.)

Missing Values. Observations that do not fit logically into a variable's meaningful categories also must be accounted for to produce a set of exhaustive categories. Those that do not fit into these "meaningful" categories are called missing values. Missing values may occur for a variety of reasons.

1. No response, no answer

2. Uncodable responses

3. Incorrect measurements or broken equipment

4. Lost data, subjects that cannot be located

Most computer programs permit special codes, called missing value codes, to allow the program to separate the meaningful responses from the missing values. The number of missing values is usually reported in a table note. When the number of missing values is added to the number of valid responses, the entire sample should be accounted for.

STEP 2: GROUPING THE DATA

The second step is to place the data for each observation (i.e., each case or subject) into one of the variable's categories. Although this is often done with a computer, it may also be done by hand tally of the frequencies in each category of the variable in question. Some examples will be presented at the end of this section.

STEP 3: CREATING A CORRECTLY LABELED TABLE

Creating a frequency distribution does not complete the process of making the distribution presentable and easily understood. The table that you create must be correctly labeled and identified. In addition, you may need to satisfy the requirements of the library or publication that will receive the information. Some general rules, consistent with APA guidelines, are presented below.

SOME GUIDELINES FOR CREATING CORRECTLY CONSTRUCTED AND LABELED TABLES

THE CONTENTS OF A COMPLETE TABLE

1. A table number

2. A table name or title that includes the name of the variable and some information about the sample or population

3. The set of mutually exclusive and exhaustive categories you have developed (the headings)

4. Frequencies, percentages, and totals (the body)

5. Notes, including the source, if the data are not original

DEALING WITH MISSING VALUES

Sometimes missing data may create a problem when constructing tables. These problems may be dealt with in a number of ways:

1. Create a category to contain the missing data

2. Footnote the number of missing values

3. Create a residual category for all unimportant values

ARE THERE GUIDELINES FOR LINE SPACING IN TABLES?

The APA guidelines require that every line in a table be double spaced; however, we have never seen a dissertation that follows this requirement to the letter. This is because the requirement is primarily for journal articles being submitted for publication. We recommend that our students use spacing to make the tables readable, and we follow that guideline in the materials presented in this chapter.

MODELS FOR THE TABULAR PRESENTATION OF COMMON DESCRIPTIVE AND INFERENTIAL STATISTICAL ANALYSES

The next several pages in this chapter provide examples of correctly labeled tables using the data from computer printouts of different statistical analyses likely to appear in dissertations. We present univariate (one-variable), bivariate (two-variable), and some multivariate examples. These examples may be used as guidelines or templates for your own analyses. For each type of example, we begin with a table that displays the options, based on whether the independent variables are discrete or continuously distributed (see Table 6.1). In addition, we consider the presentation of both the descriptive and inferential statistical material, often working directly from computer printouts. Although the potential number and variations of such tables is far too large to include all situations, we present a set of tables that covers the vast majority of dissertation presentations.

CONSTRUCTING ONE-VARIABLE (UNIVARIATE) TABLES AND STATEMENTS THAT DESCRIBE THEM FROM COMPUTER PRINTOUTS

The two examples that follow are both taken from the 1998 National Opinion Research Center General Social Survey (GSS). The GSS draws data from a national sample of all noninstitutionalized adults in the United States, 18 years of age or older. The data were processed using the Statistical Package for the Social Sciences Release 10.0.0 (September 24, 1999). Two variables are considered. The first assesses how frequently the respondent attends religious services. This variable was given the name ATTEND by those who developed the survey. The second variable, given the name AGE, assesses the respondent's age. The computer printout for ATTEND is presented in Table 6.2, and the correctly labeled table with frequencies and percentages in Table 6.3.

Note that Table 6.2 contains two sections, the first showing the number of valid and missing cases and the second showing the variable's categories, frequency, percent, valid percent, and cumulative percent.

Table 6.1

Models for the Construction of Univariate Tables

Type of Variable?	Appropriate Descriptive Statistics	Appropriate Inferential Statistics	Tables Display? (Table No. of Example)
Discrete	Proportions, percentages	Confidence interval for p; one-sample Z test	F and % of categories (Tables 6.2 and 6.3)
Continuous	Central tendency (mean, median, mode, and variability (standard deviation, range)	Confidence interval for mean; one-sample Z or t test.	F and % of class intervals (Tables 6.4 and 6.5)

The difference between the percent and valid percent columns is that the percent column contains all cases, including the missing values, and the valid percent column excludes the missing values. In this example, the missing values include 2.8% or 81 of the total of 2,904 cases. The cumulative percent column sums the valid percentages down the column. Table 6.3 presents the correctly labeled table based on the data in the computer printout (Table 6.2).

Note the differences between the computer printout and the table. First, a table number, title, and note indicating the data source have been added to the table. Second, only the frequency and percent columns have been included. Third, the full labels have been written out. Category labels are often abbreviated within computer programs, such as "MORE THN ONCE WK" for "More Than Once a Week." When space permits, as it does in this case because there are only two columns of numbers, writing out the category labels helps clarify the table. With many columns of numbers or very long labels you will often need to arrive at creative labels or provide notes to the meaning of variable names and category labels.

The following statement might be used to describe Table 6.3.

Table 6.3 presents the distribution of attendance at religious services. Approximately 24% of the sample state that they attend church at least once a week, whereas another 24% almost never attend.

Table 6.2
SPSS Printout of Variable ATTEND

Statistics

HOW OFTEN R ATTENDS RELIGIOUS SERVICES

N	Valid	2823
	Missing	81

HOW OFTEN R ATTENDS RELIGIOUS SERVICES

		Frequency	Percent	Valid Percent	Cumulative Percent
Valid	NEVER	438	15.1	15.5	15.5
	LT ONCE A YEAR	253	8.7	9.0	24.5
	ONCE A YEAR	400	13.8	14.2	38.6
	SEVRL TIMES A YR	416	14.3	14.7	53.4
	ONCE A MONTH	190	6.5	6.7	60.1
	2-3X A MONTH	271	9.3	9.6	69.7
	NRLY EVERY WEEK	160	5.5	5.7	75.4
	EVERY WEEK	486	16.7	17.2	92.6
	MORE THN ONCE WK	209	7.2	7.4	100.0
	Total	2823	97.2	100.0	
Missing	DK,NA	81	2.8		
Total		2904	100.0		

Note that the summary percentages cited above were obtained by adding and slightly rounding the first two (15.1 + 8.7) and last two (16.7 + 7.2) nonmissing categories of Table 6.3. Note also that many numbers have been left out. It is not the goal to restate every number; if you did so, why would you need a table? The goal is to point out what is perceived as notable in the table, which is in part a matter of judgment on behalf of the data analyst. In this case, the point to be made was that about one fourth of the sample almost never attend and another one fourth attend religious services at least every week.

Table 6.4 presents the computer printout and Table 6.5 the correctly labeled table of a continuously distributed variable, age at first marriage, labeled AGEWED.

Table 6.3

Frequency of Attendance at Religious Services

	f	%
Never	438	15.1
Less Than Once A Year	253	8.7
Once a Year	400	13.8
Several Times a Year	416	14.3
Once a Month	190	6.5
2 or 3 Times a Month	271	9.3
Nearly Every Week	160	5.5
Every Week	486	16.7
More Than Once a Week	209	7.2
Don't Know, No Answer	81	2.8
Total	2904	100.0

Note. Data from 1998 National Opinion Research Center General Social Survey.

The method of presentation of Table 6.5 is different from that of Table 6.3 in a number of ways. Some of these differences are optional, and some result from the fact that one variable is continuous (Age) and the other discrete, but ordinal (Church Attendance). First, note that Table 6.3 includes the missing values, whereas Table 6.5 does not (but indicates these in a table note). This is an optional decision that can be made by the researcher; however, we generally recommend exclusion and note as in Table 6.5. When missing values are excluded, always use the "valid percent" column, as this is based on the total, excluding the missing values. Second, Table 6.5 also includes a column of cumulative percentages not contained in Table 6.3. This is also an optional decision, but cumulative percentages should *never* be included with nominal level data. (Church Attendance is ordinal, Age a ratio variable.) Cumulative percentages help divide the sample into groups and are generally useful only when there is a large number of categories. Third, note that the "value" column of the printout for age in Table 6.4 contains only the numbers 1 through 7. These were replaced by age categories in Table 6.5. This is because when recoding the age categories, which originally ranged from 18 to 89, into 10-year increments, we must supply a number to represent each class interval. To present data for continuously distributed variables with a large number of categories, such as Age,

Table 6.4
Age of Respondent (Recoded)

Statistics

N	Valid	2898
	Missing	6

RECODED AGE

		Frequency	Percent	Valid Percent	Cumulative Percent
Valid	1.00	353	12.2	12.2	12.2
	2.00	644	22.2	22.2	34.4
	3.00	669	23.0	23.1	57.5
	4.00	512	17.6	17.7	75.2
	5.00	303	10.4	10.5	85.6
	6.00	242	8.3	8.4	94.0
	7.00	175	6.0	6.0	100.0
	Total	2898	99.8	100.0	
Missing	System	6	.2		
Total		2904	100.0		

the data analyst will be required to "recode" that variable into a smaller number of categories, as we have done here. The number of categories is up to the researcher, but remember these general principles.

1. The larger the width of the categories, the more data information is lost. In other words, there is more information lost in an age category of 26-45 than in two categories 26-35 and 36-45.

2. Remember to label your tables with the range of values, not the value used to represent that range. In other words, use 18-25, 26-35, etc., not 1, 2, etc.

3. Means, standard deviations, and other descriptive statistics for interval and ratio variables generally are based on the unrecoded data, which contains the most information.

Table 6.5

Distribution of Respondent's Age

Age	f	%	Cum %
18–25	353	12.2	12.2
26–35	644	22.2	34.4
36–45	669	23.1	57.5
46–55	512	17.7	75.2
56–65	303	10.5	85.6
66–75	242	8.4	94.0
76–89	175	6.0	100.0
Total	2898	100.0	

Note. Data from 1998 National Opinion Research Center General Social Survey. Age was not determined for six cases.

4. Do not destroy the original (i.e., unrecoded) data. You may want to code the data differently at some further point in your analysis.

5. Always compare the recoded and unrecoded data to make sure that no mistakes were made and that the missing values were not included in one of the valid groupings (an extremely common error).

6. Try to keep each class interval (i.e., 25-36 is a class interval) the same width. The exceptions typically are made with regard to the first and/or last categories, as illustrated in Table 6.5. Graphs based on recoded or grouped distributions containing unequal class intervals can be highly misleading and should be avoided.

HOW TO CONSTRUCT AND INTERPRET TWO-VARIABLE (BIVARIATE) TABLES

BIVARIATE DISTRIBUTIONS

Bivariate distributions, usually presented in the form of tables, are the basic ingredients of many dissertations in the social sciences, education, and business. It is therefore important to understand clearly the information these tables contain and how to construct the tables in such a way as to extract information correctly. This section concentrates on the general principles involved in constructing bivariate tables and interpreting bivariate relationships. We will discuss three types of bivariate distribution in this section. We begin with tables in which both the independent and dependent variable are categorical. These distributions are usually summarized by using percentages, and the tables are called cross-tabulations. Second, we discuss tables of means and standard deviations that summarize bivariate relationships in which the independent variable is categorical and the dependent variable a score of some sort. For example, consider gender differences in depression or differences between an experimental group and a control group on a measure of performance. Finally, we discuss tables showing the relationship between two variables, both of which are continuously distributed, such as the relationship between the amount of family violence and depression in children.

THE GENERAL FORM OF A BIVARIATE TABLE I: CROSS-TABULATIONS

A bivariate table (also called a "cross-tabulation" or "contingency" table) contains the joint distribution of two categorical variables. The categories of each variable are laid out in the form of a square or rectangle containing rows (representing the categories of one variable) and columns (representing the categories of the other variable). The general form of a bivariate table containing two variables is presented below for two variables X and Y.

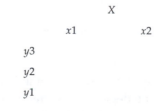

In the above example the letter X represents the variable whose categories form the columns and the letter Y refers to the variable whose categories represent rows. Thus if X represents the response to a question indicating whether or not the respondent has ever had children and Y represents attitudes toward abortion, our table might appear as follows:

| | | Ever Had Children? | |
		Yes	No
Attitudes	AW		
Toward	AAW		
Abortion	NW		

AW = Always wrong
AAW = Almost always wrong
NW = Never wrong

CELL ENTRIES AND MARGINAL TOTALS

The entries that occur in each cell will be the frequencies representing the number of times that each *pair* of values (one from each variable) occurs in the sample. These are called *cell frequencies*. The entries that occur at the end of each row or column are called *marginal frequencies* and represent the total number of times the category of the row variable or column variable occurred. By adding either the row marginal frequencies or the column marginal frequencies you obtain the total N (total sample size).

HOW TO DECIDE WHICH IS THE ROW VARIABLE AND WHICH IS THE COLUMN VARIABLE

The conventional way to construct a table is with the independent variable at the top and the dependent variable at the side of the table. Thus, as in our example above, the letter X is used to identify the independent variable and the letter Y the dependent variable.

An independent variable is presumed to cause or determine a dependent variable. If we discover that attitudes toward abortion are partly a function of parenthood (i.e., parents are more opposed to abortion than nonparents), then parenthood is the independent variable and attitudes toward abortion is the dependent variable.

A dependent variable is the variable that is assumed to depend on or be caused by the independent variable. If you find that income is partly a function of amount of education, income is being treated as a dependent variable.

SUMMARIZING THE INFORMATION IN A BIVARIATE TABLE

Table 6.6 includes frequencies for the Attitudes Toward Abortion by Parenthood table described above. What we want to do is examine Table 6.6 in such a way as to summarize the information meaningfully and to explore the hypothesis that parenthood influences attitudes toward abortion. Notice, however, that we have a different number of parent (Yes) and nonparent (No) respondents. Thus, we cannot compare the Yes with the No distributions (across the different columns) unless we standardize these distributions. The most frequently used standardizing measure is the percentage, but what is the most sensible way to form percentages from this table?

To calculate percentages, we may work within columns, within rows, or with the total sample of 1,000 observations (i.e., total N). Thus Table 6.6 may be percentaged in three different ways. Depending on how a table is constructed, only one of these ways may provide meaningful answers to the question of the relationship between the two variables. Given our recommendation to place the independent variable as the column variable, the appropriate method of percentaging is within the columns (i.e., up and down each column).

When working within columns, the column marginal total becomes the base number used for the total. For example, to find the percentage of Always Wrong (AW) answers among those with children, we take the number of AW responses in that column and divide it by the total

Table 6.6

Bivariate Table Showing the Relationship Between Attitudes Toward Abortion and Parenthood

	Ever Had Children?	
	Yes	No
AW	330	180
AAW	180	120
NW	90	100

Note. Attitudes toward abortion are coded as AW = always wrong, AAW = almost always wrong, and NW = never wrong.

number in that column and then multiply the total by 100: (330/600 × 100 = 55%).

Some texts and dissertation manuals may recommend placing the independent variable in the rows of the table. If this is the case, remember to calculate percentages within the rows (i.e., across each row).

THE CONCEPT OF ASSOCIATION BASED ON SUBGROUP COMPARISONS

The final step is to compare the conditional distributions with one another after the percentages are computed within each column. This allows us to compare the percentage responding Always Wrong, Almost Always Wrong, and Never Wrong across the Yes and No, or Parent and Nonparent, categories.

In doing this, notice that we have a definite routine in mind. We calculate percentages in one direction and make our comparisons in another direction. Because we compute percentages up and down the columns, we compare across the columns.

To examine the hypothesis that parenthood influences attitudes toward abortion, we can use a few simple rules. If each conditional distribution is identical to each other conditional distribution, then we say that the two variables involved are independent of each other or are not related to each other. If the conditional distributions are different, then the two variables are said to be related. To make this more clear, examine Table 6.7, which has been percentaged appropriately, and relabeled for clarity.

A SIMPLE STATISTIC: THE PERCENTAGE DIFFERENCE

One easy method of making a statement about the degree or amount of relationship in a table is to compare the percentages in the conditional distributions. This measure is called a *percentage difference* and is most appropriate for small tables such as Table 6.7. As an example of how this measure might be calculated and used, compare the 55% of the parents who believe that abortion is always wrong with the 45% of nonparents who believe that abortion is always wrong. The difference is 10%. You can now state that 10% more parents than nonparents believe that abortion is always wrong. A similar comparison can be made between the parents and nonparents with regard to the belief that abortion is never wrong. The percentage difference in this comparison is also 10%. An appropriate statement would be "Ten percent more parents than nonparents believe that abortion is always wrong."

GENERAL FORM OF A BIVARIATE TABLE I: PRESENTING TABLES OF GROUP MEANS AND OTHER GROUP DESCRIPTIVE STATISTICS

In addition to the presentation of tables containing frequency counts and percentages, many analyses will examine group differences on continuous variables. Continuous variables are those that can be scaled along a continuum from highest to lowest, most favorable to least favorable, healthy to unhealthy, and the like. Most psychological, sociological, political, and educational measures can be considered continuous variables. Examples are self-efficacy, alienation, political conservatism/liberalism, verbal reasoning ability, and a host of attitudes representing agreement-disagreement or approval-disapproval on a variety of issues. We have already discussed how to present the

Table 6.7
Correctly Percentaged Bivariate Table Showing the Relationship Between
Attitudes Toward Abortion and Parenthood (Column %)

Attitudes Toward Abortion	Ever Had Children?		
	Yes	No	Total
Always wrong	55	45	51
Almost always wrong	30	30	30
Never wrong	15	25	19
Total	100	100	100
	(600)	(400)	(1000)

univariate distribution of such variables by recoding, as shown in Table 6.4. Although some may argue that many of these variables constitute ordinal measurement, and thus pose problems for the computation of means and inferential statistics requiring at least interval measurement, standard practice is to utilize the techniques we suggest below with these variables. This topic is discussed further in Newton and Rudestam (1999). The logic underlying our position is that these variables are continuous at the latent level and thus, when other assumptions are met, do not pose serious problems for the social sciences.

When your goal is to compare groups on these variables, the first task will be to present the group descriptive statistics in tabular form. For example, Sangster (1991) examined the ability of a training course to improve managers' decision-making ability under conditions of uncertainty. The means and standard deviations for training type and level of management experience are presented in Table 6.8.

Note that Table 6.8 is simple and easy to understand. The independent variables are type of training and management experience; the dependent variable is decision-making ability as measured at posttest. Management experience appears to make little difference (.03), and descriptive training appears to result in higher posttest scores than prescriptive training.

The above strategy for presenting group means may be extended to a larger number of groups and a larger number of dependent variables. For example, in Richards's dissertation (1991) 16 variables believed to discriminate drug users from nonusers within secondary schools were

Table 6.8

Means and Standard Deviations for Manager's Decision-Making
Ability at Posttest by Levels of Training Type and Management Experience

Independent Variable	Decision-Making Ability (Posttest)	
	Mean	SD
Training type		
Descriptive (*N* = 42)	5.38	1.79
Prescriptive (*N* = 32)	3.75	1.85
Management experience		
Low (*N* = 33)	4.70	2.07
High (*N* = 41)	4.67	1.92

Note. Maximum possible score = 10.0; *N* = 74.

examined. For each variable, the mean and standard deviation for users and nonusers was presented (see Table 6.9). (We have shortened this table to present only the first 8 variables; the full table contains all 16 variables of interest.)

GENERAL FORM OF A BIVARIATE TABLE II: PRESENTING TABLES OF CONTINUOUSLY DISTRIBUTED VARIABLES

When both the independent and dependent variable are continuously distributed and there is only one such relationship, a correlation coefficient, presented in the text, would typically suffice. Rather than a table, a scatter plot, which is a graph, not a table, would most likely be the best way to display the joint distribution of the two variables. Such relationships can be described in the text by statements of the following type: "The relationship between age of youngest child and number of hours worked by all women in the sample was negative and statistically significant $r(75) = -.21, p = .004$."

The statistical statement indicates both the strength of the relationship (.21, a weak to moderate relationship) and its significance (.004, a statistically significant finding). The "75" in parentheses following the italicized r is the degrees of freedom associated with the statistical test and is one less than the sample size (i.e., $N - 1$).

Table 6.9

Means and Standard Deviations of Variables Discriminating
Drug Users From Non-Users by Drug Use Category

	Drug Use			
	Users		Non-Users	
Discriminating Variables	X	SD	X	SD
No. of "Ds" and "Fs"	1.57	2.67	0.27	0.85
Grade level	8.37	1.50	7.69	1.40
Importance of grades	3.16	0.83	3.41	0.75
Arguing with teachers	2.16	0.83	1.52	0.73
Absent when not sick	2.53	1.07	1.68	0.86
Ever suspended	0.37	0.50	0.08	0.27
How often angry	2.84	1.01	2.24	0.52
Fight or argue with family	2.63	1.01	2.20	0.71

When a large number of relationships is examined simultaneously it may be necessary to present the *correlation matrix* in a table. Two examples are given. The first represents a hypothetical analysis examining the relationship between three variables, X, Y, and Z. Note that it is standard to present the means, standard deviations, and sample sizes of all variables in an analysis along with their correlations. We have included these with the correlation matrix of X, Y, and Z in Table 6.10.

Note that Table 6.10 contains only the correlations below the diagonal of 1.00s. This is because correlations are *symmetrical*; that is, the correlation of X with Z is identical to the correlation of Z with X. Thus there is no need to present both the lower and upper diagonal. Note also that the 1.00s on the *main diagonal* each represent the correlation of a variable with itself.

A second example is derived from an article by Rogers, Parcel, and Menaghan (1991) examining the relationship between mother's work and child behavior problems. Rogers et al. presented the correlation matrix of 23 variables (253 unique correlations) in a single table. We present only the first 5 of these variables in Table 6.11.

A number of variations of the tables discussed above may be encountered in the literature and used by the student. First, the decimal points may be eliminated, as they are usually assumed to exist

Table 6.10
Means, Standard Deviations, and Correlations of Variables X, Y, and Z
(N = 300)

	X	Y	Z
X	1.000		
Y	0.256	1.000	
Z	0.013	0.350	1.000
X̄	3.61	2.74	4.10
S	1.23	1.66	0.93

with correlation coefficients. Second, the main diagonal of 1.0s is sometimes used to present the standard deviations, as opposed to presenting these in a separate row below the correlations as has been shown here. Third, the correlations may be asterisked and probability notes may be used. Fourth, the number of cases may be included in a note, or, when there is much variation from value to value, may be placed in parentheses below each correlation, or may be placed above the main diagonal.

TABULAR PRESENTATION OF THE RESULTS OF INFERENTIAL STATISTICS

The materials above refer primarily to descriptions of results as contained in contingency tables and tables containing means or other descriptive statistics, but they have not addressed the question of *statistical inference*. The question of inference considers whether or not the results can be generalized to the population from which the sample was drawn. In other words, this is the question of whether or not the results are *statistically significant*. Questions regarding whether or not the results are statistically significant usually follow tables describing the results, or are contained within them, but generally do not precede descriptive summaries. For example, in the bivariate table on page 134 (Table 6.7), the results seem to indicate that parents are more opposed to abortion than those who are not parents; however, this table does *not* address the question of whether or not these results are statistically sig-

Table 6.11

Means, Standard Deviations, and Correlations for Mother's Work
and Child Behavior Problems (Rogers, Parcel, & Menaghan, 1991)

	1	2	3	4	5
1 Behavior problems	1.0				
2 Mastery	−.18	1.0			
3 Maternal education	−.08	.21	1.0		
4 Child's age	−.05	−.03	−.11	1.0	
5 Hourly pay	−.10	.19	.24	.02	1.0
X̄	−.80	.27	2.07	62.51	5.58
S	11.41	12.38	1.48	10.15	2.87

Note. Correlations of .08 or greater are significant when one-tailed tests are used.

nificant. This question would be addressed with a chi-square test. These results would be added to Table 6.7 as a note and included within the text.

To facilitate our understanding of tests of statistical significance and how to present them in tabular form, we follow Newton and Rudestam (1999) and conceptualize most dissertations as fitting one of four major types of research question. Each of the four questions leads directly to a choice of descriptive and inferential statistical technique, which in turn leads to a particular type of tabular display. We recommend Newton and Rudestam (1999), Chapter 6, for a detailed discussion of how to select these different statistical techniques and models for doing so. Below we present each question followed by our recommendations for appropriate descriptive and inferential statistics and tabular display.

Research Question 1: What is the degree or strength of relationship between the independent variable(s) and dependent variable(s)?

Independent Variable: Continuously distributed.

Dependent Variable: Continuously distributed.

Descriptive Statistics: Means and standard deviations for all variables, possibly assessments of normality of distributions. Bivariate relationships expressed as Pearson or Spearman correlation coefficients. Multivariate relationships expressed as multiple R and R^2, and standardized regression coefficients. Canonical correlation less typically used to express relationships between many independent and dependent variables.

Inferential Statistics: Bivariate regression analysis and multiple regression analysis. Canonical correlation analysis less typically used. Analyses may include both statistical tests and confidence intervals.

Tabular Displays: Present univariate and bivariate statistics in a correlation matrix table (see Tables 6.10, 6.11, and 6.17) followed by multiple regression analysis summary table (see Tables 6.15, 6.17, and 6.18 and accompanying explanation).

Research Question 2: *Are there significant group differences between the groups formed by the independent variable(s) and scores on the dependent variable(s)?*

Independent Variable: Categorical.

Dependent Variable: Continuously distributed.

Descriptive Statistics: Means and standard deviations for all variables, within categories of independent variables(s). Bivariate relationships expressed as mean differences and measures of effect size including eta, eta^2, and Cohen's d.

Inferential Statistics: *t* tests and one-way analysis of variance (ANOVA). Factorial design ANOVA for multiple independent variables.

Tabular Displays: Present descriptive statistics within independent variable categories (see Table 6.8 and section on presenting tables of group means) followed by analysis of variance summary table (see Tables 6.14 and 6.15 and accompanying explanation). When many analyses exist, present descriptive statistics and ANOVA summary in the same table (see Table 6.19).

Research Question 3: *Are the scores on the independent variable(s) significantly related to the categories formed by the dependent variable(s)?*

Independent Variable: Continuously distributed.

Dependent Variable: Categorical.

Descriptive Statistics: Means and standard deviations for independent variables, possibly assessments of normality of distributions. Bivariate and multivariate relationships expressed as odds ratios. Other multivariate relationships include statistics associated with logistic regression or discriminant function analysis.

Inferential Statistics: Logistic regression or discriminant function analysis. Analyses may include both statistical tests and confidence intervals, particularly around odds ratios in logistic regression.

Tabular Displays: Present table of means and standard deviations of continuously distributed independent variables within categories of dependent variable (see Table 6.9 and section on presenting tables of group means) followed by logistic regression or discriminant function analysis summary table. (We do not present examples of these analyses because of their complexity and space limitations.)

Research Question 4: *Are differences in the frequency of occurrence of the independent variable(s) related to differences in the frequency of occurrence of the dependent variable(s)?*

Independent Variable: Categorical.

Dependent Variable: Categorical.

Descriptive Statistics: Measures of association for nominal- and ordinal-level variables: percent difference, phi, contingency coefficient, Cramer's V, Somer's D, uncertainty coefficient, and others.

Inferential Statistics: Chi-square test and other nonparametric measures as conditions dictate.

Tabular Displays: Cross-tabulation tables (see Tables 6.7 and 6.20 and the section on cross-tabulation tables).

Of course there are other types of research questions, but the purpose here is to present analyses that are likely to examine two of these major research questions, the examination of relationships and the comparison of groups. For example, research that tests the hypothesis that "The greater the amount of academic self-esteem, the higher one's grade point average" would constitute an examination of relationships, whereas research that examines the hypothesis that "Dropouts have lower academic self-esteem than those who complete their education" would constitute a comparison of group differences. It is likely that both of the above hypotheses would be examined within the same dissertation, and each hypothesis would be addressed using a different statistical procedure and presented using a different tabular structure.

As indicated above, for each research question there is a general class of analyses or analytic strategy that is typically utilized. For Research Question 1, this is correlation and regression; for Research Question 2, analysis of variance is typically used; for Research Question 3, logistic regression analysis or discriminant function analysis is typical; and for Research Question 4, cross-tabulation or multiway contingency table analysis is typical. For each type of analysis a table or set of tables usually is required, and sometimes a single table will contain a number of such analyses. Below we present additional examples directed to specific types of analyses not illustrated earlier.

HOW TO INTERPRET AND PRESENT THE RESULTS OF ANALYSIS OF VARIANCE (ANOVA)

A frequently presented type of statistical analysis is analysis of variance or ANOVA. Analysis of variance typically is utilized when the independent variable or variables form categories and the dependent variable is continuously distributed. These represent questions of the type identified as Research Question 2 above: *Are there significant group differences between the groups formed by the independent variable(s) and scores on the dependent variable(s)?* This section presents an example of an analysis of variance performed by the Statistical Package for the Social Sciences. The printout is reviewed and converted to "dissertation-ready" tables, and an example of how this information might be presented and discussed in a results section is provided. This is particularly important because the tables are intended to elaborate upon the text, not substitute for it. The text needs to stand on its own as a focus for the reader in summarizing the results of the research. We use the sample statement types discussed earlier in the section "The Nuts and Bolts of Describing Quantitative Results" to describe Tables 6.13 and 6.14.

Table 6.12, in its multiple parts, presents the results of an analysis of variance (ANOVA) with two independent variables, treatment group and race/ethnicity, and one dependent variable, a measure of depression. The treatment group variable represents a dichotomy, one group receiving an intervention, the second group (the control group) not receiving the intervention. The race/ethnicity variable contains five groups: Hispanic-English, Hispanic-Spanish, Caucasian, African American, and Asian/Other. In ANOVA language, the design can be described as a 2 × 5 factorial design. In such a design, three effects can be examined for statistical significance: the main effect of the treatment, the main effect of race/ethnicity, and the interaction of treatment with race/ethnicity. The dependent variable, labeled CESD TOTAL, represents the Center for Epidemiological Studies Depression Scale. The SPSS printout shown in Table 6.12 contains three parts, the first part showing the distribution of the number of cases in each category of each variable ("Between-Subjects Factors"), the second part presenting the descriptive statistics for each treatment by race/ethnicity combination ("Descriptive Statistics"), and the third part presenting the ANOVA summary table ("Tests of Between-Subjects Effects"). Our goal is to utilize the statistical information to provide "dissertation-ready" tables. In this example, we utilize the two-table approach, beginning with a table of descriptive statistics (Table 6.13) and following with the ANOVA Summary Table (Table 6.14). With one analysis, this approach works well. In a later section, we offer a one-table approach with a different analysis, one that combines both descriptive and inferential information into a single table of multiple analyses (Table 6.19).

What would one say about the above analysis? Clearly many numbers are presented, but what is meaningful about these numbers? The numbers are very similar, particularly in the light of an overall standard deviation of nearly 10 (i.e., 9.9), the smallest mean value being 15.3 (Hispanic-Spanish in the Control Group) and the largest being 18.8 (African Americans in the Treatment Group). Both these numbers are close to the average for all 488 cases (17.1). In addition, the F and associ-

Table 6.12

Analysis of Variance of Depression by Treatment Group and Race/Ethnicity

Between-Subject Factors

		Value Label	N
GROUP	1	A-Comparison	241
	2	B-Interv	247
RACE/ETHNICITY	1	Hispanic-English	131
	2	Hispanic-Spanish	94
	3	Caucasian	118
	4	African American	95
	5	Asian/Other	50

Descriptive Statistics

Dependent Variable: BL CESD TOTAL

GROUP	RACE/ETHNICITY	Mean	Std. Deviation	N
A-Comparison	Hispanic-English	18.17	8.89	65
	Hispanic-Spanish	15.28	11.63	40
	Caucasian	14.85	8.80	62
	African American	17.43	10.52	47
	Asian/Other	18.26	8.02	27
	Total	16.70	9.65	241
B-Interv	Hispanic-English	17.23	9.37	66
	Hispanic-Spanish	17.80	9.74	54
	Caucasian	16.52	12.15	56
	African American	18.77	9.62	48
	Asian/Other	18.04	10.01	23
	Total	17.57	10.19	247
Total	Hispanic-English	17.69	9.11	131
	Hispanic-Spanish	16.72	10.60	94
	Caucasian	15.64	10.51	118
	African American	18.11	10.04	95
	Asian/Other	18.16	8.90	50
	Total	17.14	9.93	488

(Continued)

ated *p* values shown in the ANOVA summary table indicate that none of the main or interaction effects is statistically significant. (This is evident because none of the *p* values in the far right column of the last part of Table 6.12 is less than .05, other than that for the intercept.) A short and reasonable summary of these findings might appear as follows.

Table 6.12
Continued

Tests of Between-Subjects Effects

Dependent Variable: BL CESD TOTAL

Source	Type III Sum of Squares	df	Mean Square	F	Sig.
Corrected Model	761.275[a]	9	84.586	.856	.565
Intercept	128761.632	1	128761.632	1303.066	.000
GROUP	82.861	1	82.861	.839	.360
ETHNIC	460.814	4	115.203	1.166	.325
GROUP*ETHNIC	208.687	4	52.172	.528	.715
Error	47233.250	478	98.814		
Total	191348.000	488			
Corrected Total	47994.525	487			

Note. R^2 = R squared.
a. R^2 = .016 (Adjusted R^2 = -.003).

Table 6.13 presents the means and standard deviations for level of depression by treatment group and race/ethnicity. The mean differences in these tables are quite small, varying by only one or two points from the grand mean of 17.1 ($N = 488$, $SD = 9.9$). The ANOVA summary table for these data (Table 6.14) indicates that there were no statistically significant main or interaction effects.

Statements summarizing tabular results do not need to be as brief or general as that above. For example, imagine that you were testing a specific hypothesis that the control group would be more depressed than the intervention group. This hypothesis would be statistically evaluated through an examination of the direction of the mean differences shown in Table 6.13 and the main effect of treatment group in Table 6.14. You might address this hypothesis with a statement such as the following:

Hypothesis 1 predicted that mean depression scores in the control group would be higher than those in the intervention group. As shown

Table 6.13

Means and Standard Deviations of Depression Scores,
by Treatment Group and Race/Ethnicity

	Treatment Group								
	Intervention			Control			Total		
Race/Ethnicity	N	Mean	SD	N	Mean	SD	N	Mean	SD
Hispanic-Eng.	66	17.2	9.4	65	18.2	8.9	131	17.7	9.1
Hispanic-Span.	54	17.8	9.7	40	15.3	11.6	94	16.7	10.6
Caucasian	56	16.5	12.2	62	14.9	8.8	118	15.6	10.5
African Amer.	48	18.8	9.6	47	17.4	10.5	95	18.1	10.0
Asian/Other	23	18.0	10.0	27	18.3	8.0	50	18.2	8.9
Total	247	17.6	10.2	241	16.7	9.7	488	17.1	9.9

in Table 6.13, mean differences, though small, were in the opposite direction from those predicted (Control, $M = 16.7$, $SD = 9.7$; Intervention, $M = 17.6$, $SD = 10.2$). As shown in Table 6.14, these differences were not statistically significant: $F(1, 478) = .84$, $p = .360$.

PRESENTING THE RESULTS OF MULTIPLE REGRESSION ANALYSIS

Multiple regression analysis (MRA) is a multivariate statistical technique that examines the relationship between continuously distributed independent variables and one continuously distributed dependent variable. As such, you may recognize this as a technique appropriate for the examination of questions of the type of Research Question 1 presented earlier: *What is the degree or strength of relationship between the independent variable(s) and dependent variable(s)?* In contrast to ANOVA presentations, there appears to be no standard, universally agreed upon format in which to present the results of MRA. This is not particularly surprising, given the many variations of MRA available and the complexity of the models being tested. Many of our students have used MRA in recent dissertations, and all have struggled with both the interpretation and the presentation of the results. In this section, we make some suggestions and present a few examples that may be used as guides.

Table 6.14
*Analysis of Variance Summary Table of Levels of Depression,
by Treatment Group and Race/Ethnicity*

Source	SS	df	MS	F	p
(A) Treatment Group	82.9	1	82.9	.84	.360
(B) Race/Ethnicity	460.8	4	115.2	1.12	.325
A × B	208.7	4	52.2	.53	.715
Error	47233.3	478	98.8		
Total	47985.7	487			

A wide variety of output may be generated by multiple regression analysis programs. This includes, but is not limited to, unstandardized and standardized regression coefficients (also known as *beta weights*), multiple correlations and their square (R squared or R^2), and changes in the values of R and/or R^2 in stepwise regression procedures. In addition to these statistics, there will usually be t and F statistics indicating the statistical significance of these various coefficients. We offer Table 6.15 as a model table to be used in describing the results of MRA.

Table 6.15 presents the independent variables in the rows and the regression coefficients, unstandardized (B) and standardized (Beta) in the columns. The t values associated with the regression coefficients are also presented in the columns. The R^2 value is presented at the bottom of the column, with its associated F ratio. The t values and F value are accompanied by their associated p values, as we have shown in Table 6.15. An alternative method, one that we no longer recommend, would be to asterisk these values (F and/or t) if they are statistically significant at the specified level, and to include probability notes at the bottom of the table in lieu of the column of p values.

AN EXAMPLE OF MULTIPLE REGRESSION ANALYSIS

For example, imagine a study examining the effects of education, age, and frequency of church attendance on attitudes toward premarital sex. (Clearly, other variables could also influence these attitudes, but

Table 6.15

Sample Table Template for Presenting the Results of Multiple Regression Analysis (Three Independent Variables)

Independent Variable	B	Beta	t	p
Variable 1				
Variable 2				
Variable 3				

Note. R^2 = .xxx, F(x, xxx) = xx.x, p = .xxx.

we want to keep this example simple.) Table 6.16 presents the results of a multiple regression analysis examining the effect of these variables. The results are based on data from the 1990 National Opinion Research Center General Social Survey.

Table 6.16 is composed of the following parts of the SPSS printout:

1. Descriptive Statistics: Presents the means, standard deviations, and number of cases for each independent and dependent variable.

2. Correlations: The correlation matrix of all variables, with significance level and number of cases.

3. Variables Entered/Removed: Tells which variables were entered or removed at each step in the analysis. Because there was only one step, all variables are included. (This portion is of more value when stepwise and hierarchical methods are utilized.)

4. Model Summary: Provides the R, R^2, adjusted R^2, and standard error for the overall regression model. The R^2 indicates that 22.8% of the variance in attitudes toward premarital sex can be explained by the combined influence of the three independent variables.

5. ANOVA: Presents the ANOVA summary table. This table indicates that the amount of variance explained by the regression equation is statistically significant, as shown by an F value and its associated p value.

6. Coefficients: Presents the standardized and unstandardized regression coefficients and their accompanying *t* values and level of significance. Note that, as indicated by the probability notes, all *t* values are statistically significant at *p* < .001. The beta weights provide an indication of the relative contribution of the variables to the prediction of attitudes toward premarital sex, when the other variables are controlled. Clearly, church attendance has the greatest influence, followed by age and education.

As researchers, we once again face the question of how to present these data, and as with analysis of variance, we suggest a two-table approach. The first table (Table 6.17) presents the correlation matrix and descriptive statistics. The second (Table 6.18) presents the multiple regression analysis results.

Before presenting a sample interpretation of these two tables, we return to the printout to examine how and where the information from the printout was included in the two tables. Both tables include descriptive and inferential statistics; however, the first provides only univariate and bivariate descriptive statistics, and it notes the significance of the correlation coefficients. This is the foundation upon which a multiple regression analysis is based. The second contains the MRA results that relate to the full regression equation. Note that exact probability values are not presented because these are extremely small and displayed as .000 by SPSS. Under these conditions we recommend using *p* < .001, not *p* = .000, which implies a zero probability. Space does not permit discussion of the complexities or variations of MRA. For a more complete discussion of this technique and the major issues surrounding its use, we suggest consulting Newton and Rudestam (1999). For a detailed statistical treatment, we suggest Tabachnik and Fidell (1996).

Returning to the issue of discussing the tabular results within the dissertation text, we suggest the following as a reasonable framework:

Table 6.17 presents the correlation matrix and descriptive statistics for the regression of attitudes toward premarital sex on education, age, and church attendance. Note that the correlations for both age and church attendance are negative (−.234 and −.435, respectively). Thus, as both age and church attendance increase, respondents are more likely

(Text continued on p. 151)

Table 6.16

Multiple Regression Analysis of the Effects of Education, Age, and Church Attendance on Attitudes Toward Premarital Sex

Descriptive Statistics

	Mean	Std. Deviation	N
SEX BEFORE MARRIAGE	2.87	1.21	1832
AGE OF RESPONDENT	44.80	16.88	1832
HOW OFTEN R ATTENDS RELIGIOUS SERVICES	3.78	2.67	1832
HIGHEST YEAR OF SCHOOL COMPLETED	13.40	2.92	1832

Correlations

		SEX BEFORE MARRIAGE	AGE OF RESPONDENT	HOW OFTEN R ATTENDS RELIGIOUS SERVICES	HIGHEST YEAR OF SCHOOL COMPLETED
Pearson Correlation	SEX BEFORE MARRIAGE	1.000	-.234	-.435	.093
	AGE OF RESPONDENT	-.234	1.000	.126	-.171
	HOW OFTEN R ATTENDS RELIGIOUS SERVICES	-.435	.126	1.000	.038
	HIGHEST YEAR OF SCHOOL COMPLETED	.093	-.171	.038	1.000
Sig. (1-tailed)	SEX BEFORE MARRIAGE	.	.000	.000	.000
	AGE OF RESPONDENT	.000	.	.000	.000
	HOW OFTEN R ATTENDS RELIGIOUS SERVICES	.000	.000	.	.051

(Continued)

Table 6.16
Continued

		SEX BEFORE MAR-RIAGE	AGE OF RESPON-DENT	HOW OFTEN R ATTENDS RELIGIOUS SERVICES	HIGHEST YEAR OF SCHOOL COM-PLETED
	HIGHEST YEAR OF SCHOOL COMPLETED	.000	.000	.051	.
N	SEX BEFORE MARRIAGE	1832	1832	1832	1832
	AGE OF RESPONDENT	1832	1832	1832	1832
	HOW OFTEN R ATTENDS RELIGIOUS SERVICES	1832	1832	1832	1832
	HIGHEST YEAR OF SCHOOL COMPLETED	1832	1832	1832	1832

Variables Entered/Removed[b]

Model	Variables Entered	Variables Removed	Method
1	HIGHEST YEAR OF SCHOOL COMPLETED, HOW OFTEN R ATTENDS RELIGIOUS SERVICES, AGE OF RESPONDENT[a]		Enter

a. All requested variables entered.
b. Dependent Variable: SEX BEFORE MARRIAGE.

Model Summary

Model	R	R^2	Adjusted R^2	Std. Error of the Estimate
1	.477[a]	.228	.227	1.07

a. Predictors: (Constant), HIGHEST YEAR OF SCHOOL COMPLETED, HOW OFTEN R ATTENDS RELIGIOUS SERVICES, AGE OF RESPONDENT.

Table 6.16
Continued

$ANOVA^b$

Model	Sum of Squares	df	Mean Square	F	Sig.
1 Regression	613.051	3	204.350	179.872	.000ᵃ
Residual	2076.769	1828	1.136		
Total	2689.820	1831			

a. Predictors: (Constant), HIGHEST YEAR OF SCHOOL COMPLETED, HOW OFTEN R ATTENDS RELIGIOUS SERVICES, AGE OF RESPONDENT.
b. Dependent Variable: SEX BEFORE MARRIAGE.

$Coefficients^a$

Model		Unstandardized Coefficients		Standardized Coefficients		
		B	Std. Error	Beta	t	Sig.
1	(Constant)	3.682	.147		25.005	.000
	AGE OF RESPONDENT	-1.21E-02	.002	-.168	-7.987	.000
	HOW OFTEN R ATTENDS RELIGIOUS SERVICES	-.189	.009	-.417	-20.070	.000
	HIGHEST YEAR OF SCHOOL COMPLETED	3.319E-02	.009	.080	3.820	.000

a. Dependent Variable: SEX BEFORE MARRIAGE.

to oppose premarital sex. As education increased, people became more favorably disposed toward premarital sex, but this relationship is small (.093). Table 6.18 presents the results of the MRA. Although all variables are statistically significant due to the large sample size, it is clearly church attendance that plays a major role in predicting attitudes: Beta = −.417, $t(1828) = −20.07$, $p < .001$. Almost 23% of the

Table 6.17

Correlation Matrix and Descriptive Statistics for Education, Age,
Church Attendance, and Attitudes Toward Premarital Sex

	(1)	(2)	(3)	(4)
Premarital Sex[a]	1.0			
Age	−.234	1.0		
Church attendance[b]	−.435	.126	1.0	
Education (Years)	.093	−.171	.038	1.0
Mean	2.87	44.80	3.78	13.40
Standard deviation	1.21	16.88	2.67	2.92

Note. N = 1832. Premarital sex is the dependent variable. All correlations are statistically significant at $p < .001$ except the relationship between education and church attendance, which is not
statistically significant ($p = .051$). Data source is National Opinion Research Center General Social
Survey, 1998.
a. Values for premarital sex range from 1, always wrong, to 4, not wrong at all.
b. Values for church attendance range from 0, never, to 7, more than once per week.

variability in attitudes toward premarital sex can be explained by reference to age, education, and church attendance: $R^2 = .228$, $F(3, 1828) =$
$179.87, p < .001$.

STREAMLINING YOUR RESULTS: PRESENTING
MULTIPLE ANALYSES IN A SINGLE TABLE

It is frequently the case that many similar analyses need to be presented
in a Results section. For example, if the study utilizing analysis of variance described in the previous section had also examined the relationship of treatment group and race/ethnicity to locus of control and four
dimensions of life satisfaction, each of these analyses would also need
to be presented in tabular form. If each set of means and each ANOVA
summary table were presented in separate tables, an additional 10
tables would be necessary. When such a situation arises, we strongly
recommend that you seek a means by which the results may be combined into a single table. For example, a student of ours (Paape, 1992)
examined the relationship of five health locus of control subtypes and
seven variables related to health values and behaviors. Her hypotheses

Table 6.18

*Multiple Regression Analysis of Attitudes Toward Premarital Sexual
Relations on Education, Age, and Frequency of Church Attendance*

Independent Variable	B	Beta	t	p
Age	−.012	−.168	−7.98	< .001
Church attendance	−.189	−.471	−20.07	< .001
Education (Years)	.033	.080	3.82	< .001

Note. R^2 = .228, $F(3, 1828)$ = 179.87, p − .001.

suggest that certain subtypes practice more healthy behaviors and value health more. In this study one-way analysis of variance was used to examine the differences between the five health locus of control subtypes and the multiple dependent variables. Rather than present each of the seven analyses in a separate table, she decided to combine them into a single table, as shown in Table 6.19.

Note that Table 6.19 presents the mean, standard deviation, and number of cases for each variable for each health locus of control subtype, but it does not present the complete ANOVA summary table for each analysis. It is sufficient to present only the F ratio and the accompanying probability notes (or exact probability value in some cases) to indicate the statistical significance of each analysis. Such a presentation enables the reader to examine all the results related to specific research questions in a single table, facilitating discussion and comprehension of the results.

As a second example, consider the situation in which one or more groups are asked a number of questions in conjunction with follow-up questions. You may want to present the answers to both the main questions and the follow-ups for each group in the study. An efficient way to do this is to present the results in a table that facilitates the examination of the questions and comparisons between groups. For example, in a study of psychologists and marriage, child, and family counselors, Neighbors (1991) asked each to rate the courses they had taken in the diagnosis, etiology, and physiology of mental disorder. Each area was rated as "not adequate," "adequate," or "very adequate." Following these ratings, the same groups were asked to rate their need for additional education in each area. Ratings were coded "yes" to indicate the

Table 6.19

Analysis of Variance of Health Values and Risk Mix,
by Health Locus of Control Subtypes

Variable	I	II	III	IV	V	F
			Type			
Health value						2.71*
Mean	2.9	2.1	3.0	2.6	2.4	
SD	2.2	1.5	2.2	2.2	1.7	
N	133	57	105	112	113	
Risk-mix						3.25*
Mean	2.6	3.1	2.3	2.5	2.9	
SD	1.5	2.2	1.3	1.7	1.6	
N	133	57	105	113	113	
Smoking						0.52
Mean	2.0	2.1	1.9	2.0	2.1	
SD	1.1	0.9	1.1	0.9	0.9	
N	133	57	105	113	113	
Sleep						0.81
Mean	1.7	1.7	1.7	1.6	1.7	
SD	0.6	0.5	0.6	0.7	0.5	
N	133	57	105	113	113	
Weight						1.19
Mean	0.7	0.6	0.7	0.6	0.6	
SD	0.5	0.5	0.5	0.5	0.5	
N	133	57	105	113	113	
Diet						1.04
Mean	4.5	4.6	4.3	4.2	4.5	
SD	1.5	1.3	1.4	1.5	1.5	
N	133	57	105	113	113	
Habits						4.28*
Mean	2.9	3.5	2.8	3.2	3.2	
SD	1.2	1.0	1.3	1.2	1.2	
N	133	57	105	113	113	

Note. I = Pure internal, II = Pure powerful others, III = Pure chance, IV = Double external, V =
Believer in control.
*$p < .05$.

perceived need for more education. A "no" response indicated no perceived need for additional training. Tables that present bivariate distributions such as these were discussed in an earlier section. A bivariate

Table 6.20

*Self-Ratings of Adequacy of Education and Need
for More Education, by Type of License*

| Type of Course | Adequacy of Education (%) | | | Need More | |
	Not Adequate	Adequate	Very Adequate	% "Yes"	$\chi^2(df, N)$
Diagnosis					
Psychologists	48.2	25.9	25.9 (27)	35.9 (40)	6.9 (2, 76)*
MFCCs	26.5	57.2	16.3 (49)	29.8 (57)	0.3 (1, 97)
Etiology					
Psychologists	38.5	42.3	19.2 (26)	30.0 (40)	3.9 (2, 73)
MFCCs	21.3	65.9	12.8 (47)	24.6 (57)	0.4 (1, 97)
Physiology					
Psychologists	36.0	28.0	36.0 (25)	42.5 (40)	3.5 (2, 72)
MFCCs	40.4	42.6	17.0 (47)	42.1 (57)	0.0 (1, 97)

Notes. Cell percentages for "Adequacy of Education" sum to 100 across columns. *N*s in parentheses. The first chi-square value represents "Adequacy of Education" and the second represents "Need for More Education."
*$p < .05$.

distribution could be presented for each area of training and each assessment of the need for more training, making a total of six tables. The statistical significance of each relationship was assessed with a chi-square test, creating a need to present the results of these tests also. Table 6.20 presents the results of the above analyses in a single table. Note that Table 6.20 presents the data for both questions, for each group, in a single row. Only the percentage who gave a positive (yes) response to the question regarding the need for more education is presented because the percentage who stated "no" is redundant, obtained simply by subtracting the percentage who said yes from 100. The chi-square tests, one for each question, are presented in the column labeled $\chi^2(df, N)$. A general note indicates that the first chi-square value represents the test for the adequacy of education question, whereas the second presents the test for the need for more education question.

As a final caution, it is important to point out that one can carry the quest to streamline tables too far. The result is considerable confusion rather than clarification and ease of comparison. Table 6.20 may be approaching the limits in this regard, but we believe that it presents a strategy for approaching table construction that you will find useful when composing your dissertation tables.

PRESENTING THE RESULTS OF QUALITATIVE RESEARCH

Writing an informative Results chapter for a qualitative dissertation is likely to be more challenging than doing so for a quantitative dissertation. Generally accepted guidelines exist for how to display data and summarize the results of statistical analyses in quantitative studies. This is not the case with qualitative studies. Although some sources (see Miles & Huberman, 1994) offer very specific advice on how to conduct and report qualitative data analyses, we have found no clear agreement in the literature and our students have, in fact, used a variety of formats and approaches. As with all research, the first priority is to adopt a well-organized strategy that makes sense of your data and presents them clearly and comprehensively.

Qualitative studies are likely to produce large quantities of data that represent words and ideas rather than numbers and statistics. These include, but are not limited to, interview transcripts and field notes, a wide variety of records, documents, and unobtrusive measures. The researcher may be the victim of data overload, with no idea of what to present or where to begin. Statistical program packages, such as SPSS, present quantitative data in standardized ways that permit immediate comparisons both within and across groups. Qualitative data analysis programs also exist and are becoming increasingly sophisticated (see Table 10.3), but there is considerable latitude in analyzing qualitative data, and each qualitative analysis still requires the researcher to devise his or her own method for presenting the results.

Most qualitative researchers begin their data analysis by reading and rereading in its entirety all the information they have collected, including interview transcripts and field notes, to get a feel for the whole (Creswell, 1998). They may also summarize the information in the form of memos and reflective notes. Sometimes these preliminary summaries are taken back to the participants for feedback and verification (called "member checks"). Because of the tendency for text data to be overwhelming in scope and quantity, there is almost always a need to reduce the data by developing categories or codes for sorting and refining them.

Within the phenomenological tradition, Moustakas (1994) describes two approaches to analysis. The first is a modification of van Kaam's (1966) method. The second is a variation of methods suggested by Stevick (1971), Colaizzi (1973), and Keen (1975). The following steps, adapted from Moustakas (1994, p. 122), are taken with the entire transcript from every research participant. Begin with a full description of your own (the researcher's) experience of the phenomenon. From this transcript:

1. Review each statement for how well it describes the experience.

2. Record all relevant statements.

3. Remove all statements that are redundant or overlap with others, leaving the key meaning units of the experience.

4. Organize the invariant meaning units into themes.

5. Coalesce the themes into a description of the textures of the experience and augment the description with quotations from the text.

6. Using your imagination and taking multiple perspectives to find possible meanings in the text, construct a description of the structures of your experience.

7. Create a textural-structural description of the meanings and essences of your experience.

Go through these seven steps with the complete narrative transcript of each participant of the study. Then integrate the individual textural-structural descriptions into a composite description of the meanings and essences of the experience of the entire group.

Students who select a phenomenological dissertation will need to obtain familiarity with these kinds of data reduction procedures, as exemplified in the work of Moustakas (1994). One of our students, Diane Armstrong (1994), conducted a phenomenological dissertation exploring the dreams of the blind. She relied on data from 36 interviews with congenitally blind (blind from birth) and adventitiously blind (develop blindness after a period of sight) adults. Her approach to data reduction was based on the naturalistic methods of Giorgi (1985) and led to descriptions of the sensory input, the dream setting, the dominant emotional qualities, and the content structure of the dreams. Armstrong began her Results chapter by providing a brief overview of each of her participants (a typical approach in qualitative studies), and then proceeded to present the themes that emerged from her interview data, amply illustrated and supported by examples and quotations from the participants.

Proponents of grounded theory have a slightly different way of thinking about and expressing what takes place in the Results chapter of a dissertation. Making sense of naturalistic data means processing the data through some technique of inductive analysis. Grounded theory offers a unified procedure for developing categories of information and moving from these categories to construct a narrative to connect them and generate a set of theoretical propositions. One approach involves two essential subprocesses that compose the basis of inductive analysis: unitizing and categorizing. *Unitizing* is a coding operation in which information units are isolated from the text. In the second subprocess, *categorizing*, information units derived from the unitizing phase are organized into categories on the basis of similarity in meaning. As the number of categories reaches a saturation point, the researcher attempts to write rules that define which units of information may be included or excluded from the category. This process has been called the "constant comparative method" by Glaser and Strauss (1967). The constant comparative method requires continual revision, modification, and amendment until all new units can be placed into an appropriate category and the inclusion of additional units into a category provides no new information.

The following is Strauss and Corbin's (1998) description of the steps in this inductive process:

1. Open coding: Reviewing the entire text for descriptive categories. Here the constant comparative method is used to refine each category by seeking examples of it until no new information yields additional meaning ("saturation" of the category).

2. Axial coding: Relating categories to their subcategories according to their properties and dimensions. Here the data are assessed for how major categories relate to each other and to their subcategories.

3. Selective coding: Integrating and refining the theory. Here the single category is chosen as central, and a theoretical model is generated to relate the other categories to it according to how they influence it, are caused by it, provide a context for it, or mediate it.

The resulting theory can be presented in the dissertation as hypotheses generated by the data and/or proposed as a comprehensive model, perhaps abetted by figures or tables, to understand the phenomenon in terms of both the context of the study and previous research and practice.

A dissertation example of using the grounded theory approach to work with qualitative data comes from Einhorn's (1993) goal to understand the relational aspects of women's experience in asking help from their friends. Thirty women were interviewed, both individually and in focus groups. The following comments from Einhorn reflect her attempts to cope with the tremendous amount of data she collected:

> I transcribed the interviews as soon after they were conducted as possible, and often listened to the group interview tapes before meeting with members individually so that I would remember specific areas I wanted to explore. I wrote extensive descriptions of my observations and experiences. I also talked extensively with my research consultants. . . . I began with immersing myself in the raw data (all of the interview materials and my notes); then moved to descriptions of the data (summaries of my interviews and my notes), and finally turned to understanding and interpretation—constructing meaning from the data. (p. 116)

> I employed two "subprocesses" for making sense of the data: "unitizing" and "categorizing." Unitizing involved identifying and coding the parts of the interview experiences, content and process, that were to qualify for each of the four types of data. . . . For example . . . a participant's report qualified as a "story" if it had at least two of four characteristics: time, place/situation, identified other person, and an identified kind of help. Participants' concepts about help seeking were identified as interview content that outlined beliefs, "life truths," generalizations, or assumptions *about* asking for help. The thoughts and beliefs were not quantified as units. These two types of data (stories and thoughts) proved quite distinguishable. (pp. 117-118)

Categorization was the second step. As themes began to emerge a process of sorting began: provisionally labelling categories, noticing the rules for inclusion or exclusion of particular units from one or another category, and revising categories. Themes and categories were revised until the rules for inclusion and exclusion seemed to be working, and all data "fit" a category. (p. 119)

The Results chapter of the dissertation reported the outcomes of the 247 stories Einhorn collected and categorized into the following four themes: whether and how women asked for help and received it, relationship awareness, mutuality, and empowerment. The chapter also goes into detail about the participants' thoughts and beliefs about help-seeking, as well as observations about the process among the participants in the focus groups and the process between the researcher and the participants.

In another qualitative dissertation, Dumas (1989) examined the relationship between daughters and fathers in family-owned businesses. She describes her data analysis as follows:

Data analysis for each family-business interviewed consisted of unitizing and categorizing the data collected during 40 in depth interviews averaging 2.5 hours each. I categorized these units in an ongoing manner by provisionally categorizing the cards (units) that seemed to relate to the same content. As I did this, I devised propositional statements to characterize each category's properties. I then combined these properties into rules for inclusion in each category. These rules served to justify the inclusion of each card which ultimately remained assigned to a category, to render each category set internally consistent. I then gave each category a title which was an attempt to capture the essence of the rule for inclusion of units in the category. Finally, I reviewed the entire set of categories I had formulated, including the miscellaneous cards. Some of these were eventually discarded as irrelevant. To determine when it was time to stop collecting and processing data, I used the four criteria proposed by Lincoln and Guba (1985): exhaustion of sources; saturation of categories . . . emergence of regularities . . . and overextension. (pp. 207-209)

Dumas found seven constructs that describe the essence of her interviews with fathers and daughters in family-owned businesses. She

describes these constructs as "intended to portray the situations studied, and to make the complexities of each situation apparent, as well as
indicate how these complexities interact." For example, the first construct, "Daddy's Little Girl," refers to the "roles assigned to the daughters by their fathers and the daughters themselves." According to
Dumas:

> These fathers and daughters had no previous point of reference for
> how to behave when working together. They only had their previous
> roles of father and daughter as models for how to relate to each other.
> Therefore the fathers and daughters interviewed often found working
> together confusing, unsettling and stressful. As these daughters
> indicated:
>
> > Even though I've been here a long time I still have to kiss him every
> > morning. Otherwise he'll be hurt. I don't think he's made the transi-
> > tion to seeing me as an adult. I'm still his little girl.
> >
> > I never know whether I'm talking to my dad or my boss! It drives
> > me crazy! My dad too. I just don't know when he expects me to be
> > "daddy's little girl" and when he expects me to be businesslike.
> > That makes it hard on me. (p. 237)

The work of Dumas illustrates how the results of qualitative analysis
may be reported. Following a conceptual definition of the meaning of a
category, relevant quotations that illustrate this meaning are presented.
Although some authors take the position that a case study report is primarily in written form, others, such as Miles and Huberman (1994),
suggest that the use of a wide variety of displays—presenting one's
conceptual framework, context of analysis, and results—greatly facilitates the analysis of qualitative data. They provide advice on constructing scatter plots, context charts, causal networks, and causal models.
Our students generally have chosen to utilize a combination of techniques to present their results, including written, graphic, and tabular
displays.

It is important for the qualitative researcher to describe the "context" in which a particular event takes place. Miles and Huberman
(1994) suggest the "context chart" as one manner in which to do this.
The context chart is "a network, mapping in graphic form the interrelationships among the roles, groups (and, if appropriate, organizations)

Table 6.21

Reasons for Joining a Gang for White and Hispanic Gang Members

Participants	Reasons
Hispanics	
H1	Grew up with it
H2	All my friends part of it
H3	Grew up with it
Whites	
W1	All my friends part of it
W2	Fun
W3	Hanging out

that go to make up the context of individual behavior" (Miles & Huberman, 1994, p. 102). For example, in addition to illustrating the meaning of each construct developed in her analysis, as quoted above, Dumas (1989) also presented a "genogram" and "organization chart" for each family business included in her research. The genogram (see Figure 6.1) presented the family tree as a guide to locating each interviewee's position in the family, while the organization chart (see Figure 6.2) depicted each interviewee's position in the family business.

As a second example, Leon (1991) studied motivation for gang membership among Anglo and Hispanic incarcerated juveniles. Table 6.21 presents a matrix designed to classify descriptions provided by gang members as to reasons for joining a gang. This table is based on the suggestion of Miles and Huberman (1994) to build a matrix display that organizes descriptive data categories around a particular event or experience. This matrix has been completed with a summary statement (an exact quotation could also have been used) that represents the reasons given by each participant, represented by a letter indicating their ethnicity (H or W) and an identification number (1, 2, 3, etc.) that placed the participant in the respective row.

A *causal network* is a graph displaying the independent and dependent variables in a naturalistic study. Such a graph uses arrows to represent the direction of influence (causality) and makes specific notations regarding the meaning of the connections between the arrows

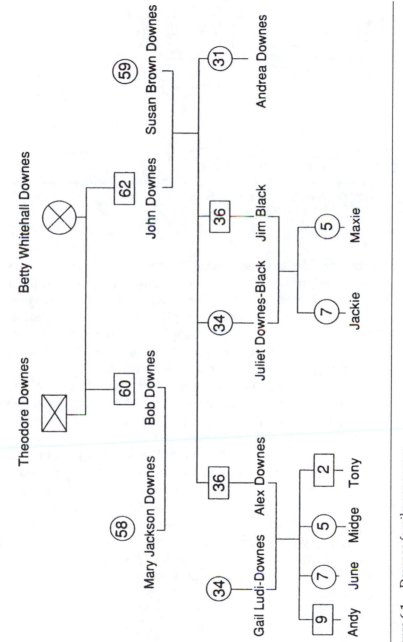

Figure 6.1. Downes family genogram.
Source. From Dumas (1989). Used with permission.

163

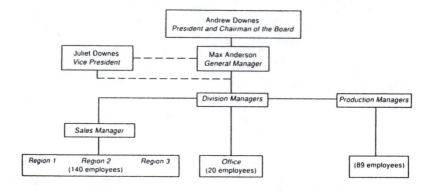

Figure 6.2. Downes, Inc. organization chart.
Source. Dumas (1989). Used with permission.

linking the variables in the analysis. This chart may serve as the basis for a conceptual framework or the development of grounded theory. For example, Williams (1989) examined the transition from individualism to social advocacy as experienced by 13 American social advocates. The descriptive model Williams developed from an analysis of interviews contained what Williams called "turning points." As Williams states, "The advocates often reflected upon significant 'markers' in their transitions and how the role of self-directed action at those markers influenced the course of the transition" (p. 240). Figure 6.3 contains Williams's representation of "marking the course," in the transition from individualism to social advocacy.

    In sum, both qualitative and quantitative analyses pose the same task for the researcher, "making sense" of the data. The methods of analyses may differ, the standards upon which reliability and validity are judged may not be the same, and the raw data upon which analysis is based assumes very different forms; nevertheless, clearly written and documented analytical summaries, the use of tables and graphs, and a careful consideration of the order and logic of presentation serve as the foundation of quality research, regardless of the researcher's method of choice.

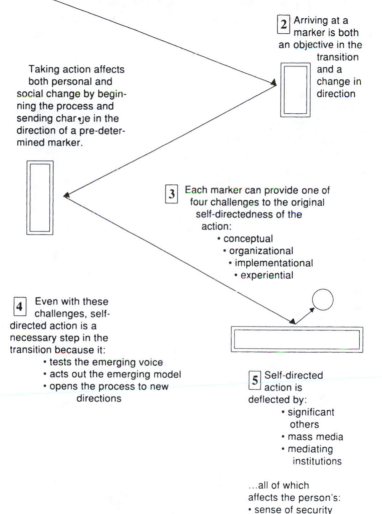

Figure 6.3. Marking the course.
Source. Williams (1989). Used with permission.

NOTE

1. The four statements for describing quantitative results were suggested by Dr. David Perkins, Department of Psychology, California State University, Fullerton.

CHAPTER 7

Discussion

By the time data have been collected and analyzed and the Results chapter of the dissertation has been completed, proceeding to write the remainder of the dissertation may seem anticlimactic. Consequently, many students do not do justice to the Discussion chapter, and it ends up being less thoughtful and comprehensive than it should be.

The Discussion chapter is an opportunity to move beyond the data and integrate, creatively, the results of your study with existing theory and research. Whereas clear guidelines exist for preparing a Method chapter and Results chapter in terms of content and format, no such formal guidelines exist for writing the Discussion chapter. A good Discussion chapter typically contains the following elements:

1. An overview of the significant findings of the study

2. A consideration of the findings in the light of existing research studies

3. Implications of the study for current theory (except in purely applied studies)

4. A careful examination of findings that fail to support or only partially support your hypotheses

5. Limitations of the study that may affect the validity or the generalizability of the results

6. Recommendations for further research

7. Implications of the study for professional practice or applied settings (optional)

Think back to the research wheel introduced in Chapter 1, which describes how the dissertation process is an evolving shift between deductive and inductive modes of reasoning, from the general to the specific and back again to the general. The Discussion chapter is largely an exercise in inductive thinking, grappling with the specific results of your study and drawing inferences to the world of theory by linking your results with the existing literature. This chapter takes over where the introduction and review of the literature left off and may be quite similar to it in style and content. Here you are forwarding your conceptual argument on the basis of the obtained data, exploring the meaning of the data from the relationships that have emerged among the variables of the study. You evaluate the extent to which your study answered the questions you posed at the outset, basing your reasoning as much as possible on the data themselves. As you marshal your own interpretation of the findings, consider the strengths and weaknesses of alternative interpretations from the literature, along with the points of agreement and disagreement between your data and conclusions in comparison with the contributions of others. A good Discussion chapter openly acknowledges and evaluates rival explanations for the results.

It is not sufficient to reiterate the findings of your study, although this is a good place to begin. One popular way of starting the chapter is by reviewing, in turn, the status of each of the hypotheses and research questions of the study now that the data have been collected and examined. Stay focused on a straightforward exposition of what you determined, taking the principal ideas one at a time. In so doing, avoid terminology that is meaningless outside the context of your study, such as referring to "hypothesis number one" or noting that "the A group scored significantly higher than the B group." Instead, use plain English and refer to the variables by name so that readers unfamiliar with the specific terminology of your study will be able to comprehend the meaning of the results. For example, the following sentence is an accurate restatement of a finding that may have been expressed more technically in the Results chapter: "The teachers who received intensive training in conflict resolution skills were significantly more successful in defusing classroom conflicts than teachers without such training."

Perhaps the most common oversight made in writing the Discussion chapter is a failure to return to the literature to integrate results of the study with other empirical studies examining the same phenomena. A good discussion embeds each result within the theoretical context that was presented in the literature review. Thus, you will need to cite some of the relevant studies that were discussed previously, as well as return to the literature to seek additional ways of understanding your results and to look for confirmatory or disconfirmatory evidence. The kinds of statements that are often found in Discussion chapters are of the following form:

> The results of this study are consistent with Jones's findings of a negative relationship between learned helplessness and efforts to seek employment and extends his findings to a nonhandicapped population.

> Unlike Smith (1999), who relied upon self-report to look for evidence of dissimulation, the current study found behavioral evidence that teenagers drink more alcohol than they admit they drink to family members.

Here are some other suggestions for writing an appropriate Discussion chapter, based on common misunderstandings:

1. The data analyses should have been thoroughly presented in the Results chapter. In the same way that findings are not discussed in the Results chapter, secondary analyses of data are not presented in the Discussion chapter.

2. Do not repeat and reformulate points that have already been made. This chapter is frequently regarded as a summary of specific findings. On the contrary, discuss the findings rather than describe them again. Focus on explaining how your data can be used to infer broader conceptual and theoretical statements by analyzing the relationships among your specific variables. An example of such a generalized statement might be, "On the basis of these findings, it appears that loss of a parent leads to an increased risk of adolescent suicidal

behavior only in those families that fail to communicate openly about their grief." Avoid speculation that is not related to empirical data or theory.

3. A common tendency among students is to list all possible criticisms of a study and to do so with an apologetic tone. It is much better to accept the study for what it is. If there are fundamental criticisms, such as attributing negative findings to a major flaw in the design of the study, it is reasonable to question why the study was conducted in the first place. At the same time, it is not unreasonable to identify flaws that were unintended or were delimitations in the study. Do so only in the context of evaluating the relative trustworthiness of your conclusions.

4. A parallel tendency is to offer a long list of recommendations for future research. This is inadvisable. It is much better to focus on one or two major recommendations. For example, to suggest that a study be extended to males, to brunettes, to 13- to 16-year-olds, and so on, is a waste of space. It is preferable to suggest the next reasonable step in forwarding a program of research in a given area of study.

5. Be careful not to offer suggestions for future research that can be addressed easily within your own study. These indicate that you have not done a thorough job of examining your own data.

6. Do not include trivial details or ramble aimlessly around the topic. This is an opportunity to think creatively, but like all other chapters of the dissertation, the Discussion chapter should be logical and focused. One specific way to maintain the balanced perspective of the scientific investigator is to avoid melodramatic or intemperate language, such as "amazing," or even "interesting" or "important." Allow your data and conclusions to be judged on their own merits and not on your amplification of them.

The mandate to present and discuss significant findings is clear. What do you do, however, when results are not statistically significant or "nearly" significant? One cannot pretend that a nonsignificant finding is significant and, strictly speaking, it should not be treated as such. On the other hand, conventions regarding significance levels (e.g., .05, .01) are somewhat arbitrary, and each field seems to have its own prevailing standards for acknowledging or ignoring trends that do not quite live up to these a priori levels. Our own position is that the size of a finding—expressed, for example, in the percentage of variance accounted for between two variables—ultimately is more informative than the presence or absence of a statistically significant effect. This is another reason not to be blinded by statistics, in terms of either overestimating or underestimating the meaning of a particular result.

Students may become particularly disheartened with nonsignificant results, when hypotheses are not validated. But nonsignificant results need not imply an inferior study. The research enterprise is a treasure hunt with an unknown outcome, and if a study is performed according to acceptable standards, negative results ought not invalidate the legitimacy of the research. Prior to collecting data it is important to anticipate how to explain the full range of empirical outcomes so that no result will be a bad result. Any result should be conceptually informative, in the sense of forwarding knowledge in a field. Negative results should, however, signal the need for a complete inquiry. Such results typically can be attributed to methodological or theoretical shortcomings. An opportunity to challenge commonly understood theory can serve as a major research contribution. Methodological shortcomings may be more difficult to handle, because it is presumed that they would have been attended to in designing the study. Nevertheless, there is usually some disparity between the best laid plans and real world events. Even the most meticulous researcher may not correctly anticipate mailings that go awry, research assistants who quit, subjects who refuse to complete a posttest, and equipment that malfunctions.

A Discussion chapter in a qualitative dissertation performs a similar function: drawing implications from the results of the study to the worlds of theory and practice. Although some researchers or some disciplines may choose to incorporate the discussion into the Results chapter, most qualitative dissertations we have seen, regardless of the particular orientation to method, have a separate chapter that is referred to as the Discussion chapter. It could be argued that a discussion of the implications of the findings is even more important in qualitative studies than in quantitative ones. The hypotheses within an experimental or quasi-experimental study are always introduced as emerging from theory and the relevant empirical literature. In most qualitative studies, there are no hypotheses as such, and the link between the research questions and the theoretical and research literature is not always as evident. The theory emerges inductively, after the data have been collected and explored. Thus, there is a compelling need to discuss the implications of new theoretical propositions and place them within the context of the existent empirical and theoretical literature at the conclusion of the study. This, as we have indicated, is the precise function of the Discussion chapter.

Dissertations do not typically contain a Summary section, although a subheading titled "Conclusions" is not unusual. This is the place to summarize concisely the principal implications of your findings in a few paragraphs. Resist the temptation to use the final pages of the dissertation as a pulpit to lament the sorry state of affairs in your area of study, your discipline, or the world at large, or, conversely, to rhapsodize about the terrific opportunities afforded to anyone willing or able to capitalize on the significance of your study. An inspired quotation or eloquent turn of phrase can add a nice touch to the conclusion, but there is a difference between forceful writing and gratuitous clichés.

ABSTRACT

Every dissertation requires an Abstract, which is essentially a brief summary of the project placed before the introductory chapter. The clarity of the Abstract should not be overlooked because it is this section of the dissertation that is generally reproduced in computerized databases as well as in *Dissertation Abstracts*. It is also the section of the dissertation that is usually read first, and it may be the only section that is read. The Abstract therefore should accurately reflect the content of the dissertation and be written in a way that makes the study seem articulate and scholarly.

It is relatively easy to put together a good Abstract after a dissertation is completed. You can almost lift two or three key sentences from each chapter of the dissertation to assemble the abstract, because the Abstract needs to provide an overview of the study's purpose, method, results, and implications. It is important to be precise and specific and not to include content that is not present in the dissertation itself.

Dissertation abstracts are generally about 150 words in length and include short statements summarizing the research problem, the subjects, the method and procedures (avoiding abbreviations and idiosyncratic terms), the results, and the conclusions and implications. Write in the past tense to report specific manipulations and procedures you employed in the study, and the present tense to describe conclusions based on the findings. Here is a sample abstract based on a dissertation (Wegmann, 1992):

This study carries forward the exploration of a link between authoritarianism and deficits in cognitive functioning. The subjects were 50 community college students and 29 registered voters recently assigned to jury duty. All participants completed Altemeyer's Right-Wing Authoritarianism Scale and three early-stage information processing tasks: (a) content recognition of a news article 2 minutes after exposure, (b) content recognition of a recorded debate 2 minutes after exposure, and (c) the selection of correct inferential statements in a set of brief paragraphs taken from the Watson & Glasser Critical Thinking Appraisal Test. The experimental setting utilized an interactive computer program that guided and monitored each subject through all phases of the study. When material to be recalled was in written format, authoritarianism interacted with reading skills to limit the recognition and retention of new information. When material was presented orally, retention was significantly affected by authoritarianism. Subjects in both samples who scored high in authoritarianism also made significantly more inferential errors. The data strongly suggest that authoritarianism covaries significantly with a lessened ability to process incoming cognitive information with reasonable care and accuracy.

TITLE

It may seem strange to position a statement about writing the title of the dissertation in the last chapter. Dissertations often have working titles that are amended when the study is completed. We are frequently amazed at how little attention students give to composing a clear and accurate title. This is in spite of the fact that the title is the vehicle that carries the meaning of the dissertation into the professional community. In constructing a title, remember to

1. Include all necessary key words to correctly and fully convey the content of the study.

2. Delete all words that are redundant or do not contribute to the essential meaning.

3. Order the words to reflect accurately the meaning you intend.

Here are some examples of titles that are problematic:

A Study of Information Processing Deficits of the Authoritarian Personality.
>   The phrase "A study of" is redundant and unnecessary. Better: *Information Processing Deficits of the Authoritarian Personality.*

The Effect of Sexually Abused Children Testifying in Court.
>   The word order makes it unclear who is being affected by the testimony. An alternative order: *The Effect of Testifying in Court on Sexually Abused Children.*

An Exploratory Study of the Interrelationship of Loneliness, Obesity, and Other Selected Variables Within Two of Bruch's Obesity Subgroups and a Control Group.
>   Much too long and cumbersome. Try to reduce your title to no more than 12-15 key words that summarize the main idea. For example: *The Role of Loneliness in Bruch's Obesity Subgroups.*

Predicting Acting-Out Behavior From the Achromatic-Chromatic HTP.
>   Do not use abbreviations in the title. Accurate indexing of the dissertation depends upon writing out all variables. Better: *Predicting Acting-Out Behavior From the Achromatic-Chromatic House-Tree-Person Test.*

BOX 7.1

Student
Suggestions

1. You can't always rely on standard manuscript and publication guides to give you the exact format needed for your dissertation. Since dissertations are submitted to your graduate school, and not to a journal, you will need to consult your program's requirements for preparing the final manuscript. There seem to be departmental differences, for example, on whether or not to include a Summary, whether or not to include applications in the Discussion chapter, and how to format references.

2. It was tempting to think of my dissertation as finished when the data were collected and analyzed. I had to get my second wind to write the Discussion chapter. I recommend allotting sufficient time and energy to think about the meaning and implication of your results. Don't set unrealistic deadlines for completing this chapter! In many ways it becomes the most important chapter of the dissertation.

PART III

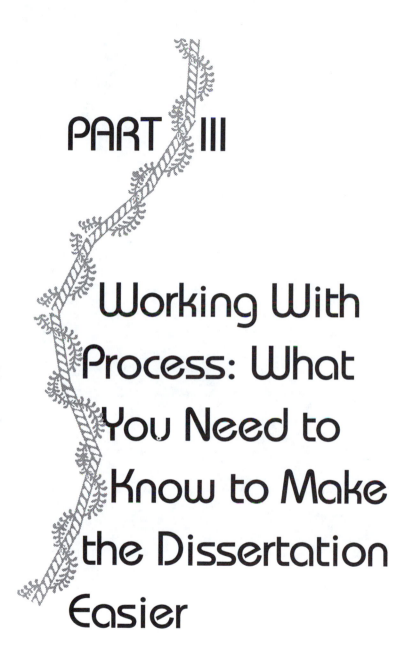

Working With Process: What You Need to Know to Make the Dissertation Easier

CHAPTER 8

Overcoming Barriers:

*Becoming an Expert While Controlling
Your Own Destiny*

Throughout this book we have interspersed firsthand suggestions from some of our students to streamline the task of completing the dissertation successfully. In this chapter, we take up six specific types of issues that, when unattended, can lead to complications in the dissertation process. They are

➤ working with your committee

➤ emotional blocks

➤ task blocks

➤ getting organized

➤ depending upon others for data collection and data analysis

➤ dissertation orals

Awareness of these issues can go a long way toward the prevention of subsequent trouble.

WORKING WITH YOUR COMMITTEE

Each dissertation committee becomes its own social system. Under the best circumstances all the committee members work together smoothly, communicate frequently, and support the student through the dissertation process. That's the ideal scenario. In real life things rarely happen so fortuitously. Committee members disagree and squabble, each member has his or her personal axe to grind, and at least one recalcitrant or neglectful member holds up the completion of the dissertation in an inexcusable fashion.

Students in most graduate programs have the opportunity to choose most, if not all, of their committee members. Certainly the rumor mill in most academic departments provides enough data about this selection process. It may be tempting for you to choose "easy" committee members, that is, faculty who may let you get away with an inferior product and not offer much in the way of feedback—helpful or not. In our experience there is little advantage in avoiding difficult committee members, if by *difficult* one means not obstinate or unreasonable, but those who give rigorous feedback and demand the highest quality product. We have found that students who are willing to invite, insist upon, and manage thorough, sometimes critical, feedback early in the dissertation process end up not only with superior studies but also with proposals that glide smoothly through almost any knowledgeable reader's hands in the later stages. The way to get through many challenging educational hurdles, as well as situations in life, is being able to manage negative feedback with grace and nondefensiveness. It is a skill worth cultivating.

We would be remiss, however, if we did not note that one can cogently argue for choosing a very competent and supportive chair, working closely with that person, and selecting additional committee members who are not likely to provide much substantive input and, hence, slow down the dissertation process! With this cynical but possibly pragmatic strategy, you would be encouraged to circulate drafts of the dissertation to committee members as infrequently as possible and rely on the wisdom and support of your chairperson for major input and guidance. Whether or not this strategy seems appropriate should depend in part upon your assessment of the political climate of your department.

One aspect of the skill of managing feedback is how to deal with instances when committee members differ among themselves and make contradictory recommendations. Certainly faculty have their own tastes and preferences and their own vested interests. One committee member suggests using a particular scale while a second committee member nominates another scale; one person says to delete a section while another person says to expand it. This is to be expected, and no committee will ever be in total agreement. You need to stay in charge of your own project and negotiate with each faculty member. It is vital to know which suggestions are critical and which are window dressing. There is no point in being obstinate about making minor changes to please someone who possesses a vote on your academic future. At the same time, you need to maintain your integrity on important issues and argue them persuasively, based on facts and logic, not emotional resistance. When committee members have divergent opinions that seem nonnegotiable, it is time to appeal to your chairperson for support and perhaps to turn the dilemma over to the faculty themselves to resolve. Never, however, play faculty members against one another.

The constitution of the committee is significant. Always begin by selecting a chairperson and then consulting with your chair before inviting the other members. All faculty have a "short list" of colleagues they either enjoy working with or abhor working with. In a general sense, you want committee members who will promote rather than hinder your progress. Beyond this universal guideline, one way to think about the composition of a dissertation or thesis committee is in terms of the roles the participants play. If your study concerns the fears of Asian immigrant children, it makes sense to have at least one committee member representing expertise in each of the major variables: fears, phobias, or anxieties; Asian culture and immigration; and children or developmental issues. If you are fortunate, all these characteristics may be wrapped up in one or two persons (such as when a study is derived from a faculty mentor's ongoing research program), but it may require three distinct individuals. Be sure to include at least one committee member who has sufficient expertise in the kind of methodology and analysis procedures you anticipate using. Finally, do not forget the important need for social support in the dissertation process. We suggest the inclusion of a committee member who can provide some emotional sustenance during inevitable periods of frustration.

Be mindful of typical committee procedures. Remember that faculty are inevitably busy people, so that you must provide sufficient lead time for them to make responses to drafts and inquiries. It is very reasonable to ask when a response might be forthcoming. Furthermore, you cannot assume that faculty will guard your proposal or dissertation drafts with the same vigilance that you would. Make copies of all documents under all circumstances, including backups of computer files. Our experience, exemplified by a student who recently lost all existing copies of her dissertation materials in a fire, suggests that backup copies should be stored in a different location. It is truly tragic whenever a manuscript or data are "lost" and there is no surviving record.

EMOTIONAL BLOCKS

We have discovered that technical supervision and consultation with graduate students is not the only kind of support instrumental in facilitating successful completion of the dissertation. The task itself also has a way of stimulating emotional issues that can, if overlooked, stymie the process. It is not unusual for the dissertation process to elicit all kinds of blows to self-esteem. Along the way it is quite common to feel that you will never reach the end of the trail. Some students don't know when to give up on a dead-end idea and switch trails to another topic, whereas other students fail to stay on a trail long enough to negotiate its necessary pitfalls. It is not unusual to question a choice of topic or method and to torture oneself about it. If you are overly compulsive, you will inevitably think that you have left something out, and the dissertation will never feel finished. Students need to maintain a perspective that allows them to know that frustration is predictable and that this too will end. One way of maintaining this perspective is to do the dissertation in small steps by selecting definable targets along the way and by calling on others for emotional support when feelings of failure loom large.

The challenge of completing an acceptable dissertation may also invoke deeply felt beliefs about incompetence and the inability to master this task. In our experience, the dissertation process more often than not stirs up a student's most basic behavioral patterns and emotional vulnerabilities. Here is a sample of the kinds of issues that have been presented by students we know:

➤ The belief that completing the dissertation and obtaining the doctoral degree will be a sign of disloyalty to parents and family members who never came nearly so far in their own educational pursuits

➤ The belief that completing the dissertation and obtaining the doctoral degree will bring a greater sense of responsibility and promise of future achievements that seem scary and unattainable

➤ The belief that completing the dissertation and obtaining the doctoral degree will cost a marriage or relationship due to the threat of living with a "doctor," especially if one is a woman

➤ The belief that the intelligence it takes to complete a dissertation is way beyond my capacities

➤ The belief that I am an impostor, only "pretending" to be capable of completing a dissertation

➤ The belief that there is no end in sight, that the dissertation will never be accepted as complete

➤ The belief that I will have to give up my ideals and sell my soul to complete the dissertation

This list of beliefs may seem trivial or inappropriate for students at the doctoral level of graduate education. On the contrary, we are convinced that these feelings and attitudes are more common than we usually admit and that they frequently stand in the way of progress on the dissertation. In our program we use supervision groups that encourage students to share not only their substantive research ideas with one another and with faculty, but also their fears and doubts about themselves in the process. We have found that sensitive exploration of these blocks can often forward the process as much as technical support. We have also been gratified to discover that students can generally identify and access significant coping skills that they may never have realized they possessed.

TASK BLOCKS

Writing a dissertation is a time-consuming, fundamentally lonely act that generally takes in the neighborhood of 2 years from start to finish. No matter how secure your social support system, you will need to generate great persistence to complete it. Some compulsivity helps, but so does preparatory organization of space and time.

A block that is part emotional and part cognitive is the inability to manage time. It should come as no surprise that our universities are full of A.B.D.s, that is, students who have satisfactorily completed all requirements for the doctoral degree other than the dissertation. One of the most common reasons for this state of affairs is the inability to deal with time constraints adequately. To be sure, the dissertation is the singular most time-consuming graduate requirement. Because the completion of courses generally relies upon the structure of a graduate program, the indeterminate freedom of the dissertation may be a cause for alarm and paralysis. Here are some tips for arranging your life to conform to the task of completing the dissertation:

1. Give yourself privacy and quiet. Arrange a space or area of your house or office that is identified with studying and only studying. This is particularly important in the dissertation process. Make this space sacred so that you engage in other tasks, such as writing bills and talking on the telephone, in other areas. This is a straightforward application of the behavioral principle of stimulus control.

2. Taken as a whole, a dissertation can seem like a forbidding and overwhelming challenge. Use the principle of successive approximations to divide it into manageable slices. Tackle the dissertation one step at a time—the review of the literature, the research question and statement of the problem, the method, the results, and the discussion.

3. Get your thoughts on paper. Don't allow yourself to obsess and mull over ideas too long without putting those ideas down in type. Seeing words on a page or on a computer screen has a way of generating momentum. Don't worry at the outset if your words aren't polished. The important thing is to develop a pattern of producing some output on a regular basis.

4. Talk your ideas over with others. Some people, especially extroverted individuals, seem to do their best thinking through discussing ideas with others. Other people prefer to get away by themselves and listen to their own inner voice. In either case, discussing your ideas with friends and colleagues can help you view your work from a fresh perspective and keep you motivated.

5. Establish a regular weekly schedule that allows for several hours of concentrated dissertation time. Many of our students recommend reserving some time each day for the dissertation. Your own schedule will, of course, be influenced by your other commitments, but the important thing is the structure and the regularity. A firm schedule will help guide you through the inevitable stages when ideas are not forthcoming, when obstacles arise, or when temptations lure you to greener pastures.

6. Recognize that even the most productive plowhorse needs a break now and then. Give yourself some time off for enjoyable distractions and do so in a way that reinforces progress. If you find yourself violating your schedule and taking a brief vacation from your dissertation, be gentle and forgiving.

Inevitably, many ordinary life activities will be put on hold during the dissertation. It is crucial to be sensitive to family members because you will no doubt have to negotiate time off from normal responsibilities and contact with them. In our experience, when students graduate with their doctoral degrees, they are most appreciative of the unrequited support and tolerance of their family members in dealing with the impact of the dissertation. Moreover, a negative, impatient spouse can sabotage your progress. One way of encouraging ongoing support is to keep one's partner fully informed about the status and content of the dissertation. Otherwise, it is too easy to feel left out and neglected when a significant other is engaged in a scholarly project that may seem arcane, trivial, or simply interminable.

GETTING ORGANIZED: A CASE STUDY

One of the major tasks of completing a dissertation is maintaining control of the sheer magnitude of the project. You may be testing multiple hypotheses, with different instruments using numerous statistical analyses. In this section we report on how one student managed the project. This student, Helen Barrett, Ph.D., lives in Alaska and was unable to meet with her committee on a regular basis. Therefore, it was extremely important for her to develop clear and informative presentations of research design and hypothesis testing procedures. Barrett was interested in the relationship between learning style, adult self-directed learning, and personal computer competency. Her dissertation (Barrett, 1990) involved the testing of 10 hypotheses and a number of subsidiary questions. Data collection required questionnaire and interview strategies, and data analysis included both quantitative and qualitative methods. To make her plans clear to both her committee and herself, Barrett developed two tables, which are reproduced in their entirety here. The first, "Hypotheses, Instruments, and Statistical Analysis," is presented as Table 8.1.

Note that the hypotheses are included in their entirety in the left-hand column and form the rows of the table. Barrett utilized four instruments plus personal interviews to obtain her data. These instruments consisted of a questionnaire that Barrett designed to assess specific aspects of computer use, a Personal Computer Competency Inventory (PCCI), the Kolb Learning Style Inventory (LSI), the Self-Directed Learning Readiness Scale (SDLRS), and personal interviews.

Each of these is listed in columns following the hypotheses. By examining the cells formed by crossing the hypothesis with the instruments, one can determine which instruments will be used to examine which hypotheses. The pound sign (#) is used to indicate a specific item number on an instrument. If particular subscales or factor scores derived from an instrument are used, these are indicated in the cells.

Table 8.1

Hypotheses, Instruments, and Statistical Analysis

Hypothesis	GQ	PCCI	LSI	SDLR	Variables	Stat Test
H1.1: Competent computer users spend more than 70% of the time learning their computer using self-direct learning strategies	#17				IND = Level of PCC DEP = % of Time SDL	Mean & St. Dev.
H1.2: Competent computer users will have a higher level of self-directed learning readiness than beginning computer users				Total Score	IND = Level of PCC DEP = SDLRS Score	ANOVA
H1.3: Computer users with intrinsic motivation to learn how to use a personal computer have a higher relative level of personal computer competency than those with extrinsic motivation to learn	#3 & 4	Total Score			IND = Source of Motivation DEP = PCCI Score	ANOVA & Chi-Square
H1.4: Computer users with a foundation for learning will have a higher level of personal computer competence	#9, 5, 6, 10, 31, 30, 15, 16, 21	Total Score			IND = Prior Experience, Sources of Assistance, Hours spent, typing speed, user group, PC ownership DEP = PCCI Score	ANOVA & Chi-Square
H2.1: Computer users with an active learning style will have a higher relative level of personal computer competence than those with a reflective learning style		Total Score	AE-RO		IND = Learning Style DEP = PCCI Score	ANOVA
H2.2: Computer users with an abstract learning style will have a higher relative level of personal computer competence than those with a concrete learning style		Total Score	AC-CE		IND = Learning Style DEP = PCCI Score	ANOVA
Subsidiary Question: What is the relationship between learning style and readiness for self-directed learning?			Four Styles	Total Score	IND = Learning Style DEP = SDLRS Score	ANOVA

Source. From Barrett (1990). Reprinted with permission.

Note. GQ = General Questionnaire; LSI = Learning Styles Inventory; SDLR = Self-Directed Learning Readiness; IND = Independent Variable; DEP = Dependent Variable; PCCI = Personal Computer Competency Inventory.

(Continued)

Table 8.1
Continued

Hypothesis	GQ	PCCI	LSI	SDLR	Variables	Stat Test
H3.1: Computer users with a concrete learning style preference will favor the Graphical User Interface	#33		AC-CE		IND = Learning Style DEP = Interface Preference	Chi-Square
H3.2: Computer users with an abstract learning style preference will favor the text-based user interface	#33		AC-CE		IND = Learning Style DEP = Interface Preference	Chi-Square
H3.3: Competent users of graphical user interface computers will use more types of applications than competent users of text-based systems	#8	No. of Apps			IND = Level Expertise DEP = # of Applications	2-Way ANOVA
H3.4: The type of computer learned has a greater impact on learning strategies than the learners' preferred learning style	#10, 18, 14	Total Score	AC-CE		IND = Learning Style IND = Type of Interface DEP = Strategies	ANOVA Chi-Square

Source. From Barrett (1990). Reprinted with permission.
Note. GQ = General Questionnaire; LSI = Learning Styles Inventory; SDLR = Self-Directed Learning Readiness; IND = Independent Variable; DEP = Dependent Variable; PCCI = Personal Computer Competency Inventory.

Following the instruments is a column of variables, which lists the independent and dependent variable for each hypothesis. In the last column, Barrett presents the type of statistical analysis that will be used to examine each hypothesis. By examining this table one can determine exactly how Barrett is proposing to test each hypothesis in her research. This was not all that Barrett did to make things simple for her committee. She also developed an "Overview of Research Design," which is presented as Table 8.2.

In Table 8.2, the columns are formed by the concepts of her study (learner characteristics, computer competency, learning style, self-directed learning, and learning strategies). For each major concept, Barrett has provided the instrument to be used, the type of data gathered, and the type of scores produced. The remaining space was used to present her proposal for a final synthesis and summary of the findings.

We have not polished these tables to make them acceptable for presentation in this book; they are presented exactly as Barrett constructed them. These tables allow Barrett, committee members, statistical consultants, and anyone else with an interest in this research to obtain immediately a picture of the study in question. We offer this example as a model for use in making your own research clear to yourself and to others.

COLLECTING AND ANALYZING DATA: DEPENDING UPON OTHERS

It is one thing to control your own behavior and quite something else to manage the behavior of others. There are at least two occasions when helpers or consultants predictably may become involved in the dissertation. One is in setting up the study and collecting the data; the other is in analyzing the data. Many dissertations require the cooperation of agencies and institutions, particularly to access pools of available and suitable subjects. Sometimes it is possible to graft a dissertation onto an ongoing research project of greater scope and magnitude.

There is much to be said for this strategy. Much of the best research in any field is collaborative and involves a team of professionals coming together to complete a set of studies. If someone is currently engaged in a large research project, particularly one with grant funding

Table 8.2

Overview of Research Design

Adult Self-Directed Learning, Personal Computer Competency and
Learning Style: Models for More Effective Learning

COMPONENTS OF STUDY

	Learner Characteristics	Personal Computer Competency	Learning Style	Self-Directed Learning Readiness	Learning Strategies
Instrument	General Questionnaire	PCCI Bersch/ Barrett Personal Computer Competency Inventory	LSIKolb Learning Style Instrument	SDLRS Self-Directed Learning Readiness Scale	Optional Additional Questions
Type of Data Gathered	Quantitative Demographic Data	Quantitative (Single response on list of 60 competencies)	Quantita-tive (12 questions with forced responses to 4 words/ phrases)	Quantita-tive (58 Likert Scale responses)	Qualitative Responses to open-ended questions
Type of Scores Produced	Single item indicators	Total Score plus ten clusters of computer application skills	Two polar-ity scores (AE-RO and AC-CE) plus one of four Learning Styles	Total Score plus eight Self-Directed Learning Factors	Analysis of responses by question

Final Synthesis and Summary of Findings:
1. Report findings related to hypotheses
2. List of questions found to warrant further study
3. Graphic model of learning process
4. Suggested methods for "learning how to learn" personal computers

Source. From Barrett (1990). Reprinted with permission.

and institutional support, that can be a great advantage. A subjects pool is available, and it is often possible to add some additional measures or interventions to those that already constitute the focus of the study. If you choose and have the opportunity to go this route, a number of considerations should be kept in mind:

1. Remember that a doctoral dissertation must be your own project, both in concept and in design, and that you need to retain ownership over it. This means that the data must be available to you to analyze as you see fit and that you must be free to describe whatever conclusions you reach, regardless of anyone's special interest or investment in the project as a whole. Do not rely on vague promises made in passing, particularly by those not in a position to guarantee you the use of a data set or population. Make your needs explicit, and elicit promises regarding your involvement in a project and your use of the data from those authorized to make such promises. You also need to have the freedom to be able to publish the results in your own name.

2. Sometimes the scheduling of someone else's study may not conform to your own needs. We have found that students who collect dissertation or thesis data prior to having a completed, approved proposal do so at considerable risk. Method and procedures need to be in place and agreed upon prior to the start of data collection. This may be difficult if you are joining a larger study. It can also be tricky if your need for collecting data is governed by external considerations, such as the availability of schoolchildren at the beginning of the academic year or the established starting date of a program or group that you need to evaluate. The antidote to this problem is to plan ahead and assume that it will take longer to establish procedures than you imagine. Some very good research studies capitalize on the occurrence of unanticipated events that are ripe for data collection (e.g., a political revolution or ecological disaster), but they rarely result in doctoral dissertations.

3. It should go without saying that you and your committee are the final arbiters of the research questions and procedures of your study. It is not unusual for other people's large-scale projects to use measures or procedures that do not exactly measure what you intend to measure. Be certain that you have the freedom to make methodological changes that are critical to ensuring the quality of your study. If you

determine, for example, that the only measure of weight loss available to you is not a sufficient indicator of fitness, the setting for your proposed study may not be right.

A different kind of issue concerns the employment of peers to collect or code data. Many students have had the experience of serving in this role as research assistants. When graduate students use research assistants, however, they may not hold the same authority over them as do professors. In our experience, raters and other assistants often quit or do not reliably follow through on their commitments. It pays to be careful and conscientious in hiring assistants and have backup strategies available if plans go awry. It is also important to train and supervise assistants thoroughly at every step of the process. What seems obvious to you, being totally immersed in your study, may not be so obvious to someone else. A frequent problem is obtaining low interrater reliability on coding data because the raters have not been trained sufficiently.

Finally, whenever you collaborate with faculty or consultants, remember to take and maintain responsibility regarding your own dissertation project. We have witnessed many instances where students, either unwittingly or manipulatively, attempt to shift responsibility to others for problems for which they are responsible. In one prime example, a student had a fixed deadline for completing her dissertation proposal in order to receive committee authorization to collect data that could only be obtained within a one week time period in order to avoid a six month wait for another data collection opportunity. She promised her committee that she would complete her proposal three weeks in advance of this date. As the deadline rolled by, she made panicked telephone calls to her committee to move the deadline forward. The committee agreed to extend the deadline by a week. After expressing the need for "just a few more days," the student submitted her proposal 10 days before the collection date. Subsequently, one committee member believed that the student needed to make some changes in her data collection procedures, but there wasn't sufficient time to make the revisions within her window of opportunity. Rather than respecting the extra effort the committee member made to read the draft of her proposal, she summarized the situation by claiming that "Dr. X wouldn't let me collect data." We urge you to avoid this distortion of responsibility attribution in all its numerous forms.

Students also shift blame to consultants, particularly statistical consultants, when things go wrong. While it is sometimes helpful to rely upon an experienced statistician to "crunch your numbers," you should never lose control of your analysis to this person, despite the appeal of discharging this responsibility to someone else and thus making that person accountable. At times it may be proper to utilize statistical consultants to conduct analyses and assist with the interpretation of results, but this should not be seen as a means of avoiding the need to learn and apply statistics. Take direct responsibility for all phases of the data collection and analysis process and never place yourself in the position of confessing, "I don't know, my consultant was in charge."

DISSERTATION ORALS

The tradition of the final oral defense of the doctoral dissertation is long-standing and likely to engender some anxiety in most doctoral students. The defense ranges from a congenial ritual in which the student publicly presents his or her findings to an assemblage of receptive "colleagues," to a more excruciating examination of the quality of the dissertation and grilling of the candidate by an unsympathetic faculty committee. In our view, no student should be allowed to schedule a final dissertation oral defense if the dissertation is not regarded as complete by the committee. Consequently, part of the function of the defense is a formal "coming out" of the student into the community of scholars, a celebration of the completion of a major scholarly achievement, and a symbolic rite of passage to the awarding of the doctorate. In the best of cases, the oral defense is an opportunity to think about and articulate the implications of your study to your own discipline and to be challenged by your committee to claim your right to sit among them as an acknowledged expert in your field of study.

You can make a number of reasonable preparations to make the experience a positive one. Certainly, being fully familiar with your study is crucial. It is likely that by the time of the oral defense you will be a leading authority on your particular topic. The more familiar you are with the details of your study, including the relevant literature in the area, the more you will appear as the expert. The role that the committee can rightly play is to provide some new lenses through which to view your work because it is likely that by this time you have stood so close to your own study that it may be difficult to gain perspective and appreciate it from other vantage points.

In the best of circumstances, your committee will be aligned with your own goals of presenting your study as a colleague-to-be. Sometimes, unfortunately, the orals become an opportunity for faculty to build up their own egos at your expense. One recommendation for meeting this challenge is to take control of the situation as much as possible and move out of the victim position. One student we know scouted the site of his orals beforehand, rearranged the furniture in the room according to his preferences, and then greeted his committee personally as they entered the room.

Typically, students are asked to spend anywhere from 10 to 45 minutes providing an overview of their study at the outset of the orals. Think carefully about this task beforehand. Try to boil your presentation down to the essentials so that you do not overwhelm your audience with minutiae. Audiovisual materials can help organize and illustrate a presentation, and slides and overheads are particularly effective ways of supporting a talk. Do not plan to chew up your allotted time with a long, drawn-out oral presentation in the hope that there will be no time for questions. Your committee is too smart for that and will assume that you are insufficiently knowledgeable for meaningful discussion of your work.

The presentation of the summary of the study is followed by questions and comments from the various committee members. On the basis of these comments, which can be benign or intimidating, the committee will determine their recommendations. In the best of circumstances, these rounds of questions can generate lively and enjoyable discussion about the study and the topic that will further establish your credibility as a professional. The more you can frame the final oral defense of the dissertation as an opportunity to present your research publicly, the better the experience is likely to be. The more you take a proactive, nondefensive position, the less likely it is for your committee to humiliate you. Count on being asked a few questions you will not be able to answer. That does not mean the end of the world. It may even be wise to "save something for the committee" so that they can make an acknowledged contribution to the completion of the project.

The most likely outcome of any dissertation orals is a pass with the request for minor revisions. Minor revisions are changes to the dissertation that do not impugn the central thesis, perhaps some additions to the bibliography, some further analyses, or some elaborated discussion. Major changes are more substantive alterations to theory and method and thus are more troublesome. The general antidote to the request for major changes is to keep your committee fully informed about the dissertation throughout the process by inviting them to read every chapter as it comes off the press. The more you request feedback during the 2 years or so of dissertation work, the less likely it is that a committee member will sabotage the entire dissertation at the orals stage. Be wary of the committee member who remains on the fringe of your project and does not have time to read your dissertation. This person is likely to ask questions about statistics, because asking these sorts of questions does not require knowledge of your field or even the content of your dissertation. Have a good understanding of why you used each statistic for each analysis. Then you will be prepared for questions such as, "Well, Mr. Jones, why did you use an analysis of variance to assess Hypothesis 3?"

There tends to be a significant letdown for students at the conclusion of successfully defending their dissertations. Often this emotional letdown includes not wanting to see the dissertation ever again. We encourage you to respond to the request for changes as soon as possible. Otherwise, completion of the dissertation may drag on interminably. Moreover, we have found that if a student does not make a concerted effort to publish the results of the findings shortly after the orals, in either book or journal article form, it is unlikely that it will ever happen. Some departments attempt to counteract the resistance to publishing quality dissertations by accepting finished dissertations in publication form, perhaps including a broader review of the literature and discussion as appendices. In any case, for all those graduate students who have precipitously forgotten their dissertations on the way home from the orals, there are others who have launched their careers by distilling the dissertation into one or more promising publications.

The doctoral dissertation is likely to be the singular most ambitious research project of most social scientists' careers. As such, it not only

has the potential for providing entrée into a field of professional practice and scholarship but also serves as an ongoing source of self-esteem
and intellectual achievement. It is a transformative experience. Para-
doxically, whereas most students look back upon their dissertation
experience as grueling, overwhelming, and oftentimes aversive, students also evaluate the experience as confirming, life-changing, and an
important transition into the world of the professional scholar.

CHAPTER 9

Writing

Jody Veroff

Knowing how to express ideas in written form is an essential skill for the researcher. From the beginning of any research project to its final report, most researchers will spend more time writing about their ideas, their understandings of previous theory and research, and their own procedures, findings, and conclusions than they will spend actually conducting experiments or performing statistical analyses. It is easy to ignore how much of "science" depends on the communication of ideas in written form. It is also easy to ignore how much the ability to write clear and interesting prose contributes to the success of any research you may undertake. Well-written proposals are more likely to be

- ➤ Received positively by funding agencies or dissertation committees
- ➤ Accepted for publication in professional journals
- ➤ Understood and appreciated by the audiences they reach

Thus, the ultimate impact of any research you undertake is likely to be much enhanced if you can write well about your work.

You can learn a good deal about "how to write a research report" by referring to books and articles explicitly focused on this topic. I have listed some references in the bibliography at the end of this chapter. These will teach you conventional approaches to organizing and formatting your work and will help you mirror the characteristic logic and development of research writing. You can also study the writing style and organization of articles in professional journals that publish research reports in areas related to your topic. Modeling these probably will ensure that your report complies sufficiently with that journal's requirements to be acceptable.

Unfortunately, many models available in professional journals are masterpieces of indirection, obfuscation, and sheer boredom. Some existing models support the suspicion that the writer has specifically aimed to make the report impossible for the average reader to understand, intending to speak only to an elite audience whose existing understanding of the topic is complete enough to permit them to interpret and translate what has been written. Indeed, this approach to writing about research is so prevalent that we might give it the label "gobbledygook." If you use such writing as your model, you may convince some readers that your work is important and profound because they cannot understand anything you have written, but you will also lose the opportunity to inform and communicate with a readership that is not already in the inner circle.

At one time or another most of us have been deeply affected by a scientific article because it helped us understand something we previously could not understand or because it engaged our own thinking and emotions in a way that stimulated our thinking about the topic. If you wish your writing to affect readers in this way, it is important to pay attention to your writing style and to learn to express your ideas with clarity, with energy, perhaps even with grace. You will need to learn how to

➤ Write what you mean

➤ Choose words and ways of putting them together that convey your understandings directly

➤ Avoid scientific jargon and stylistic "gobbledygook"

➤ Identify with your potential readers and to try to imagine their process of understanding what you have written

Learning how to write this way seems to me to be no different from learning how to write for any other purpose. Because, for many of us, something about both the realities and myths of "scientific writing" turns our minds to stone or slush and makes us feel awkward, stupid, and convoluted in our very thinking process, it may be easier to learn how to improve our writing in general than to begin with the specific demands of research writing.

PAST EXPERIENCES WITH WRITING

One way to demystify the process of writing is to retrace your history as "a writer." Remembering your own experiences may help you understand current pleasures you have as a writer as well as negative feelings and writing problems. Although the joys and sorrows of your own past experiences with writing undoubtedly are unique, there are communalities in human development and similarities in educational structures that typically influence the way most of us learn to write. A brief review of these may help you retrieve some of your own past experiences and may help you understand current feelings and difficulties you may have with writing. Remembering and reappraising these experiences may also suggest ways to change your feelings and take steps to remedy your difficulties.

LEARNING TO DISTANCE YOUR SELF FROM WRITING

Your writing career probably began at a tender age when you learned how to write your own name. This is a triumphant accomplishment even when the process is laborious and painful and the final product misshapen and awkward. Writing your name may not seem like "real writing" because it has only do with learning how to shape letters, but it is the beginning of being able to express your self on paper, the beginning stage of a new way to communicate with others about your thoughts and feelings. Unfortunately, subsequent education can encourage you to put more and more distance between your writing and your self, so that you learn to devalue your own voice and may even conclude that it is an inappropriate presence in your writing. You may learn to ignore personal ownership of your writing or any real connection between what you write and who you are or what you think or feel.

This distancing of the self from writing is perhaps inevitable, given the predictable lag between conceptual abilities and the skills required to render thoughts on paper. Stubby little fingers can rarely keep up with the complex ideas that young children may want to express; the spoken vocabularies they command usually are far more extensive and sophisticated than the reading or writing vocabularies they master in the first few years of school. Learning to write "Run, run, run" or "See Betty catch the ball" may be a significant achievement for a first-grade child, but one that is essentially mechanical, having little connection with his or her own thoughts or the way he or she talks about the world.

Distancing writing from the self may also be a consequence of the typical educational priorities, which tend to focus on the development of essential skills such as penmanship, spelling, and grammar. Children *do*, of course, need to master these skills before they can use writing to communicate their ideas in writing, but there is considerable risk that the disconnection between such skill-learning and the child's ongoing experience will teach him or her that writing does not have much to do with one's self and the things he or she might like to say on paper. Even when writing skills are essentially in place, later school experience may continue to reinforce a separation between the child's own thoughts and feelings and the process of writing. Writing projects are often geared toward teaching children how to use libraries and reference materials and requiring them to demonstrate the facts learned from their "research."

In my schooling years, students had little choice about topics for writing projects; when your geography class was studying the New England region, you could write about "The Principal Products of Lowell, Massachusetts" or a similar topic from a limited list. Although I hope and think that children currently have more choice in the topics they must write about, public libraries are still full of young children straining their eyes over encyclopedias, keeping their place with one hand while they write down information with the other. It is easy to imagine that they are writing, just as I did, papers on "The Honey Bee" or "The Mountains of Peru" or "Diphtheria," without much interest in their topic and without much inclination to go beyond recording the information provided in the encyclopedia.

LEARNING TO THINK OF WRITING AS A BORING ACTIVITY

Using writing projects to augment standard classroom learning or to assess whether children have mastered the skills required to collect information about a topic is a reasonable way to teach children important academic skills. A regrettable conclusion that children may draw, however, is that the purpose of writing is to write down someone else's information about a subject that is not very interesting. Part of their learning may be that writing is a tedious and unrewarding activity to be put off as long as possible. The experience of understanding more about a topic by writing about it and the pleasure of writing about something of personal interest and importance can be rare and unusual for the average child going through school. It is not surprising, then, that so many of us grow up to view writing as burdensome.

LEARNING TO FEEL INADEQUATE AS A WRITER

In the later years of grade school and on through high school and college, teachers become increasingly evaluative of their students' writing and are particularly alert to errors in grammar, punctuation, and spelling, sometimes to the exclusion of attention to the content or the way ideas have been developed. Most of us can remember the sinking sensation we experienced when writing assignments were returned, covered with red ink and graphically showing how many errors we had made on every page. We searched in vain for any evidence that the teacher liked what we said or the way we said it and found instead that the comments in the margins informed us only of where we had been unclear, illogical, or awkward. Whatever pleasure or excitement we might have felt about the original writing assignment was usually diluted and tarnished. Some of us may remember feeling so stupid and unskilled that we began to be afraid to write papers at all. Although students with some "natural" gift for writing well and those with more compassionate teachers may escape such aversive experiences, many people respond to less affirming school experiences by learning to be afraid to write. As teachers, especially at the college level, become more and more concerned about the inability of many students to write at even a minimally acceptable level, they are likely to redouble their efforts to point out error and will be less and less inclined to notice or reward the ideas the student has expressed.

This review of common educational experiences around writing has focused on those that foster the following beliefs:

➤ It is not quite appropriate to write about your own ideas.

➤ Writing is primarily a boring rehash of other people's ideas.

➤ What has been written will be read vigilantly by evaluators seeking primarily to find mistakes.

For those of us whose experience was tilted in this way, the surprising thing is that we did not give up on writing altogether once we finished high school or college. It is not surprising if we learned to be afraid to write or to have difficulty in getting ourselves to sit down and write, or to believe we cannot write. Yet most of us continue to write. We write down lists of things to do today; we write directions to the baby-sitter or the plumber; we write business letters, letters of complaint, letters of explanation, letters of sympathy and condolence, and occasional letters of thank you. Although the writing of friendly letters is mourned by some as a dying art, some of us still write to our mothers or our children or our friends who live in distant places. If our work requires it, we write progress reports, project proposals, memos, and instructions, all without crippling anxiety or resistance. The old aversive feelings about writing emerge most dramatically when we must write something that someone else will receive and evaluate as "serious" writing. Writing about theory or research may provoke the most intense concern; not only are there conventions and myths about conventions for this kind of writing that limit our freedom of expression, but in addition writing about more abstract topics is generally difficult, especially if we do not fully understand the ideas we are writing about. Although the very process of struggling to write about ideas is often clarifying and can promote deeper comprehension, it is tempting to circumvent this struggle by stringing words, phrases, and clauses together in a way that is sufficiently obscure so that no one will be able to detect our gaps in understanding.

If you are burdened with anxiety about your writing, or by a perpetual reluctance to begin to write, or by a conviction that the demands of writing well require a gift that you do not have, do not despair. If you can think and if you can speak about what you think, it is almost guaranteed that you can learn to write. You are even a good candidate for learning to enjoy writing. The major obstacles that you need to overcome are (a) *fear*, engendered by past unpleasant experiences associated with writing; (b) *boredom*, resulting from not caring enough about what you are writing about; (c) *perfectionism*, which makes you labor too hard over each word you use, worry too much about evaluation, or try to report in full detail everything that has ever been said about your topic; (d) *disenfranchisement* from your own voice and your own ideas that makes you feel unentitled to express your ideas in a form that others can examine and evaluate; (e) *impatience* that allows you to imagine that writing should be effortless, an activity that doesn't require the time and effort ordinarily required to learn to do anything well; and (f) *excessive pride* that makes you believe that your public expressions should be wonderful, thus making you unwilling to reveal that sometimes they are not. Additional obstacles may reside in difficulties with spelling, grammar, and sentence structure, but these obstacles usually can be overcome by learning the rules of the grammatical structure of English, by enlisting an editor or proofreader, by employing word processing programs designed to pick up such errors, or by using a dictionary and a guide to common grammatical and spelling errors.

OVERCOMING OBSTACLES

Overcoming the obstacles created by negative experiences and unrealistic expectations sounds like a formidable challenge that might require a substantial therapeutic intervention to achieve. It is not always easy to lay anxiety to rest or to give up perfectionism or concern about evaluation. Reflections of successful writers on their work suggest that these problems continue to haunt even the best of writers, many of whom suffer from writer's block for extended periods of time and often struggle on a daily basis to keep themselves writing. Most writers emphasize the importance of regular writing and describe strategies they employ to make sure they do this. Many would agree that it is often easier not to begin to write, just as it might be easier not to do the dishes or go jogging or practice the piano. But all skills require regular practice, and most of us are accustomed to imposing sufficient discipline in our lives to attend to the things we consider important. Writers often schedule daily blocks of time they will spend or set goals for the number of pages they will complete each day. They take their work as writers seriously enough to organize their lives so that their writing time is at least as sacred as the time they allot to other activities. If you want to learn to write, it is essential to make writing a regular and routine activity that is at least as important to you as brushing your teeth or reading the newspaper. There will be no better way to increase your skill and your comfort.

GETTING STARTED

MAKING LISTS

Resolving to write as a part of your daily routine may not necessarily protect you from the depressing circumstance of staring at a pristine yellow legal pad or the blinking cursor on your computer screen, wondering how in the world to begin. Even when you urgently need to complete a writing project, you may find yourself quite literally at a loss for words. Sometimes it helps to fall back on the kinds of writing most of us do every day. You might, for example, begin by making a list of ideas that seem important to address in your paper. List-making is a familiar and comfortable activity that does not have to be any more profound and meaningful than writing a shopping list or a list of things to do today, yet just as these prosaic lists help to organize your thoughts and priorities, a list of ideas that seem important can begin to organize the shape of the piece you want to write. A good list can be played with. You can put the items in order of importance, so that your list can remind you of what needs most to be included, just as a list of things to do today reminds you of the priority of paying the electric bill before the lights are turned off. You can also organize a list by establishing which things should be first and last and somewhere in the middle, just as a list of errands might remind you to take the casserole out of the freezer first and buy the ice cream last. A list can help you take into account the way some of the ideas are related to others and need to be clustered together, just as a useful shopping list groups lettuce, apples, and potatoes together, separate from butter, eggs, and milk. Playing with your list of ideas in this way can give you a structure for your writing project that will allow you to get started and to know where you are going.

CLUSTERING

If the linearity of lists stultifies you and you have never been able to make an outline until you have written your piece, a different way of beginning may be more in tune with your thinking style. In her book *Writing the Natural Way*, Gabriele Rico (1983) describes a method she believes helps writers to access the natural structuring tendencies of the human brain. She calls this method "clustering."It begins with a free associative task that involves writing your topic somewhere in the middle of a piece of paper and then writing words and phrases that come to mind around that central topic, with no conscious attention to their spatial placement. As more and more apparently random associations are recorded, you can begin to draw lines between ideas that seem connected and gradually fill in the "map" of associated thoughts. Rico contends that at some point a structure emerges that will allow you to write a reasonably well-formed paragraph about your topic that represents your current understanding of your topic, linking and organizing your ideas in a coherent form. I have used this exercise in writing workshops; it does seem to allow most participants to produce a meaningful paragraph in a very short period of time. A few people in each group have found this method so liberating and helpful that they feel their approach to thinking and writing has been virtually transformed. If you are stuck and cannot get yourself to begin to write, you will risk little by trying this method, and you may be lucky and discover that it is uniquely compatible with your way of thinking.

WRITING A LETTER TO A FRIEND

Another way to trick yourself into beginning is to pretend you are writing to a friend to tell her about your topic and what you have learned about it. Suppose you are interested in exploring whether or not men and women go through different processes in deciding to run for political office. If you were writing about this interest to a friend, you probably would want to tell her why you were interested in this topic, why you think it is important, and what hunches you have about differences that might exist. Imagining what you would need to tell her to help her understand your ideas may help you begin to write and organize your thoughts about the topic without feeling as intimidated as you might if you were imagining your reader to be your dissertation chair or the review committee of a funding agency. Because you may know already what your friend thinks and knows about gender differences or running for political office, you will be able to imagine how she might receive and react to what you have written. You can foresee some of the arguments you may have to present to convince her that this is an important issue to study.

Beginning as if you were writing to a friend will highlight the communicative aspect of writing and remind you of the importance of your self in the communicative relationship that is created by writing. It will encourage you to write about your ideas in simple, direct, and nontechnical language. It also may allow you to make connection with why you care about your topic. If your "letter to a friend" instead adds fuel to your fear that your topic is so boring that no one could possibly want to read about it, perhaps the exercise will help you decide to find a better topic.

JOURNALISTIC DEVICES

Introductory classes in journalism suggest another trick that may help you get started. Fledgling reporters are instructed to begin every news story with a paragraph that tells the reader "who?" "what?" "why?" "when?" and "where?" (An additional query—"how?"—is a useful addition in writing about research.) Reporters learn to put this essential, bare bones information in the lead paragraph so that a coherent account of the news event will still remain if the editor decides to cut the remainder of the story. This journalistic device is useful for getting started on any writing project even when you have no reason to fear that your audience will not read beyond your first paragraph. This format may help you get started because it describes a small and delimited task that will help organize your writing and remind you to include the information necessary to tell your reader what your article will be about. It can often become the introductory paragraph of your paper. If you wish, for example, to write about the problem of inner-city violence in adolescents, a good introduction might be this:

> (what?) Escalating violence among inner-city adolescents is becoming a major social problem (why?) that exacts an enormous toll in young lives and crime control costs. Understanding the causes of this escalation is, thus, an imperative research agenda. (where?) This study will survey a sample of 15- to 19-year-old adolescents (who?) attending school in Detroit, Michigan (when) in the fall of 1999, (how?) using attitude questionnaires to identify their perceptions of the causes of violence in the schools.

The relatively simple task of answering the journalistic questions results in an introduction that states the purpose and approach of the study clearly and directly and prepares the reader for the elaborations that will follow. Your reader can then make a decision about whether or not he or she is sufficiently interested in your topic and your approach to read further.

WRITING STORIES

If you are a person who likes to tell stories, you might find it useful to write about your topic in story form. The story of how you came to be interested in your topic might be a natural way to begin. Or you might tell the story of how you learned more about your topic. Most of us learned the basic structure of a story when we were very young and know by heart the convention that begins with "Once upon a time" and ends with "and they lived happily ever after." In between the beginning that sets the stage and the ending that brings things to a satisfying conclusion, we know that characters must be introduced and that some kind of problem must be posed that leads to some kind of action that allows for the "happy ending," with enough tension and suspense built in so that the reader cares to keep on reading.

You may find it a bit odd to think of writing a research report as if it were a story, but some of the most engaging and interesting examples of scientific writing have qualities similar to a good detective story. The writer describes the "mystery," tells you how she developed her "clues" and how she went about collecting the evidence, and how she ruled out various "wrong" solutions on her way to discovering a convincing answer to the mystery. This device is especially useful in writing about research findings and theories in social science, where the phenomena under consideration are often complex and potential "causes" are both multiple and interactive. Researchers and theorists often begin with a relatively simple hypothesis such as, for example, that increased stress will be associated with illness. The plot soon thickens, and researchers must attend to other factors that influence this relationship, eventually constructing a "cast of characters" that play a role in how stress affects well-being. Writing the "story" that describes the hunches that have been followed up, the "red herrings" in the case, the new clues that emerge, and the new evidence that must be collected would be an engrossing way to present the literature relevant to this topic, and it might in itself generate new insights.

Each of these devices for getting started provides a way to organize your thoughts and ideas that should allow you to put some words on your pristine piece of paper or your blank computer screen. You may also be able to see where the rest of your writing project will be going and the kind of structure it will have, because each of these devices creates a purpose for what you are writing:

- ➤ To order your ideas

- ➤ To recognize the connections between ideas

- ➤ To make sense of your ideas in ordinary language

- ➤ To persuade someone to follow your way of thinking

- ➤ To provide your reader with essential information

- ➤ To tell the story of the development of your ideas

If your writing does not initially seem to have a purpose beyond satisfying the requirements of an assignment, these devices may help you generate other purposes that will facilitate the writing process and make it more interesting.

TOPIC AND PASSION

If you have any choice at all about topics for your writing, one of the most important things you can do to facilitate your writing is to choose one that you care about and are interested in. Although some advisers warn against choosing topics with high personal relevance on the grounds that your appropriate objectivity will be impaired, this danger is small compared to the problems that arise when you try to write about something entirely divorced from your personal experience, concern, or interest. The energy required to sustain effort, to endure frustration, and to think creatively flows most readily from passion for your topic. This may be a passionate desire to find answers to puzzling questions or a passionate curiosity to learn as much as possible about a topic of interest or a passion to communicate to others the important things you have discovered and learned. Passion not only provides energy that will propel your writing project onward but also helps guarantee that you will interact with the materials you are writing about, testing the ideas and information of others against your own thoughts and ideas and experiences. Thus, what you write will be both more integrative and more likely to generate new insights for yourself and for your readers. Your evident investment in your topic will almost inevitably make what you write interesting to others. The energy derived from your passion and interest will be evident in your writing and will make it exciting for almost any reader.

Sometimes even a randomly chosen topic can inspire interest and passion as you learn more about it. Evidence of growing interest or even passion for a topic exists if you begin to wonder about something you have read or to want to argue with its author or become eager to pursue the topic in greater depth. These are exciting moments in intellectual development, and you should not eliminate such possibilities in your search for a topic. Especially when you are writing to fulfill an assignment in a class, you may find it initially difficult to think about anything you care very much about. Doing some general reading relevant to the course content before you select a topic for a writing project with special attention to ideas that stimulate questions or connections or curiosity will be useful in identifying a topic sufficiently interesting to sustain your writing momentum.

Even when you care about your topic, you may not be able to generate the kind of passion I have been describing if you limit yourself to reporting what is known about the topic. Such writing often becomes a kind of laundry list of what others have discovered or said about the subject and just as often is both boring to write and boring to read. The "detective mode" usually is more effective in communicating the excitement you feel about your topic. By this I mean the organization of your writing around questions that you have sought to answer and the possible answers that have presented themselves. The difference between writing about a *topic* and writing about *questions* could be described as the difference between reviewing what is known about a topic and identifying the relevance of what is known to the questions at hand. Although both approaches will communicate essentially the same information, the detective mode engages the writer in interacting with available information and is likely to engage the reader to interact similarly. Whenever you find yourself wondering why something is the way it is or how it works, or who might be affected, or whether it always happens this way or instead depends on something else to set it off, you have more than likely identified a good topic for both research and writing. Your questions will make you care about finding answers and will make it easier for you to write a well-organized and interesting paper.

AUTHORSHIP AND VOICE

Much of what I have said about caring and passion is directly related to another important attribute of good writing that I call "claiming your authorship." Excluding your self from your writing is a good way to make your writing boring to yourself and to others. The unfortunate tendency to exclude oneself as knower, scholar, interpreter, and discoverer in writing is often learned very early, in ways I already have described. Educators, in their eagerness to educate, often emphasize the need for children to demonstrate *what* they have learned. Children take tests or write papers to demonstrate that they have the requisite knowledge of literature, geography, history, science, and all the other things they might not know if they were not taught. Less often do educators encourage students to think about what they have learned, to share those thoughts, or to write about what they may know from experience or from sources other than standard textbooks and reference materials. It is easy for children to conclude that "received knowledge" (see Belenky, Clinchy, Goldberger, & Tarule, 1986) is more true, more valuable, and more rewarded than any other kind of knowing. Received knowledge, by definition, comes from the authority of others. When the measurement of children's learning is their ability to recite the knowledge they have received, it is difficult for them to perceive themselves as entitled to be authors of knowledge.

Scholarly writing about theory and research generally requires the writer to go beyond recording received knowledge. Authors of such writing have almost always thought about issues, reached conclusions on the basis of available evidence, and interacted with their information in order to organize and integrate it. Yet, many theorists and researchers persist in using a style that suggests that it is inappropriate for writers to acknowledge their authorship or involvement with what they have written. Conventions of referring to the self in the third person, never using the word "I," and predominantly using the passive voice suggest that even a writer who is discussing his or her own discoveries or theories must pretend it was someone else who thought or discovered or concluded. Of course, when writers say "It was discovered that. . . ." or "It is reasonable to conclude that. . . ," we all know that they mean "I discovered this" and "I conclude that," but the language style suggests that the knowledge they are presenting was received from somewhere else and did not really involve the researcher.

I came across an embarrassing example of the extent to which prevailing conventions encourage writers to disown what they have written in this way when I recently reread my doctoral dissertation, written in 1959. Throughout this document, I had disowned not only my authorship but also my gender by referring to my ideas in the masculine third person. Although current emphasis on nonsexist language probably protects young women writing today from such absurd constructions, they were not uncommon in those days, and they provide graphic examples of how this convention of "scientific writing" influences the relationship of the writer to her writing. This kind of depersonalization is motivated not only by a reluctance to claim authority but apparently also by an attempt to demonstrate objectivity by underplaying the fact that there is a real and potentially fallible person who has written about his or her own ideas and conclusions. It serves to reinforce the fears of many that they are not entitled to have ideas or to think about topics or to draw their own conclusions. Claiming authorship requires taking responsibility for what you write; although this may be intimidating, it is also empowering.

Although the stylistic rules of your publisher may require you eventually to disembody yourself in your writing, there is no rule that says you can't begin by openly acknowledging that "I wondered about this, I think these ideas are unsupported by evidence, I surveyed the literature, I designed a study, and I concluded that. . . ." To do so will make you very aware that you are the author of what you write, responsible for what you say, and entitled to communicate your own ideas and understandings. If you must remove the "I" from your writing to satisfy the demands of others, it will be easier to find ways to do this that do not deny your authorship if you have first written more personally. The *Publication Manual of the American Psychological Association* (1994) makes the following observation: "Inappropriately or illogically attributing action in the name of objectivity can be misleading. Writing 'The experimenter instructed the participants' when 'the experimenter' refers to yourself is ambiguous and may give the impression that you did not take part in your own study" (p. 29). Although many journals and advisers continue to insist on the disembodied voice, it is likely that these observations by a major arbiter of style will eventually influence changes in the requirements imposed by journal editors.

Developing a "voice" as a writer depends on a strong sense of yourself as the possessor of knowledge and ideas who is entitled to speak about these to others. The voices of writers such as Ernest Hemingway, Marcel Proust, Mark Twain, or Sigmund Freud are easily recognized (and can be easily parodied) by readers familiar with their work. If you claim authorship in your writing and practice doing so, your voice will become distinctive in much the same way as is your fingerprint or your way of walking. In this sense, developing your voice not only lends authority to your writing but also tends to make writing a more "natural" process in which ways of expressing ideas or constructing sentences flow more easily without requiring as much conscious and deliberate effort.

No one develops a writing voice overnight, and the steps that might hasten the process are not easy to describe. Peter Elbow struggles to describe voice through a whole chapter in his book *Writing With Power* (1998), expressing dissatisfaction with people who see it as similar to *authenticity, sincerity,* or *authority.* He says,

> Voice is what most people have in their speech but lack in their writing—namely, a sound or texture—the sound of "them." We recognize most of our friends on the phone before they say who they are. A few people get their voice into their writing. When you read a letter or something else they've written, it has the sound of them. (p. 288)

Elbow contends that conscious work on voice and help from someone else in distinguishing between passages in writing that have voice and those that do not encourages students to do more experimentation in their writing and also to include more about themselves in what they write. In addition to attending to your own thoughts, feeling, and characteristic modes of expression, I believe acquiring a writing voice also depends on developing your sense of entitlement to have ideas and to write about them. Perhaps, however, the development of a sense of entitlement of this sort could be equated with the development of voice.

A part of your voice resides in the kind of words you like to use, the rhythm of your "natural" speech or writing, the way you use metaphor and images to convey your ideas, and the very organization that seems most natural in structuring your thoughts. Sometimes, you can become aware of the absence of your voice by reading what you have written out loud. It is often easier to hear than to see the false notes, the awkward expressions you would never use when speaking, as well as the absence of rhythm and flow. By listening to what you have written, you become the observer of what you have written with an outsider's perspective, and you may become more aware of the dissonance between what you have written and what you intended to communicate.

An exercise that may be useful in alerting you to elements of your voice involves writing about a randomly chosen topic for several minutes with the explicit goal of writing whatever comes to mind and not allowing yourself to stop writing. Such "free writing" unmediated by conscious attention to content or "proper" form can provide helpful insights about your natural style of expression on paper.

An entertaining way to further explore issues of voice involves writing about a given situation from several different perspectives. For example, reviewing a research report of a psychological experiment would be illuminating. In the characteristic mode of objective science, the report would most likely be written from the perspective of a disembodied, anonymous third person who presumably aims to report the facts about the experiment. Try writing about the experiment from the perspective of one of the subjects of the experiment, usually referred to as "S." Then write about the experiment from the perspective of the experimenter, trying to imagine his or her thoughts and feelings while conducting the experiment. Finally, write a description of the experiment from your own perspective as a reader. The differences among your resulting descriptions reflect different voices and can help liberate your own voice. A fringe benefit of this exercise may be new insights about what really happened during the experiment and what interpretations you may want to draw from it.

CONCERN ABOUT AUDIENCE AND EVALUATION

I have stressed the importance of recognizing that writing is a form of communication that involves not only the writer but also the potential reader. It is important to write with some awareness of your potential readers so that you can foresee what they will need to know to understand your ideas. Imagining the needs and interpretive skills of your reader is a way to provide yourself with critical feedback necessary to make sure that your writing communicates what you want to say in the clearest possible fashion. Writing with this kind of awareness of your potential readers is also a good way to retain the kind of liveliness and energy that often characterizes conversation.

There is, however, another kind of awareness of your potential readers that can be a serious obstacle in writing. When you allow yourself to become preoccupied with how the readers of your work will evaluate what you have written, you are likely to stifle the flow of your writing, sometimes to the point of suffocation. If you try to guess what your reader expects or wants you to say, it will be difficult to feel free enough to say what you *want* to say in a way that honestly reflects your own thinking and ideas. If you focus on trying to impress your readers with how much you know or how elegantly you can write about what you know, you will have lost sight of the real purpose of your writing, which presumably had something to do with ideas you wanted to express. A preoccupying focus on how your writing will be evaluated by its readers may be one cause of writer's block because it encourages you to strive for a "perfect" piece of writing. Because it is impossible to foresee what someone else will see as perfect, you have set yourself an impossible task, and it is not surprising that you cannot go forward. For the extreme perfectionist, no sentence put down on paper is quite good enough, and no choice of words exactly captures the idea the writer has in mind. Whenever you find yourself stuck on the first paragraph of a writing project, writing and rewriting your introduction, it may be helpful to ask yourself whose expectations you are trying to meet. Turning off the "editor in your head" may provide you with enough freedom to begin and even to complete a first draft which will be a more useful basis for corrections and revisions than a page full of false starts.

I can personally attest to the writing problems caused by over-concern with an evaluative audience. In the process of writing this chapter I have struggled at length and to no particular advantage with both the things I have written and the way I have written them because I imagined it would be highly presumptuous to write about writing if I could not demonstrate that I am a really good writer, qualified to advise other people about their writing. I know that all that I can do is to write what I believe to be true about the challenge of writing, the obstacles that may emerge, and the strategies I have found useful to deal with these; however, my acute awareness that I have exposed myself to public evaluation of my ideas, my writing style, and my logic has continuously impeded my progress and interrupted the flow of my thinking and my writing. It is both consoling and sobering to realize that some members of my audience may actually be relieved to see that a person writing about writing sometimes fails to write clearly or gracefully, but this does not entirely relieve the inhibition caused by overconcern with my audience.

My experience suggests that it is sometimes very difficult to turn off "the editor in your head." The need to do so is signaled when you find yourself struggling for a long time to think of the best way to express an idea or when you realize that you have been working and reworking a passage endlessly without achieving any sense of progress. At such times, it may help to resort temporarily to one or another of the "getting started" strategies I described earlier. Sketching in a passage by listing key ideas that you will return to on another day may allow you to move on. Shifting the focus of your attention from an evaluative audience by pretending you are writing to a friend or are writing a story may reduce your anxiety sufficiently to quiet your concern about all the potential editors out there. Another useful strategy is to conjure up an alternative audience who may benefit in some way if only they have a chance to learn what you know and think about your topic. These tricks will probably afford only partial relief for a severe case of "editor anxiety" but may get you through the worst stage of total paralysis.

Goldberg (1991), in her engaging book about writing, *Writing Down the Bones*, suggests still another strategy. When "the editor is absolutely annoying," she suggests that you write out your most damning version of what the editor will say about your work in full and gory detail. She observes that "the more clearly you know the editor, the better you can ignore it" (p. 26).

REVISION

Despite all of my cautions about not striving for perfection in your writing, I do want to stress the importance of rereading and revising what you have written. It is unlikely that any one of us can execute a first draft of a writing project that

- ➤ Says exactly what we want to say

- ➤ Provides all the information our readers need to understand what we have written

- ➤ Does not contain awkward sentences or grammatical constructions

- ➤ Cannot be significantly improved upon reconsideration

Reading aloud what you have written is an excellent way to *hear* the awkward phrases and grammatical errors that inevitably creep into any piece of writing. Because once you have committed your ideas to paper they are apt to seem complete and logical, asking someone else to read what you have written may be a way to get help in identifying places where your development of ideas is confusing or insufficiently supported by evidence even though it seems to make sense to you. It is easy to leave out crucial steps in an argument; we count on readers to follow our thought processes even when these have not been fully stated, and sometimes we expect them to be able to read our minds. A friendly reader can help us see when we have expected our audience to know more than they do and to fill in gaps in our writing that they cannot possibly manage to do. At the other extreme, problems arise from beating an argument to death by repeating essentially the same point over and over in slightly different form. Someone coming fresh to the writing piece is almost always more sensitive than the author himself to problems of either omission or redundancy.

Douglas Flemons (1998) provides a gold mine of examples of how to improve sentences and paragraphs by thoughtful editing and revision in his chapter "Social Science Papers" (pp. 30-77). This chapter is also extremely valuable because of its clarity in defining the essential parts of a social science paper and at the same time stressing that writers should adapt standard procedures to fit with their own intentions. This is a liberating message and should be encouraging to students who find themselves trying to adapt their own ideas, methodologies, and interpretations to a mold that doesn't quite fit.

In the days before word processing, writing successive drafts of a paper was a time-consuming and laborious task. Writers' wastebaskets overflowed with crumpled sheets of paper containing false starts and discarded passages. Each draft usually involved extensive retyping of the previous draft, and only the most persistent and committed writers could discipline themselves to undertake the multiple drafts that might lead to a final version they found fully acceptable. Composing papers from the start on the computer allows for continuous revision and for free writing of sections that may ultimately fit best many pages later (or that may be deleted with the stroke of a key). This is an extraordinary boon to many writers, although I still occasionally hear of writers who use their computers only for typing their final drafts. If you prefer to revise a completed draft rather than changing things as you go, you may still want to experiment with the freedom afforded by computers to write anything that comes into your mind and consign it to oblivion in the next second or to save ideas that are not yet fully developed but that may become important as your writing project develops.

My use of my computer has made me much more sensitive to my writing problems and much more willing to work to correct these; I hope and believe that it has resulted in considerable gains in my writing fluency. Although everyone may not find this tool as indispensable as I have, I do recommend at least experimenting with it. The freedom first to detach from overconcern about what you are writing or how you write, and afterward to reconstruct and revise what you have written so readily, is likely to make first drafts easier to write and at the same time to increase your willingness to subject your work to the kind of revision that is almost always necessary.

CONCLUSION

There are many steps between the beginning stages of getting started, choosing a topic, and developing passion and voice and the final stages of revision and completion of the writing project. These will be shaped by your writing purpose, your topic, and your audience and cannot easily be addressed in a single chapter about writing. At the end of this chapter, I have included a number of references that discuss "how to write" from different perspectives and for different purposes. The following list of "tricks" that summarize what has gone before may also help you keep your momentum from the beginning of your efforts to their successful completion.

TWELVE TRICKS TO KEEP YOU GOING WHEN YOU WRITE

1. At least in your first draft, use the first person singular to keep you in touch with *your* ideas, *your* reactions, *your* beliefs, and *your* understandings of what other people have written. Enjoy your voice as AUTHOR. Speak as straightforwardly as you can. Avoid the passive

voice whenever possible. If the requirements for publication or whatever dictate some other form, you can always revise later on.

2. Write as flamboyantly as you like in your first draft to give voice to
   your passion. If you like adverbs and adjectives, use them
   generously.

3. If it makes you nervous to assert your own position, qualify it as often
   as possible in your first draft. Brave statements seem less dangerous
   with lots of phrases like "in my opinion," "I think," and "it seems to
   me," as well as "probably," "not infrequently," "perhaps," and "in
   some instances." It is better to get your words on paper than to get
   hung up by anxiety about whether you have the right or sufficient
   knowledge or adequate proof to make strong statements.

4. In the beginning, try to forget how your audience might evaluate
   what you write or how you write it. There will be plenty of time later
   on to worry about the feedback that editors, publishers, or faculty
   advisers inevitably will give you. In the beginning, worrying about
   pleasing evaluating audiences is likely to lead to obsessing about
   each word you write, and you will often end up trying to impress
   your evaluators with your erudition, intellect, or elegance of phrase.
   This wastes a lot of time and energy.

5. Try to write in short sentences, especially in your first draft, so that
   you don't get tangled up in long, convoluted sentences that can
   obscure your meaning. Much writing time is wasted trying to
   straighten out grammatical absurdities that will never exist in the first
   place if you try to put just one idea in one sentence.

6. Try to find your own comfortable writing style and way of developing ideas. Be respectful of your style. If it is easy and useful for you to
   outline your ideas and then develop the outline into an essay, do
   that. If you spend more time making an outline than it would take to
   write the whole piece, don't let anyone convince you that you should
   make an outline. If you like to write in the middle of the night, do it. If
   you need to write around and around your topic until you finally get
   to the center of it, do it.

7. Do not be afraid to use the writing of others as a model. This is not a
   fraudulent act, but rather one that acknowledges how much we can

learn from master craftspeople. When you come across a piece of writing that seems especially clear, forceful, and enjoyable to read, pay attention to how that writer organizes and communicates ideas.

8. Introduce discipline into your writing task by committing yourself to spend a given number of hours (or minutes) writing or to produce a given amount of written text every day. If it is hard to do this, set your goals low and don't allow yourself to exceed them in the beginning. Set an alarm clock, if necessary, and even if you are in the midst of an interesting idea, stop when the alarm goes off. You will soon find yourself more and more frustrated by having to interrupt your work and more and more eager to extend your writing time just a few more minutes. It is safe to do this, but feel free to go back to your time limits if you find yourself staring at your paper or out the window very long. If you write only a few paragraphs a day, you will proba-bly have six or seven pages to show for your effort at the end of a week. This is much more encouraging to most of us than spending 4 or 5 hours a day with nothing but aimless jottings or a wastebasket full of crumpled paper at the end of each work session.

LATER ON, WHEN YOUR FIRST DRAFT IS FINISHED AND YOU ARE READY TO REVISE YOUR WORK

9. Remove all the adverbs and adjectives you so joyously put in your first draft and restore only those that are absolutely necessary to your meaning. If you have been outrageously emotional or have put your-self far out on a limb with your assertions, weed out some of the color and make sure you can defend with evidence what you have said.

10. Eliminate all your qualifying statements and restore only those that are necessary to be honest and to retain your meaning. Now that you are at the end of your project, you will feel braver about what you have written and will not need so much to hide behind disclaimers.

11. If all your short sentences sound choppy and telegraphic, combine some of your sentences to make a better flow. Be careful when you do this. If you can't combine two sentences without making a ponderous

and incomprehensible whole, leave your short sentences alone. It is preferable to suffer a little choppiness than to leave your reader perplexed about what you mean to say. The rhythm that results from varying the length of your sentences can contribute variety and momentum to your writing that will make it more exciting to read.

12. Don't accept any of the foregoing rules or any other rule of writing that can't be broken or doesn't work for you. To paraphrase Julia Child's immortal words about making bread, remember that you are the boss of your writing.

REFERENCES

Belenky, M., Clinchy, B., Goldberger, N., & Tarule, J. (1986) *Women's ways of knowing: The development of self, voice and mind.* New York: Basic Books.

Elbow, P. (1998). *Writing with power: Techniques for mastering the writing process* (2nd ed.). New York: Oxford University Press.

Flemons, D. (1998). *Writing between the lines: Composition in the social sciences.* New York: Norton.

Goldberg, N. (1991). *Writing down the bones/Wild mind.* New York: Quality Paperback Book Club.

Rico, G. L. (1983). *Writing the natural way.* Los Angeles: J. P. Tarcher.

SUGGESTED READINGS

American Psychological Association. (1994). *Publication manual of the American Psychological Association* (4th ed.). Washington, DC: Author.

Ballou, S. V. (1970). *A model for theses and research papers.* Boston: Houghton Mifflin.

Beale, W. H. (1982). *Real writing.* Glenview, IL: Scott, Foresman.

Becker, H. (1986). *Writing for social scientists.* Chicago: University of Chicago Press.

Campbell, W. G., & Ballou, S. V. (1977). *Form and style: Theses, reports, term papers* (5th ed.). Boston: Houghton Mifflin.

Cox, S. (1981). *Indirections for those who want to write.* Boston: David Godine.

Davis, G. B., & Parker, C. (1979). *Writing the doctoral dissertation.* Woodbury, NY: Barron's.

Graves, R., & Hodge, A. (1966). *The reader over your shoulder.* New York: Collier Books.

Hall, D. (1973). *Writing well.* Boston: Little, Brown.

Hilbish, F. M. (1952). *The research paper.* New York: Bookman Associates.

Howard, V. A. (1986). *Thinking on paper.* New York: William Morrow.

Jacobi, E. (1976). *Writing at work: Do's, don'ts, and how-to's.* Rochelle Park, NJ: Hayden.

Madsen, D. (1983). *Successful dissertations and theses.* San Francisco: Jossey-Bass.

Modern Language Association. (1977). *MLA handbook for writers of research papers, theses and dissertations.* New York: Author.

Mullin, C. J. (1977). *A guide to writing and publishing in the social and behavioral sciences.* New York: John Wiley.

Pugh, G. T. (1963). *Guide to research writing.* Boston: Houghton Mifflin.

Zinsser, W. (1988). *Writing to learn.* New York: Harper & Row.

Zinsser, W. (1990). *On writing well* (4th ed.). New York: HarperCollins.

CHAPTER 10

Computing:

Using a Personal Computer Effectively

In the first edition of this book, we extolled the virtues of personal computer use as a time-saving tool for data analysis, writing, literature searching, and organization, but we suggested that it might be possible for someone to complete a dissertation without actually using a personal computer. Given the tremendous advances in computerized literature searching, quantitative and qualitative data analysis software, word-processing and bibliographic management software, and, of course, the Internet, it is now Victorian to suggest that anyone attempt to complete a dissertation without a personal computer, a host of software, and Internet access.

This chapter is designed to provide you with information about the available software that performs numerous tasks that make the dissertation process more efficient. We describe what the software does and how it may help you. We organize the chapter in a manner reflecting the steps in a typical dissertation journey, represented by the saga of Jon and Ron, described below. We begin with suggestions on how to use the computer to assist with formulating an idea and reviewing the literature. Second, we review software for controlling your bibliography. Next we consider questions of data analysis. We summarize programs that perform both qualitative and quantitative analysis. Finally, we consider other options for data collection using a computer. If the possibility of completing a high-quality dissertation without ever leaving your computer seems farfetched or unrealistic, please read on: Our students have completed dissertations in just that manner, and more are doing so all the time.

IN FAIRNESS TO SOFTWARE MANUFACTURERS

In the following pages, we mention a large number of software programs and reference dozens of Web sites. We do not claim to know which programs are "best" or to provide a comprehensive review of the pros and cons of these programs. Which is "best" is more often a function of the fit between project goals and user skill than it is universal agreement that one program is better than another. What is wonderful for one user may be totally unworkable for another. We make no claims to have reviewed all the software available, and we apologize to those software developers whose programs may have been excluded. We considered publishing the costs of various software, but our own experience is that the ready availability of student or educational discounts is not evident from the material available on Web sites, and prices change almost monthly. Like shopping for a car, you can shop for software. What we offer is a strategy for utilizing your computer to facilitate a successful dissertation; you, the reader, can and should obtain more information, particularly by downloading and "test-driving" those programs you are considering.

TWO SCENARIOS

Both Jon and Ron began the dissertation process at about the same time. Neither was totally clear about the exact project focus, so both went to the library to examine the literature in their general area of interest, and both found themselves in the reference section. Jon, however, went to the virtual library by logging onto his campus computer system from home. From there he was able to examine his university library's on-line databases and access the holdings of libraries throughout the world. Ron, on the other hand, physically went to the library to access this information. Each, after exploring a number of different databases, discovered 234 articles, books, and dissertations published in his general area of interest, and each narrowed the search by selecting only those materials dealing with the one topic area that particularly interested him. Each discovered that there were 36 articles, books, and dissertations that focused on his specific topic. This seemed a reasonable place to start, so Jon simply downloaded the abstracts, with references, into his computer. Ron placed his disk in the library's computer and copied the abstracts and references of the 36 documents onto this disk. He then went home to examine these on his personal computer. The total time involved for Jon was less than 30 minutes. Ron, on the other hand, had to first determine the library's hours and then make the trip from home to the library and back. While at the library, he was required to wait for his "turn" to use the library's CD-ROM database holdings and had to honor a half-hour "time limit" at the library's overcrowded workstation.

Later, both Jon and Ron carefully examined the content of each abstract on their personal computers. Both determined that there were six journal articles, two dissertations, and two books that were worthy of a complete reading. Ron was able to download the full text of four articles and used a document delivery service to obtain the last two. He decided to purchase two recent dissertations for delivery to his home, and he used the library's electronic hold request to have the books placed on reserve for later pickup, after electronic notification that the items had arrived. Ron returned to the library to make copies of all six articles; however, one journal was missing and another was not part of the library's holdings. Because he was not aware that he could reserve books or make interlibrary loan requests on-line, he had to place his request in person and wait 2 weeks for the items to arrive.

Both Jon and Ron were required to create a short preliminary literature review for the chair of their committee. Both authored their review using the same word processing software; however, Jon was able to interface his word processing software with citation management software, and did not have to type references, which were correctly formatted directly from the references downloaded earlier and automatically checked against the citations within the text. Ron had to retype each reference and visually ensure that the format was correct and that each reference listed in the text also existed in the references.

Eventually both Jon and Ron were given approval to collect their data by their dissertation committee. Jon designed an Internet survey, which he sent via electronic mail to 300 persons, with reminder letters automatically e-mailed at 2-week intervals. Ron used a mail survey to send his survey to the same sample. Because Jon's response rate was higher and his data arrived in electronic form, he was able to begin data analysis almost immediately after ending data collection, 4 months sooner than Ron. Ron had to enter each response by hand into a data-base and had to send two reminder letters to each respondent, a process that required considerable additional time and cost.

After collecting data, both decided to use the services of a statistical consultant to help with the computerized analysis of the data. Because Jon had purchased a copy of the statistical software, he was able to work directly at his desk with the consultant, trying different analysis options and discussing the results. Ron received all of his output in hard copy format (i.e., on paper), and each minor modification required another meeting with the consultant. After deciding which output would serve as the basis for the tabular presentation, Jon was able to access this information with his word processor and add the necessary titles and labels. Ron, working from the hard copy, typed all the information onto separate pages. Once again, Ron spent many more hours than Jon completing this stage of the process.

Both Jon and Ron reached the final draft stage. Jon used his bibliographic reference management software to guarantee that every article cited in the dissertation was contained in the reference list and vice versa. As this list had grown to more than 200 citations, the task of cross-checking references and formatting them correctly had grown tremendously. He then had the list printed in the correct format. Ron, however, had to examine each reference on every page to make sure that the reference was included in the bibliography. Then he had to retype the bibliography in the correct format, using his computer.

Both Jon and Ron finished their dissertations, and both produced high-quality work. Jon finished 8 months earlier than Ron. Despite spending considerable money and time learning how to use a number of different software programs, Jon saved 8 months of tuition, which more than made up for the time and expense required to purchase and master software. Jon was able to give more time to the intellectual and creative aspects of his dissertation because the clerical and repetitive tasks were made easier. His dissertation reflects the fact that he was able to spend more time thinking about the content issues and less about format issues.

Finally, Jon brings to the labor market a number of highly generalizable computer skills that can be used to publish his dissertation in the form of a book or articles, to conduct new research and to keep records, to write letters and memos, to keep track of clients, and to organize his complex life. Ron, on the other hand, remains frozen in the world of those who know only how to do word processing, a virtual computer illiterate in the world of the 21st century.

The point of the above two scenarios is that the entire process of completing a dissertation, from the initial formulation of an idea, through data collection, to the preparation of the final draft, complete with references in the correct format and margins to satisfy the university librarian, can be streamlined with the aid of your personal computer. Data can be collected and analyzed, literature can be searched and articles downloaded, reference lists and citations can be automatically formatted to any style desired, and your computer will check to make sure that every citation in your dissertation has a corresponding reference in your bibliography. High-quality, user-friendly quantitative and qualitative data analysis programs abound. As one of our students states,

> I found that the electronic tools that I used kept me organized and motivated throughout the entire process over 2 years. The [Macintosh computer] that I used was fun to use and intrinsically motivating as a thinking tool. Appropriate computer technology reduces the "unauthentic labor" associated with the entire process: that unnecessary effort that gets in the way of conceptualizing, organizing, and presenting information. (Helen Barrett, personal communication)

WHAT KIND OF COMPUTER USER ARE YOU?

In their software sourcebook for qualitative data analysis, Weitzman and Miles (1995) ask their readers to consider the following four key questions when contemplating the selection of a software program:

1. What kind of computer user am I?

2. Am I choosing software for one project or the next few years?

3. What kind of project(s) or database(s) will I be working on?

4. What kind of analyses am I planning to do?

Although the above key questions refer to selecting software for qualitative data analysis, they are relevant for any software purchase. We would include one additional question: "What kind of computer user do I want to become?" Are you a beginner who wants to learn more? Are you at ease with the prospect of exploring new software? Do you consider yourself a sophisticated user and relish the prospect of becoming acquainted with as much software as possible? Do you spend more time with your computer than your friends?

As a starting point, we recommend that you consider two critical issues. First, what software is "standard" for your academic department? You may be a comfortable user of SPSS (Statistical Package for the Social Sciences), but if your department, particularly your dissertation chair, is a dedicated SAS (Statistical Analysis System) devotee, you should plan on learning SAS. Second, can you get help? By "help" we mean hands-on assistance from experienced users, not technical help from the software vendor's help lines. The availability of on-line technical assistance is important, but such help is designed to cope with difficulties of installation, "bugs," "patches," and technical problems, not hands-on training. If you consider yourself a beginner, we recommend "computer friendliness" as a primary consideration. Many programs may "wow" you with their capabilities, but you may use only 20% of those capabilities. If a program is difficult to use and includes obtuse manuals, no matter how powerful, it may not be a good choice. It is also important to consider where you hope to end up after completing your dissertation. If you plan on working in a highly computer-oriented environment, conducting research and teaching others, sophistication with a wide variety of software is essential. If you plan on entering a work environment not heavily involved in research, such as that of a nonresearcher clinical psychologist, and you find learning software generally difficult and uninteresting, you may want to minimize your software purchases and investment of time in learning. Whatever your situation, we recommend picking a program to suit your needs and sticking with it. That means your choice should consider your future needs, the ability of the software you choose to meet those needs, and the likelihood that the software and the company that supports it will still exist in 5 years. For example, much of the software reviewed in the Weitzman and Miles (1995) book, mentioned above, is no longer available or being supported by a vendor. It is sometimes more difficult to switch programs than to learn a new program that accomplishes similar functions. (Think of learning to touch-type using a new keyboard with letters in different places.) Your first choice should be a good one.

Weitzman and Miles's third and fourth questions above can be considered as one. Try to make the software fit the project rather than force a project to fit software for which it was not designed. Word-processing software will "search," but it was not designed for qualitative data analysis. Spreadsheet programs will compute statistics, but they were not designed with anywhere near the statistical analysis capabilities of most statistical software. It is not uncommon for software vendors to "add in" routines to support the claim that their programs can accomplish the same task that their competitor can accomplish with ease; however, actually getting the software to do so is often cumbersome. This is true for both qualitative and quantitative data analysis programs, which may claim to accomplish everything but clearly do some things better than others. The task of weighing the overall capabilities of a program against its ability to accomplish a specific task is difficult. If you choose too narrowly, you may need to buy more software to accomplish other tasks. If you choose too broadly, you may find diminished ability to easily accomplish a critical function.

USING YOUR COMPUTER AS A LITERATURE SEARCHING AND BIBLIOGRAPHIC MANAGEMENT TOOL

The standard reply of a dissertation adviser when faced with a student's vague notions regarding a research topic is "Go to the library and find out what information exists on this subject." A thorough literature review is an absolute requirement for a dissertation and can be the most time-consuming of all dissertation challenges.

The task before you can be broken down into a series of distinct but overlapping steps:

1. First, you must obtain a comprehensive collection of the literature relevant to your dissertation topic.

2. Second, you must obtain copies of the articles you find most relevant to your topic.

3. Third, you must read these articles and take notes on the material for later incorporation into your dissertation literature review.

4. Finally, you must produce a bibliography or reference list that is formatted correctly and in perfect synchronization with those materials as referenced in your dissertation.

Fortunately, at least three major software packages allow you to do these tasks easily and efficiently: Citation, EndNote, and Procite. Table 10.1 provides basic information and Web site locations for these programs. We strongly recommend that you familiarize yourself with one of these programs. From the locations in Table 10.1 you can obtain extensive information about the programs and their capabilities, download trial versions, or purchase and download the complete programs.

In short, you can accomplish the following tasks with any of these programs:

➤ Search on-line databases by opening connection files that permit access to hundreds of remote bibliographic databases, university card catalogs, and the Library of Congress. From these locations you can drag and drop references directly into your bibliographic database in one step.

➤ Create a large number of databases with thousands of references per database with hundreds of bibliographic styles. (That should do it!)

➤ Create one-step bibliographies in MS Word, WordPerfect, and a number of other word processors, including RTF and HTML formats.

➤ Search your own database of references, keywords, and notes.

In the following material we describe these steps in the process and refer you to these programs.

Table 10.1

Software for the Management of Bibliographic Information

Program	Developer	Web Site	Comments
Citation	Oberon Development Ltd.	www.oberon-res.com	Nice Web site. Check out teaching notes and library links.
EndNote	Institute for Scientific Information	http://www.endnote.com	
Procite	ISI Research Software	http://www.procite.com/pchome.html	

In the preliminary stages, the most you probably want are references and abstracts; only after much culling of information will you want complete articles. Bibliographic databases, either Internet or CD-ROM–based, are ideal for this purpose. The key to being successful with this process is twofold. First, you need a "portal" or "gateway" from within which to access these databases; second, you need to develop "search skills." This means that you understand how to use the software effectively and that you have a good understanding of the appropriate search terms to use with your topic. Dissertation students often miss critical articles because they do not understand how to search, not because the articles are not contained within the databases they search. Below we suggest some strategies for making use of your library and referencing some of the most popular databases available via on-line and CD-ROM.

DATABASES: USING YOUR LIBRARY'S COMPUTERIZED SEARCH CAPABILITY

The above information about bibliographic search and management software discusses savings in time, but it does not cover the monetary costs associated with searching some databases. Some are free, but it is expensive to maintain up-to-date lists of anything, and most require a paid subscription to defray those costs. This is where your university library becomes important. Information vendors sell information to information providers such as Silver Platter, Online Computer Library Center (OCLC), and Ovid. Most university libraries then contract with these providers to allow library users, free of charge, to access reference materials from compact disks (CD-ROMs) or the Internet, frequently from home rather than the library workstations. In other words, your library pays the fee. Students and faculty are then permitted to search topic areas and obtain lists (either hard copy, on disk, or sent directly to the user's e-mail address) of references and abstracts related to their topic of interest. These lists can be accessed, edited, and organized by the software referenced in Table 10.1.

One of the most effective on-line reference services to which many libraries subscribe is Online Computer Library Center (OCLC) FirstSearch. FirstSearch calls itself a "Web-based online reference service." It provides access to more than 85 databases, more than 3.3 million full-text articles, and 2,100 electronic journal titles. You may check out the OCLC home page at www.oclc.org/oclc/menu/home1.htm. From there you will be able to access FirstSearch or NewFirstSearch, or take the guided tour, which we highly recommend.

A few of the hundreds of available databases are described below.

ERIC (Educational Resources Information Clearinghouse): ERIC is a database of education-related materials collected by the Educational Resources Information Center of the U.S. Department of Education. ERIC covers books, reports, unpublished documents, and approximately 750 journals in education.

ABI INFORM: ABI INFORM is a database of business information consisting of bibliographic entries and abstracts to more than 800 different journals. The database includes the most recent 5 years and is an excellent source of information on companies, products, business conditions, management techniques, and so on.

PsycINFO : The American Psychological Association's PsycINFO® database, with more than 1.5 million records, is the comprehensive international database of psychology. It covers the academic, research, and practice literature in psychology from more than 45 countries in more than 30 languages. PsycINFO® includes relevant materials from related disciplines such as medicine, psychiatry, education, social work, law, criminology, social science, and organizational behavior. It is an essential tool for researchers, practitioners, and students in psychology and its numerous related disciplines. PsycINFO® provides indices to journals, dissertations, book chapters, books, technical reports, and other documents from 1887 to the present, including the optional Historic PsycINFO® and archive file database. PsycINFO® includes Hot Links between book and chapter citations, as well as field-specific author and journal title indices.

Sociological Abstracts: Sociological Abstracts provides access to the latest worldwide findings in theoretical and applied sociology, social science, and policy science. Produced by Cambridge Scientific Abstracts, Sociological Abstracts features journal citations and abstracts; book, chapter, and association paper abstracts; and book, film, and software review citations. The database also contains major and minor descriptors. Entries cover sociological aspects of 29 broad topics, including anthropology, business, collective behavior, community development, disaster studies, education, environmental studies, gender studies, gerontology, law and penology, marriage and family studies, medicine and health, racial interactions, social psychology, social work, sociological theory, stratification, substance abuse, urban studies, and violence. Sociological Abstracts is fundamental for interdisciplinary research on social science issues and for practitioners seeking the sociological perspective on various disciplines.

Political Science Abstracts: Political Science Abstracts, produced by IFI CLAIMS® Services, has been an important source for political science articles published since 1976. The database contains abstracts of materials from professional journals, major news magazines, and books devoted to North American and international politics and political analysis. Topics include political institutions, processes, and behavior; international law and politics; public policy; public administration; political theory; and political economics. The database is a valuable resource for students, policy makers, and decision shapers charting political issues, processes, and public policy worldwide.

PAIS International: PAIS International, from Public Affairs Information Service, is an important index to political, economic, and social issues in current debate. The database covers the public and social policy literature of business, economics, finance, law, international relations, public administration, government, political science, and other social sciences—with emphasis on issues that are or might become the subjects of legislation. Dating from 1972 to the present, PAIS International contains abstracts of journal articles, books, statistical yearbooks, directories, conference proceedings, research reports, and government documents from all over the world. The materials indexed are published in 60 countries in six languages—English, German, French, Spanish, Italian, and Portuguese. All subject headings and abstracts are written in English. PAIS International aids public policy researchers in academic, government, corporate, and community settings.

EMBASE: Geriatrics & Gerontology: A subset of EMBASE, EMBASE: Geriatrics and Gerontology includes abstracts and citations relating directly to geriatrics and gerontology. Citations are selected from top geriatrics and gerontology journals, including 3,600 biomedical journals published in 110 countries. This database covers clinical aspects of aging and experimental work on the aging process, as well as the diagnosis, medical and surgical treatment, rehabilitation, hospitalization, and welfare of the aged. Additional topics covered include mental and emotional problems of the aged and social and organizational aspects of care of the aged. Also included are abstracts from other clinical and basic disciplines which have relevance to geriatrics and gerontology.

Social Work Abstracts Plus: Social Work Abstracts Plus, from the National Association of Social Workers, provides two separate databases on one disc: Social Work Abstracts and The Register of Clinical Social Workers. Social Work Abstracts contains information on the fields of social work and human services from 1977 to the present. The database provides exceptional coverage of more than 450 journals in all areas of the profession, including theory and practice, areas of service, social issues, and social problems. The Register of Clinical Social Workers is a directory of clinical social workers in the United States. It contains information such as name, address, telephone number, employer, education, and employment history, as well as type of practice and licensing information. Practitioners and researchers in areas such as social sciences, gerontology, welfare, public health, criminology, and education will benefit from this database.

Mental Measurements Yearbook: Mental Measurements Yearbook, from the Buros Institute, contains descriptive information and critical reviews of more than 2,000 commercially available standardized English-language educational, personality, aptitude, neuropsychological, achievement, and intelligence tests. Each entry includes test name and classification, author(s), publisher, publication date, price, time requirements, existence of validity and reliability data, score descriptions, levels, and intended populations. Mental Measurements Yearbook contains the text of the Buros Institute's Ninth, Tenth, Eleventh, Twelfth, and Thirteenth Yearbooks and is updated every 6 months to ensure timely access to current information. A valuable resource for academic and professional libraries, the Yearbook provides a convenient tool for educators, counselors, psychologists, personnel directors, lawyers, and medical professionals to locate and evaluate testing instruments.

Current Contents Search®: Current Contents Search® is the electronic version of Current Contents, the highly regarded current awareness tool from ISI. Providing unlimited access to tables of contents and bibliographic data from more than 7,000 of the world's leading scientific and scholarly journals and 2,000 books, Current Contents Search® provides users with up-to-date research information. Each journal meets stringent qualitative and quantitative standards, such as impact factor, timeliness, depth and breadth of coverage, and editorial integrity. Complete bibliographic information is provided, including English-language author abstracts (for approximately 85% of the articles and reviews in the science editions), author keywords, KeyWords Plus®, reprint and research addresses, and full journal information.

Social Sciences Index: The SSI provides subject access to 300 major English-language periodicals published in the United States and abroad, in these and related areas of the social sciences: anthropology, black studies, economics, environmental sciences, geography, international relations, law and criminology, planning and public administration, political science, psychology, public health, sociology, urban studies, and women's studies.

The library card catalog is also becoming a thing of the past. Card catalogs are now maintained as computer databases or Online Public

Access Catalogs. These provide complete bibliographic information (e.g., author, title, publisher, date, etc.), location, call number, and circulation status of every item in the library. Even if you know only the approximate title or part of the author's name, the on-line catalog will search for close approximations and return all references that come close. Most on-line catalogs can be searched from your personal computer via a modem and telecommunications software.

DATABASES CONTAINING COMPLETE ARTICLES

Wilson Social Sciences Abstracts Full Text: Social Sciences Abstracts Full Text contains abstracting and indexing coverage for all 513 periodicals included in Social Sciences Index as well as the full text of more than 150 periodicals, offering instant access to information from publications such as *Adolescence, Africa Today, Alcohol Health and Research World, American Demographics, American Journal of Economics and Sociology, American Journal of Psychotherapy, Annual Review of Anthropology, Annual Review of Psychology, Annual Review of Sociology, Anthropological Quarterly, Asian Affairs, Behavioral Science, British Journal of Psychology, Canadian Review of Sociology and Anthropology, Contemporary Economic Policy, East European Quarterly, Futurist, Health Care Financing Review, International Journal of Social Psychiatry, International Labor Review, International Social Work, Journal of Aging Studies, Journal of Applied Behavior Analysis, Journal of Comparative Family Studies, Journal of Contemporary Asia, Journal of Economic Issues, Journal of Psychology, Journal of Social History, Public Management, Social Science Journal, Social Theory and Practice, Sociological Quarterly, Women & Environments,* and *World Affairs.* Subjects include anthropology, crime, economics, law, medicine, planning, political science, psychology, public administration, social sciences, and sociology.

Online Periodical Article Delivery: CARL UnCover (http://uncweb.carl. org): CARL UnCover is an on-line periodical article delivery service that indexes nearly 18,000 English-language periodicals in its growing database. There are currently nearly 9 million articles available which have appeared since Fall, 1988 (an additional 5,000 are added daily). You may search this database for free, and articles can be sent to your fax machine within 24 to 48 hours. An article costs $10 plus a copyright royalty fee. For $25 annually you can automatically receive the table of contents of up to 50 journals and the results of predesigned search strategies via e-mail. Visit the home page above for information about the products and services available from CARL and to search its databases.

ADVANTAGES AND DISADVANTAGES
OF COMPUTERIZED LITERATURE SEARCHING

There are both advantages and disadvantages of computerized search strategies as compared to the "old-fashioned" method using printed indexes and abstracts. Clearly, using a computer speeds things up. On-line indices are also likely to be more up to date. Another big advantage is the ability of the computerized search to examine titles and abstracts for keywords. For example, Mann (1987) notes that in the early 1980s *Psychological Abstracts* did not contain the word *burnout* as a heading or cross-reference, but searching for *burnout* as a keyword produced more than 200 items in such varied areas as occupational stress, occupational adjustment, and employee attitudes. Some databases also permit unique search strategies that allow access to review articles, letters to the editor, articles written only in English, and articles written only after (or before) a certain date. Finally, computerized searches permit the crossing of terms. For example, if you are interested in suicide among adolescent males, a computerized search may permit the crossing of suicide with adolescent, with male (or gender).

Despite the tremendous advantages cited above, there are also some costs and frustrations likely to be encountered with computerized searches. First, on-line searching may not be free, but typically access through your library is free. Second, you may want to search several databases, but each may need to be searched in a different manner, as search processes are not necessarily the same across all databases. Third, books are not as likely to be referenced as journal articles, and the indexing of books may not be as thorough. Fourth, older articles may no longer be referenced on computerized databases. For example, the print version of Psychological Abstracts begins in 1927, whereas the CD-ROM version (PsychLIT) begins only in 1967. Fifth, if you utilize a library search technician you are relinquishing control to another person, who is not as likely to understand your topic or its related terms. The potential to miss references is very real. Finally, searches may uncover articles containing the correct words but in the wrong area. Mann (1987) mentions that a search to locate articles on "Venetian blinds" may also uncover references on "blind Venetians."

In sum, computerized reference location takes the drudgery out of finding what is available on a topic, but it is not a guarantee. A bad search can be conducted with the computer as well as without it. Like all aspects of the dissertation process, literature searching takes care and patience.

READING AND RECORDING: HOW TO TAKE NOTES WITH YOUR COMPUTER

Assume that you have obtained a number of articles that you wish to pursue in greater detail. As you begin reading these articles, you will want to keep a record of the complete bibliographic reference, the major points, the methods of data collection and analysis, and so on. There are four basic methods to accomplish this task: index cards, word-processed notes, bibliographic management software, and database managers. Index cards offer an "old-fashioned" alternative and are easily portable but are difficult to sort and search. Database management programs allow you to retrieve and reorder the information in a variety of ways but may be expensive and have a slow learning curve. Thus, it may not be worth your time to learn a complete database manager if your only goal is to use these skills for note taking. Using your word processing program may mean no learning curve or expense, but it is not designed for sorting and searching. The ideal solution, from our experience, is a database manager designed for use with text-based material that can be used to record notes, to conduct content analyses, and to manage bibliographies. Citation (www.oberon-res.com) fits this solution extremely well. It works with word processing software to let you enter both research notes and bibliographic information on books, articles, and other sources, using notecard-like forms. You are prompted by the program for citation information as well as keywords that can be searched using an extensive array of search strategies.

BIBLIOGRAPHIES: A SPECIAL CASE

Constructing bibliographies used to be a particularly troublesome and time-consuming aspect of any research. It is critical that bibliographies be in the correct format and contain the correct information, yet one of the most frequent complaints of those who read others' dissertations is that the references are incorrect. Four methods for dealing with bibliographies are currently available. First, some word processing software, such as Note Bene and the APA program, Manuscript Manager, are designed for professional writing and have built-in methods for handling citations and bibliographic references. Second, any database manager has the ability to format bibliographic information, but predefined templates for doing so may not be available. Third, you can simply use your word processor to manage your bibliography. Fourth, the programs referenced in Table 10.1 are designed specifically for professional researchers to aid with the referencing process. These are the programs we recommend as best suited to the process of creating a complete and accurate bibliography.

WRITING, SPELLING, AND GRAMMAR

Faculty members like to talk about the "old days" when we had to continually type and retype each dissertation chapter numerous times to please the whims of every member of a dissertation committee. A high proportion of the total time involved in producing the final product was consumed with these chores. Word processing has changed the process drastically, and for the better. It is not reasonable or sensible to undertake any major writing task, particularly a dissertation, without a word processor. But even in the recent past, word processing programs were often insufficient to handle our needs for spelling and grammar checking or our need for a thesaurus. Every major word processing program today includes these functions and a host of others. Our advice is simple: Pick one and learn to use it effectively. Dissertation committees are well aware that students have powerful spelling and grammar checking programs available at the touch of a key. Work that is riddled with spelling and grammar mistakes makes it all the more obvious that students have not committed themselves to quality work. Though not "polished," even a "rough draft" should be checked for spelling and grammar, as well as carefully proofread.

SOFTWARE FOR QUANTITATIVE AND QUALITATIVE ANALYSIS

SHOULD I CONDUCT MY OWN STATISTICAL ANALYSIS?

The scariest part of the dissertation for many students is statistical analysis. There are many reasons for this. First, statistics is frequently equated with mathematics, and many behavioral scientists feel incompetent with mathematics. Incompetence with math may generalize to similar feelings of helplessness with statistics. Second, statistics is viewed as the purview of a relatively few "high priests" who are the only ones who can understand it. The average person is not *supposed* to understand statistics. Third, statistics courses often reinforce students' beliefs regarding the intractability of statistics. Statistics typically is taught in the abstract. Statistics courses may focus on mathematical proofs, require the memorization of formulas, and rest heavily on probability theory. The truth of the matter is that statistics is merely a tool. Although it is true that statistics must be "calculated," and thus require mathematics, virtually no full-time researchers calculate statistics. Calculation is a job best left to computers. Statistics are meaningful only in the context of social science research when applied to a particular question. It is our experience that when students are fully aware of what that question is, they are able to understand, and discuss, the sorts of answers to that question that statistics provide. Just as one does not need to understand the internal combustion engine to drive a car, or the silicon chip to operate a computer, one does not need a strong mathematical background to use statistics in an efficient and intelligent manner.

Given the above points, how does one learn enough about statistics to use them as a tool in the dissertation process? There are a number of answers to this question, and the correct one often depends on the nature of the institution that a student is attending. Students at large research universities will be required to take a number of statistics and computer courses, will often serve as research assistants on faculty projects, and will be trained in a tradition of research that requires the mastery of quantitative (or qualitative) analysis to achieve success. These students will frequently approach the dissertation with sufficient experience, and enough additional sources of expertise, to analyze and interpret their dissertation data.

But what about everybody else? For these students, a number of potential sources of assistance are available. A patient and understanding faculty member may play the role of "statistical educator." It is a good idea to select a committee that contains at least one person willing to be of assistance with analytical issues. In this context we must recommend our own text, *Your Statistical Consultant: Answers to Your Data Analysis Questions* (Newton & Rudestam, 1999). This text, based on years of questions from our students, was specifically designed to address the "issues" that confront the young statistician, including how to select the appropriate statistical test, how to deal with issues of normality, the meaning of statistical significance, and many others. Second, independent reading of others' work is often of value. Many students "model" their analyses on similar analyses done by others. By reading how one person presents the results of analysis of variance or regression analysis, students learn how to present their own. There are many texts that do a good job of presenting elementary statistics to students, but only a few that present complex multivariate methods in a clear, intuitive manner. One of these is Sam Kash Kachigan's *Statistical Analysis: An Interdisciplinary Introduction to Univariate and Multivariate Methods* (1986).

SHOULD I BUY MY OWN STATISTICS PROGRAM?

There are numerous software programs for quantitative analysis. Table 10.2 shows 11 of the major players and their home page addresses. We recommend against purchasing a small, less sophisticated package available for the personal computer. Often these are so

Table 10.2

Quantitative Data Analysis: A Sampling of Programs

Name	Developer	Web Site	Download Demo?	Comments
Statistical Package for the Social Sciences (SPSS)	SPSS Inc.	www.spss.com	No	Grad pack inexpensive and contains full program. Many stat texts and users' guides from other publishers. Most widely used in the world.
Statistical Analysis System	SAS Institute	www.sas.com	Yes	Not recommended unless departmental standard. Obtuse manuals (but see StatView below). Large company with many software titles.
MicroCase	MicroCase Inc.	www.microcase.com	Yes	Very user friendly; student version free with text.
GB Stat	Dynamic Microsystems	www.scolari.com www.gbstat.com	Yes	Distributed by Scolari, the software division of Sage Publications.
Stata	Stata Corporation	www.stata.com	Yes	Great user support. Known for exploratory data analysis (EDA) capabilities.
Systat	SPSS Inc.	www.spss.com/software/science/systat	Yes	Known for graphics capabilities; owned by SPSS Inc. Expensive.

MiniTab	MiniTab Inc.	www.minitab.com	Yes	Large and long-standing company. Many stat texts and users' guides from other publishers. Widely used in business.
Statgraphics	Statgraphics Inc.	www.statgraphics.com	No	As name implies, very graphics intensive.
Number Cruncher Statistical System (NCSS)	NCSS Statistical Software	www.ncss.com	Yes	Also produces PASS, a $250.00 power analysis and sample size program.
Software and Alternative Media (SAMtitle)	Lawrence Erlbaum, Inc.	www.erlbaum.com	NA	Explore this site for a host of software for all sorts of analysis.
StatView	SAS Institute	www.statview.com	Yes	Published by SAS Institute. Originally a Macintosh-based program, now fits all platforms.

limited as to make very simple changes very time-consuming, if not impossible. The problem with inexpensive programs is that they reach their limitations very quickly, and you can probably purchase an extremely powerful program for about the same price. You should think ahead about flexibility, which is very difficult to do if you are not experienced. It is a mistake to spend a lot of time learning a program that has little flexibility. The large statistical packages, such as SPSS, permit extraordinary flexibility in terms of what can be accomplished with your data. They have the ability to handle thousands of cases and hundreds of variables. Although these programs were quite expensive, intense competition has brought the price down considerably (especially for students), and sometimes these programs, when purchased through a university bookstore, are cheaper than less well-known programs purchased on-line. For example, the "graduate pack" of SPSS, a fully functioning CD-ROM–based program, can be purchased (with student identification) at any California State University bookstore for under $200. When purchasing "student versions," be aware that these are often very limited and may be designed only for a "statistics course," not a dissertation analysis. This may mean that only a limited number of cases or variables can be processed, or that some features are missing, such as time series analysis. All of the vendors we mention offer downloadable trial versions and an e-mail address. The larger sites also offer numerous guides and references for using their products. We highly recommend that you make use of these to make an educated decision about what is best for you.

WHAT ABOUT QUALITATIVE DATA ANALYSIS?

The explosion of qualitative dissertations has been accompanied by the development and refinement of a group of excellent programs for qualitative data analysis. Programs for qualitative analysis are generally more expensive than those for quantitative analysis and are more similar in price, but remember to look for student discounts and educational versions. Table 10.3 lists seven possibilities, all distributed by Scolari, the software arm of Sage Publications. The table provides refer-

Table 10.3

Qualitative Data Analysis: A Sampling of Programs

Name	Developer	Web Site	Comments (all from manufacturer's Web sites)
ATLAS.ti	Scientific Software Development	www.scolari.com www.atlasi.de	ATLAS.ti is a powerful software workbench for the qualitative analysis of large bodies of textual, graphical, audio, and video data. It offers a variety of tools for accomplishing the tasks associated with any systematic approach to "soft" data.
Ethnograph	Qualis Research	www.scolari.com www. qualisresearch.com/	The Ethnograph v5.0 for Windows PCs is a versatile computer program designed to make the analysis of data collected during qualitative research easier, more efficient, and more effective. You can import your text-based qualitative data, typed in any word processing software, straight into the program. The Ethnograph helps you search and note segments of interest within your data, mark them with code words, and run analyses that can be retrieved for inclusion in reports or further analysis.
HyperRESEARCH	Research Ware	www.scolari.com www. researchware.com	HyperRESEARCH's ability to work with multiple data types, such as text, graphics, audio, and video sources, provides the flexibility to integrate all of the data necessary to conduct your research. Specifically designed for ease of use, this program has a menu-driven "Point & Click" interface that allows you to focus your time on the project, not on running the program.
Code-A-Text	Dr. Alan Cartwright	www.scolari.com www.codeatext. co.uk	The Code-A-Text Multi Media System is a software package that has been designed to facilitate the analysis of dialogues. It aids the analysis of text, sound, or video, making available a range of quantitative and qualitative methods. The new help system has more than 50 videos illustrating the tutorials.

(Continued)

Table 10.3
Continued

Name	Developer	Web Site	Comments (all from manufacturer's Web sites)
QSR NVivo	Qualitative Solutions & Research	www.scolari.com www.qsr-software.com	With QSR NVivo, qualitative data will no longer be bound by black and white textual boundaries. NVivo is a very richly featured and highly advanced program for handling qualitative data analysis research projects. It combines rich, editable text and multimedia capabilities to help you bring your data alive.
winMAX	Dr. Udo Kuckartz	www.scolari.com www.winmax.de/heade.htm	The winMAX program is a powerful tool for text analysis that can be used for Grounded Theory–oriented "code and retrieve" analysis as well as for more sophisticated text analysis, enabling both qualitative and quantitative procedures to be combined. The program has a simple and easy-to-use interface of four main windows showing the texts already imported, the list of codes, the list of coded segments, and the text itself.
QSR NUD*IST	Qualitative Solutions & Research	www.scolari.com www.qsr-software.com	QSR NUD*IST set out to do exactly what the acronym claimed—to assist researchers handling Nonnumerical Unstructured Data by Indexing, Searching, and Theorizing. QSR NUD*IST 4 is a major upgrade from NUD*IST 3 and includes the separate program QSR Merge.

246

ence to the Scolari site as well as the manufacturer's site. You can easily link between Scolari and the manufacturer from either location; however, the manufacturer's site always contains more information about the program, offering more links, examples, and advice. In addition to obtaining downloadable trial versions, you might learn a lot about how to invest your money by considering the quality of the site itself. For example, compare the site of Qualis Research (www.qualisresearch. com), which produces Ethnograph, with the site of Scientific Software Development (www.atlasti.de), which produces ATLAS.ti. Spending a few hours exploring the sites listed in Table 10.3 not only will give you some ideas about what type of program may work best for you but will also give you an education in qualitative analysis.

OTHER DATA ANALYSIS SOFTWARE

The software listed in Tables 10.2 and 10.3 will certainly get you through most quantitative and qualitative data analysis projects, but these programs do not cover the full range of data analysis needs one might have. For example, none of the programs mentioned in Table 10.2 will perform power analysis or analyze a structural equation model. For these analyses, specialized software is necessary. Power analysis is designed to answer the question, "How many subjects do I need?" A number of programs will accomplish this type of analysis. SPSS, Inc. offers SamplePower (http//www.spss.com/software/ spower/overview.htm), Lawrence Erlbaum offers Power and Precision (http//www.erlbaum.com/html/1167.htm), and NCSS Statistical Software offers PASS 2000 (http//www.ncss.com/pass.html). A thorough search of these Web sites is recommended, and pricing varies widely. For example, PASS 2000 is currently offered for $199.95 and offers an additional student discount; Power and Precision is currently offered for $495 with no discounts. We recommend that you explore the SAS, SPSS, and Erlbaum sites for a thorough education on the wide range of statistical software available.

WHAT ABOUT DATA: CAN I OBTAIN
MY DISSERTATION DATA USING ON-LINE
DATA COLLECTION METHODS?

It is possible, and not unrealistic, to obtain all the information you need
to complete a dissertation directly from the Internet. There are a number of ways to do this, and we will discuss each. First, recall the difference between "primary" and "secondary" data analysis. Primary data
analysis refers to the analysis of data collected by the researcher or by
the researcher's trained observers or interviewers. Secondary analysis
draws on data collected by other researchers, often for other purposes,
or data created by nonresearchers outside the specific context of
research. For example, data from the U.S. Census; data collected by the
Gallup, Roper, or Field polling organizations; data collected by feder-
ally funded research grants; and data from numerous other sources frequently find their way onto the Internet, typically for the explicit purpose of making these data available to researchers.

There are several reasons for making use of secondary data sources,
not the least of which is the fact that the costs of collecting primary data
often are greater than the resources of most graduate students, even
those with substantial funding. Moreover, the quality of secondary
data is frequently higher than that of the data a single graduate student
would be able to collect on his or her own. Below we briefly discuss
strategies for the use of the Internet to acquire both primary and secondary data.

Use of e-mail and/or the Internet as a primary data collection
resource is not unreasonable given some preliminary considerations.
First, are you comfortable enough with your computer skills to work
through the inevitable difficulties that will arise? Second, do you have
an extremely clear idea of the population to be sampled and how you
can reach this sample through your computer? Third, is your dissertation committee accepting and supportive of your proposed data collection strategy? Given positive answers to these questions, you may wish
to consider data collection via the Internet. Two good resource books
are Don Dillman's *Mail and Internet Surveys: The Tailored Design Method*
(1999) and Dale Nesbary's *Survey Research and the World Wide Web*

(1999). Both books offer a wealth of information on good survey design and how to use the Internet to collect survey data. Although neither book can be described as a technical manual on the use of HTML or other software, the final two chapters of Nesbary's book present a step-by-step tutorial on building Web surveys in MS Front Page. You may need to consult an expert to accomplish this, but the costs are typically less than those associated with mail surveys. A less technical method is simply to send the survey via e-mail and ask respondents to put an "X," "check," or written response in the appropriate space and return it to you. Although this is less sophisticated, it may get the job done, given a motivated and cooperative sample. To see examples of both strategies in action and complete an open-ended questionnaire, go to The Question Factory (http://users.erols.com/bainbri/qf.htm). To read an article on quantitative Web-based surveys, go to http://users. erols.com/bainbri/rel.htm. This article is a section of a book chapter titled "Web-Based Research Approaches," written by William Sims Bainbridge (2000).

Conducting secondary analyses of data downloaded from a Web site is becoming commonplace for scientists from all disciplines, not just students engaged in dissertation research. The typical framework for this activity involves first locating the site containing the data you need; second, obtaining the necessary passwords, if any; third, mastering the download format or data extraction system; fourth, downloading the data; and fifth, accessing the downloaded data with your statistical program (the data could also be textual, which would make the process easier). For example, the holdings of the U.S. Census can be found at http://www.census.gov/main/www/access.html, and instructions for downloading can be found at http://www.census. gov/DES/www/inst.html. We also recommend IPUMS (Integrated Public Use Microdata Series) at the University of Minnesota Population Center (http://www.ipums.umn.edu). There you will find a national census database from 1850 to 1990 and an international database containing census data from around the world. Finally, the world's largest archive of computerized social science data is available from the Inter-university Consortium for Political and Social Research (ICPSR) located within the Institute for Social Research at the University of Michigan (http://www.icpsr.umich.edu/). There you will find information about how to join and download data from the ICPSR's huge database holdings, as well as a list of member institutions, training activities, and other data archive material.

A short tour of the Web sites described above will illustrate the growing viability of "downloading" existing data to conduct secondary data analyses. A more thorough treatment of secondary analysis can be found in *Research Methods in the Social Sciences*, by David Nachmias and Chava Frankfort-Nachmias (2000; see especially chapter 13). We hope you will give Web-based data collection serious consideration as a primary research approach and not just as a secondary option when traditional methods of data collection fail.

HOW TO PROTECT YOUR WORK

We would like to relate two brief dissertation nightmares regarding dissertations lost to the unpredictability and naïveté of computer users. The first is a tale of a student who asked Professor Newton if she could use his printer to print a final draft of her master's thesis. The student arrived and produced a badly worn floppy disk, complete with strands of hair, dust, and dirt accumulated from the bottom of her purse. When asked if that was her only copy, she replied "Yes." Of course the disk wouldn't work, and the student's own carelessness resulted in her having to retype the entire thesis from a previous draft.

The second story is from a student of Professor Rudestam, who on a rainy afternoon went to the airport to pick up her husband. Upon returning, she found that lightning had struck her home, destroying everything, including extensive transcripts from interviews, all the interview tapes collected from around the world, and all computer equipment.

The message is clear: Anything can happen, so follow a few rules. First, make backups of everything that is important, and do so regularly. Second, always make copies that you store somewhere else: at work, at school, with your best friend, or on your major professor's computer. Below we offer some advice on how to prevent computer disasters and streamline your computer operations.

UTILITIES: SOFTWARE TO STREAMLINE AND PROTECT YOUR SYSTEM

Disk utility libraries or "utilities" are special software programs designed to make living with your computer easier. They allow you to perform hundreds of operations that facilitate working with your system. These include checking disks and files for errors, recovering files that have been deleted inadvertently, and most important, protecting your computer against viruses. Most computer purchases today include a virus protection program, such as McAfee VirusScan, but most do not offer a complete suite of programs to protect, optimize, and repair your PC. For example, McAfee Office Pro2000 contains programs to scan for viruses (VirusScan), uninstall programs (Uninstaller), update programs from the Internet (Oil Change), provide Internet privacy (Guard Dog) and e-mail privacy (PGP), and prevent system crashes or implement repair after a crash (First Aid 2000). Norton SystemWorks 2000, from Symantec, does much the same thing with Norton AntiVirus, Norton Utilities, Norton CrashGuard, and Norton Cleansweep. You can check out the latest prices and updates from a number of on-line vendors, including www.pcconnection.com (voted the best mail order site eight times).

HOW MUCH COMPUTER DO I NEED?

Computer technology is changing at a tremendous rate, and it is risky to make recommendations regarding what a student or colleague needs today when these needs are likely to change tomorrow. A potential consumer should ask a few basic questions before starting to look for a computer system. We feel that the most essential of these is, "What computer configuration is being used by my department and by my committee members?" A second, related question is, "What computer software is my committee familiar with?" It is very important to be "compatible" with your academic department and committee. This allows you to seek advice regarding the use of software and the interpretation of computer output, particularly from quantitative and qualitative data analysis programs.

We have only three basic recommendations. First, if your computer is more than a few years old, you are probably better off starting your dissertation with a new one. Second, never buy a computer without a written guarantee. We think that a good guarantee should cover parts and labor for at least 1 year after purchase. We recommend against buying a computer with only a 90-day guarantee. One reason for buying a computer from an established vendor (e.g., Costco, Circuit City, Best Buy, Dell, Gateway) is that they are likely to remain in business, and most allow you to purchase an "add-on" warranty that will guarantee repairs for up to 3 years. A guarantee is only as good as the stability of the company that supports it. Computers assembled in someone's garage often work fine, but when they "crash," most computer dealers refuse to touch them. Third, always buy a computer with a tape or Zip drive that will allow you to back up your work. We prefer Zip drives, but *anything* is better than nothing.

SHOULD I COPY MY FRIEND'S PROGRAM
AND SAVE SOME MONEY?

Many people will obtain a "bootlegged" program from a friend or acquaintance who happens to have a copy of a program they desire to own. This is not a particularly difficult thing to do because most software manufacturers have responded favorably to consumers' complaints regarding the difficulty of making backup copies and installing "copy-protected" software. We recommend against the copying of licensed software on moral, legal, and practical grounds. Morally, the copying of software is taking the intellectual creativity, time, and money of another person without paying for it. This is no different from recording the music, copying the writing, or videotaping the films of another person. Second, copying of software is illegal. One is not simply copying software, one is *illegally* copying software. Third, there are practical reasons for not copying software. Software needs documentation. Copied software may not include the documentation needed to install, run, troubleshoot, and understand the capabilities of the program. Moreover, software copied illegally may be contaminated by a virus. When software is passed around, the probability of picking up one of these viruses increases. Finally, software copied illegally has no user support or guarantees. When you purchase software you will be asked to send in a license agreement. This agreement guarantees your program against bugs and allows the vendor to communicate with you regarding updates, add-on enhancements, and other related programs. In some cases the agreement also permits phone assistance, usually free, sometimes for a fee, and, unfortunately, often very poor. In sum, buy your own software and feel good about it.

CHAPTER 11

Guidelines for the Presentation of Numbers in the Dissertation

Many dissertations require that the manuscript be typed in the format of the professional association representing the discipline of the dissertation. For example, in a department of psychology it is likely that the dissertation will present tables and figures, and describe these in the text using guidelines presented by the American Psychological Association (APA). This section describes the rules that one is likely to encounter when discussing numbers in text. Numbers may be expressed as words (five) or as figures (5), but when do we use a word as opposed to a figure? This section addresses nine areas of concern as outlined by the *Publication Manual of the American Psychological Association* (1994). We use the guidelines presented by the APA because they are complete, likely to cover a wide range of issues, and not idiosyncratic to the single field of psychology.

EXPRESSING NUMBERS AS FIGURES

General Rule: Use figures to express numbers 10 and above and words to express numbers below 10 (APA, 1994).

EXAMPLES:

Correct	Incorrect
only about 13%	only about thirteen percent
a 22 mm line	a twenty-two millimeter line
four subjects	4 subjects
three out of five groups	3 out of 5 groups

Exceptions:

1. All numbers below 10 that are grouped for comparison with numbers 10 and above, and appear in the same paragraph, are also expressed as figures (APA, 1994).

Correct	Incorrect
5 of 32 groups	five of 32 groups
	five of thirty-two groups
when ranked, the 3rd and 12th	when ranked, the third and twelfth
	when ranked, the third and 12th
8 of the 30 cases	eight of the 30 cases
	eight of the thirty cases

2. Numbers that immediately precede a unit of measurement are expressed as figures, regardless of size (APA, 1994).

Correct	Incorrect
a 5 mm line	a five millimeter line
	a five mm line
a mean of 36.22 cm	a mean of thirty-six and twenty-two one hundredths centimeters

3. Numbers that represent statistical or mathematical functions, fractional or decimal quantities, percentages, ratios, and percentiles and quartiles are expressed as figures, regardless of size (APA, 1994).

Correct	Incorrect
a mean of 3.54	a mean of three point fifty four
	a mean of three and fifty-four one hundredths
subtracted from 5	subtracted from five
4 3/4 times as many	four and three fourths times as many
0.44	point forty-four
	.44 (must precede a decimal with 0)
a 5 kg weight	a five kilogram weight
scored in the 4th percentile	scored in the fourth percentile

4. Numbers that represent time, dates, ages, sample or population size, scores and points on a scale, exact sums of money, and numerals as numerals are expressed as figures, regardless of size (APA, 1994).

Correct	Incorrect
4 persons in each sample	four persons in each sample
seven 9-year-old children	seven nine-year-old children
	7 9-year-old children
in 7 years	in seven years
study began in 1984	study began in nineteen eighty-four
prior to April 1	prior to April first
no group lasted longer than 3.5 hours	no group lasted longer than three and one half hours
a score of 6 or greater	a score of six or greater
each subject was paid $7.50	each subject was paid seven dollars and fifty cents

5. Numbers that denote a specific place in a numbered series, parts of books and tables, and each number in a list of four or more numbers are expressed as figures, regardless of size (APA, 1994).

Correct	Incorrect
sample 4	*sample four*
Figure 1	Figure One
page 60	Page sixty
Chapters 2, 5, 6, 8 and 23	Chapters two, five, six, eight and 23

EXPRESSING NUMBERS AS WORDS

General Rule: Use words to express numbers below 10 that do not represent precise measurements and that are not grouped for comparison with numbers 10 and above (APA, 1994).

EXAMPLES:

Correct	Incorrect
about seven or eight	about 7 or 8
one of the first	1 of the first
	1 of the 1st
only two persons	only 2 persons
two surveys	2 surveys
one-way ANOVA	1-way ANOVA
two-tailed *F* test	2-tailed *F* test

Exceptions:

1. The numbers *zero* and *one* when the words would be easier to comprehend than the figures, or when the words do not appear in context with numbers 10 and above, are expressed in words (APA, 1994).

Correct	Incorrect
one-on-one session	1 on 1 session
only one subject	only 1 subject
the concept of zero	the concept of 0

2. Any number that begins a sentence, title, or heading should be expressed in words. (Whenever possible, reword the sentence to avoid beginning with a number [APA, 1994]).

Correct	Incorrect
Five studies support	5 studies support
Twenty-six percent of . . .	26% of . . .
	Twenty-six % of . . .

3. Common fractions are expressed as words (APA, 1994).

Correct	Incorrect
one half the sample	1/2 the sample
	1 half the sample
exactly one fifth	exactly 1/5

4. Honor universally accepted usage (APA, 1994).

Correct	Incorrect
the Twelve Apostles	the 12 Apostles
the Ten Commandments	the 10 Commandments
the Fourth of July	the 4th of July

COMBINING FIGURES AND WORDS TO EXPRESS NUMBERS

General Rule: Use a combination of figures and words to express rounded large numbers and back-to-back modifiers (APA, 1994).

EXAMPLES: Rounded Large Numbers

Correct	Incorrect
About 3 thousand	About 3,000
	About three thousand
A net loss of $1 billion	A net loss of one-billion dollars
	a net lost of $1,000,000

EXAMPLES: Back-to-Back Modifiers

Correct	Incorrect
3 one-way interactions	three one-way interactions
2 two dollar bills	2 $2.00 bills
	2 2 dollar bills

ORDINAL NUMBERS

General Rule: Treat ordinal numbers (except percentiles and quartiles) as you would cardinal numbers (APA, 1994).

EXAMPLES:

Correct	Incorrect
the first sample	the 1st sample
the 11th grade	the eleventh grade
the 2nd and 12th	the second and 12th
	the second and twelfth
the second	the 2nd
the 12th	the twelfth

DECIMAL FRACTIONS

General Rule: Place the decimal point on the line, not above the line. Use a zero before the decimal point when numbers are less than 1 (APA, 1994).

EXAMPLES:

Correct	Incorrect
0.45 mm	point forty-five millimeters
	.45 mm
a 0.2 s interval	a .2 second interval

Exception: Do not use a zero before a decimal fraction when the number cannot be greater than 1, as in correlations, probability values, proportions, and levels of statistical significance (APA, 1994).

$r = .44, p < .01$.

ARABIC OR ROMAN NUMERALS

General Rule: Use Arabic, not Roman, numerals whenever possible (APA, 1994).

Exception: If Roman numerals are part of an established terminology, do not change to Arabic numbers; for example, "Type II error" (APA, 1994).

COMMAS

General Rule: Use commas between groups of three digits in most figures of 1,000 or more (APA, 1994).

Exceptions:

Page numbers	page 2134
Binary digits	001101010
Serial numbers	571606999
Degrees of temperature	2349° F
Acoustic frequency designations	3000 Hz
Degrees of freedom	F(35, 1100)
Numbers to the right of a decimal point	6,750.0748

PLURALS OF NUMBERS

General Rule: To form the plurals of numbers, whether expressed as figures or as words, add "s" or "es" alone, without an apostrophe (APA, 1994).

EXAMPLES:

Correct	Incorrect
the early 1960s	the early 1960's
from the 30s and 40s	from the 30's and 40's

APA REQUIREMENTS FOR STATISTICAL AND MATHEMATICAL COPY

1. Your Responsibilities
   You are responsible for selecting the correct statistical method and the accuracy of all supporting data. Raw data should be retained for 5 years following publication (APA, 1994).

2. Should References for Statistical Analyses Be Presented?
   Statistics in common use are not referenced. Less common statistics not commonly found in textbooks should be referenced. When a statistic is used in a unique or controversial manner, or when the statistic is itself the focus of the research, references should be given (APA, 1994).

3. Presenting Inferential Statistics in Text
   Give the symbol, degrees of freedom, value, and probability level. In addition, give the mean or other descriptive statistic to clarify the nature of the effect (APA, 1994).

EXAMPLES: *F* and *t* tests

$F(2, 34) = 67.22, p < .001$

$t(35) = 3.71, p < .001$

EXAMPLES: Chi-Square Statistics

$\chi^2(4, N = 78) = 11.15, p < .05$

4. Should Symbols or Word Terms Be Used in the Text?
   Use the term, not the symbol (APA, 1994).

EXAMPLES:

Correct	Incorrect
The means were	The Ms were
	The Xs were
The standard deviations were	The Sds were

5. How Do I Express the Number of Subjects?
   Use an uppercase *N* to designate the number of members in the total sample and a lowercase *n* to designate the number of members in a limited portion of the total sample (APA, 1994).

EXAMPLES:

a total sample of $N = 130$

$n = 50$ in each group

6. How Do I Express Percentages?
   Use the symbol for percent only when it is preceded by a numeral. Use the word "percentage" when a number is not given (APA, 1994).

EXAMPLES:

21% of the sample

the percentage of the sample

Exception: In table and figure headings and legends, use the % symbol to conserve space (APA, 1994).

This completes our discussion of the presentation of numbers in text, but the details of APA and other formats include considerably more than just the above set of rules. In addition, the American Psychological Association has an excellent guide to assist students with the use of the APA publication manual. *Mastering APA Style: Student's Workbook and Training Guide* (Geftand & Walker, 1990) includes instruction and exercises covering references and citations, tables, statistical and mathematical copy, and other topics.

Finally, it is advisable to begin using your discipline's style at the very beginning of the dissertation process. This gives you considerable time to master the intricacies of the style and prevents you from having to "fix" hundreds of pages of text at the very end.

The Library of Congress
will mark its 200th birthday
on April 24, 2000, as a
celebration of all libraries
and the important role they
play in community life.

200

LIBRARY OF CONGRESS
BICENTENNIAL
1800 – 2000

Visit our web site: www.loc.gov

CHAPTER 12

Informed Consent and Other Ethical Concerns

All universities have ethical standards for conducting research with human beings, most have formally established research ethics committees, and many have institutionalized procedures to guarantee that informed consent is obtained prior to initiating all research. It is the student's responsibility to become knowledgeable about the university's requirements, obtain the necessary documentation, and follow the university's guidelines. This should be done prior to collecting data, as early as possible after the research procedures are established. One important reason for meeting these expectations in a timely fashion is that you may be required to obtain an authorizing signature from the research ethics committee, and these committees tend to meet infrequently, particularly during academic breaks and summers.

COMMON ETHICAL CONCERNS

The two main ethical issues that pertain to using subjects in social science research are the need for fully informed consent to participate and the need to emerge from the experience unharmed. Ultimately, the value of a study is determined by balancing the potential benefits, in

terms of generalizable knowledge, with the costs and potential ri
recurrent problem is the failure of students to reflect conscien
upon how particular subjects are likely to experience the study
cannot cavalierly assume that experimental manipulations, interv
questionnaires, or even feedback of results will not be upsetti
some participants. It is permissible for research to carry some ris
it is imperative to anticipate such risks beforehand.

Perhaps the most controversial type of research design is one
employs concealment or deception. The issue here is whether
straightforward, alternative procedures are available and whethe
deception is justified by the theoretical or applied value of the st
Field studies may raise important ethical concerns when the inves
tor deviously manipulates variables in the environment or whe
research component is covertly introduced into an everyday situat
such as gathering data from unwitting employees in the course of t
work. The rule here is to seek informed consent whenever there is m
than minimal risk of harm to the participants. In any case, full disc
sure needs to be given to participants as soon as possible after the d
have been obtained. Over the course of time, the biggest drawbac
the use of concealment or deception is probably the gradual erosion
public trust in the research enterprise.

The American Psychological Association has a clearly stated set
guidelines for research with human participants. We reproduce the
guidelines in their entirety in Box 12.1. Other disciplines may opera
with somewhat different standards, but this is a relatively complete l
that well represents the ethical concerns voiced by researchers in t
social sciences. The APA guidelines form the foundation for obtainin
informed consent according to the 11 points discussed below.

INFORMED CONSENT

One key element of conducting ethical research involves obtainin
informed consent from your participants. Informed consent is require
in most cases, unless there is "minimal risk." Examples of methodolo
gies that typically do not require informed consent include secondary
analyses of data, archival research, and the systematic observation o
publicly observable data, such as shoppers in a suburban mall. There is

(Text continued on p. 270)

BOX 12.1

Ethical Principles of Psychologists

Principle 9

The decision to undertake research rests upon a considered judgment by the individual psychologist about how best to contribute to psychological science and human welfare. Having made the decision to conduct research, the psychologist considers alternative directions in which research energies and resources might be invested. On the basis of this consideration, the psychologist carries out the investigation with respect and concern for the dignity and welfare of the people who participate and with cognizance of federal and state regulations and professional standards governing the conduct of research with human participants.

a. In planning a study, the investigator has the responsibility to make a careful evaluation of its ethical acceptability. To the extent that the weighing of scientific and human values suggests a compromise of any principle, the investigator incurs a correspondingly serious obligation to seek ethical advice and to observe stringent safeguards to protect the rights of human participants.

b. Considering whether a participant in a planned study will be a "subject at risk" or a "subject at minimal risk," according to recognized standards, is of primary ethical concern to the investigator.

c. The investigator always retains the responsibility for ensuring ethical practice in research. The investigator is also responsible for the ethical treatment of participants by collaborators, assistants, students, and employees, all of whom, however, incur similar obligations.

d. Except in minimal-risk research, the investigator establishes a clear and fair agreement with research participants, prior to their participation, that clarifies the obligations and responsibilities of each. The investigator has the obligation to honor all promises and commitments included in that agreement. The investigator informs the participants of all aspects of the research that might rea-

(Continued)

BOX 12.1

Ethical Principles
of Psychologists

sonably be expected to influence willingness to participate and explains all other aspects of the research about which the participants inquire. Failure to make full disclosure prior to obtaining informed consent requires additional safeguards to protect the welfare and dignity of the research participants. Research with children or with participants who have impairments that would limit understanding and/or communication requires special safeguarding procedures.

e. Methodological requirements of a study may make the use of concealment or deception necessary. Before conducting such a study, the investigator has a special responsibility to (i) determine whether the use of such techniques is justified by the study's prospective scientific, educational, or applied value; (ii) determine whether alternative procedures are available that do not use concealment or deception; and (iii) ensure that the participants are provided with sufficient explanation as soon as possible.

f. The investigator respects the individual's freedom to decline to participate in or to withdraw from the research at any time. The obligation to pretest this freedom requires careful thought and consideration when the investigator is in a position of authority or influence over the participant. Such positions of authority include, but are not limited to, situations in which research participation is required as part of employment or in which the participant is a student, client, or employee of the investigator.

g. The investigator protects the participant from physical and mental discomfort, harm, and danger that may arise from research procedures. If risks of such consequences exist, the investigator informs the participant of that fact. Research procedures likely to cause serious or lasting harm to a participant are not used unless the failure to use these procedures might expose the participant to risk of greater harm, or unless the research has great potential benefit and fully informed and voluntary consent is obtained from each participant.

The participant should be informed of procedures for contacting the investigator within a reasonable time period following participation should stress, potential harm, or related questions or concerns arise.

h. After the data are collected, the investigator provides the participant with information about the nature of the study and attempts to remove any misconceptions that may have arisen. Where scientific or humane values justify delaying or withholding this information, the investigator incurs a special responsibility to monitor the research and to ensure that there are no damaging consequences for the participant.

i. Where research procedures result in undesirable consequences for the individual participant, the investigator has the responsibility to detect and remove or correct these consequences, including long-term effects.

j. Information obtained about a research participant during the course of an investigation is confidential unless otherwise agreed upon in advance. When the possibility exists that others may obtain access to such information, this possibility, together with the plans for protecting confidentiality, is explained to the participant as part of the procedure for obtaining informed consent.

some lack of clarity and need for judgment about the standard of minimal risk. For example, the criterion of minimal risk could pertain to research involving brief questionnaires that do not address questions likely to be disturbing to the participants. Questions regarding favored sports or preferred television programs are probably not disturbing; questions regarding childhood victimization probably are. One way to think through the potential impact of your research procedures is to reverse roles and imagine what it would be like to be a participant in your study (Research Ethics Committee, The Fielding Institute, 1999). What concerns would you have regarding confidentiality? What information about the study would be important for you to know? Would you feel free to decline to participate if others in your selected group did participate?

The elements of informed consent are outlined below.

Tell the participant who is conducting the study.

This is usually the student; however, other persons, such as friends, spouses, or paid employees may also be used to collect data. Include the institutional affiliation of the researcher, as well as the supervisor of the dissertation or thesis.

Why was the particular person singled out for participation?

Answer the "Why me?" question. For example, "You have been selected to participate in this project because you have recently experienced the birth of your first child. We are particularly interested in your experience of. . . ." Sometimes not all potential participants are chosen to be included in the study. If this is the case, you need to sensitively communicate inclusion and exclusion criteria to those who were not selected.

What is the time commitment?

Let the participant know about how long it will take to complete his or her involvement. For example, "Pretesting with these instruments indicates that it takes approximately 45 minutes to complete all forms."

Are there any benefits to be expected?

Be reasonable, but don't oversell the study. Typically, there are few or no advantages to participating in most research, although greater self-awareness, monetary remuneration, and/or an enhanced sense of altruism might apply. The researcher can hope that a potential participant will feel good about helping someone collect data, but this is not a particular benefit.

Are there any potential risks, and how have these been managed?

Let the participants know what the potential risks are. This includes any possible emotional, psychological, physical, social, economic, or political difficulties or harm that might ensue from participating. What will you offer participants who experience difficulties attributable to participating in your study? For example, "Some people may experience negative emotions when discussing parental alcoholism. If you would like to discuss these with someone, please feel free to call the study director at the number below." In the case of studies with no foreseeable risks, state "there are no known risks associated with participation in this research."

Explain the study and offer to answer questions.

This should be done in lay language easily understood by your subject population. If you cannot share the purpose of the study fully because it would compromise the integrity of the research, describe what the participant is expected to do and provide the purpose during the debriefing. Offer to answer questions about the study then.

Participation is always voluntary.

Subjects should not be subtly pressured to participate by your assumption of social status or the scientific establishment to lend more authority to the project. Moreover, the participant has a right to withdraw from the study at any time.

When conducting research in any setting where the participant is likely to experience pressure to participate, it is important to make this point explicit. For example, "Your participation in this research is not required and will have no effect on your grade in this course. You may choose to withdraw from the research at any time without penalty." In some settings, a person may be apprehensive that his or her social standing, job security, or friendships would be affected by participating or by not participating. In these situations it is of particular importance that decisions to participate, to decline to participate, and to withdraw be confidential.

Provide the participants with a copy of the informed consent form.

The participant should be given a copy of the "informed consent form" (if relevant) and asked to sign another copy for the researcher. For example, "If you would like to participate in this study please sign one copy of the attached consent form and return it in the enclosed envelope. Keep the other copy for your records."

Payment

Will the subject receive compensation for participation? Let the subject know what payment he or she can expect, if any.

Confidentiality

Let the participant know the limits of confidentiality. *Confidentiality* refers to the treatment of information that a participant has disclosed in a relationship of trust, with the expectation that it will not be divulged to others without permission in ways that are inconsistent with the understanding of the original disclosure. Confidentiality is different from anonymity. *Anonymity* means that no one, including the researcher, will know the participant's identity, whereas confidentiality means that the participant's identity will be preserved, at all costs, by the researcher. For example, if your data are transcribed or analyzed by a third party, how can you guarantee confidentiality? Typically, summary statistics based on data will be public. In funded research the data may also be public, but identifying information is removed, and there is too little relevant information available to identify specific individuals.

Debriefing

If there is to be a debriefing, let the participant know how you will do it. Typically, all participants deserve to have the opportunity to learn about the results of the study. You may choose to describe the purpose of the study in more detail at the end, as in a study that involves deception, or you may offer to send a summary of the results to those who wish to receive it. For example, "If you would like to receive a summary of the results of this research, please write your name and address in the space provided at the end of the questionnaire." (In this case, the respondent would yield anonymity, but his or her confidentiality may be preserved.) Feedback in the debriefing should be in lay language and general enough to be informative without being harmful. In general, summarized, aggregate data rather than individualized test results should be given to participants.

We have included in this chapter a sample letter of invitation (see Table 12.1) to participate in a dissertation study and a sample informed consent form (see Table 12.2). Note that some groups are simply not able to provide informed consent on their own. These include (but are not limited to) persons under 18 years of age, the mentally retarded, and the psychologically disabled. In these situations the informed consent form should be signed by the participant's parent or legal guardian.

Finally, Table 12.3 presents a list of questions to guide you in determining whether or not you have attended to all relevant ethics principles in administering your study.

BIAS-FREE WRITING

We conclude this chapter with a brief discussion of ethical issues in scholarly writing. Throughout the dissertation it is important to avoid language and materials that are oppressive or discriminatory to any group of people. Questionnaires and measures should be checked scrupulously to be certain that they do not imply that it is "normal" or "right" to belong to a specific ethnic group, have a particular sexual preference, or engage in a particular lifestyle.[1] Writers need to stay current with language that is sensitive to diverse groups because what was acceptable terminology yesterday may not be acceptable today. Here are a few guidelines to keep in mind to eliminate bias.

(Continued on p. 276)

Table 12.1
Sample Letter of Invitation to Participate in a Research Project

CHILDHOOD TRAUMA AND PERSONALITY

I am currently involved in a research project addressing clinical issues related to childhood trauma and personality. The project examines the relationship of certain childhood experiences to specific heightened abilities. The study is performed as partial fulfillment of the requirements for my Ph.D. degree in clinical psychology at the University of the North Pole.

Your participation in this project will provide useful information on this topic. You qualify for participation if you are between the ages of 18 and 65. You will be asked to complete five (5) brief true-false instruments that will take about 30 minutes. You will also be asked to fill out a background questionnaire and a childhood history survey that will take approximately 20 to 30 minutes.

Participation in this study is strictly voluntary. You may withdraw from the study at any point without penalty. Participation is not associated with your class grade. All data from this project are confidential and will be used for research purposes only. Data from questionnaires and instruments are anonymous. Names of participants will not be connected to information and scores.

Although there are no foreseeable risks to the participant, the childhood history survey contains detailed questions regarding family violence and abuse. If you feel questions of this type would upset you, please feel free to decline from participation at any point in this project.

Thank you for your assistance.

(Signature)
Name of researcher
Telephone number

Table 12.2

Informed Consent for Participation in Research Project

This study considers the relationship between childhood experiences and personality. It is performed as a partial fulfillment of the requirements for the researcher's Ph.D. in clinical psychology at the University of the North Pole.

There are no foreseeable risks with this research. The main potential benefit is in contributing to scientific knowledge on this topic. No costs or payment are associated with participating in the study. If any discomfort should arise regarding material addressed in the study, participants can call the number listed on this letterhead to ask questions or discuss their feelings. A more complete statement of the nature and purpose of the research will be available when the data collection is completed.

I agree to participate in this research project and I understand that:

1. The time required for this study is about 60 minutes.

2. The nature of my participation includes complete five (5) self-report measures, a background information questionnaire, and a childhood experience questionnaire.

3. My participation is entirely voluntary. I may terminate my involvement at any time without penalty.

4. All my data are confidential. All research measures will be destroyed within five (5) years after completion of the study.

5. All data are for research purposes only and will not affect my course grade.

6. If I have questions about the research, or if I would like to receive a copy of the aggregate findings of the study when it is complete, I can contact the researcher by calling (telephone number) or writing to:

Name of researcher _____

Address of researcher _____

Signed _____ Date _____   Signed _____ Date _____
     (participant)   (researcher)

Table 12.3

The Five C's of Research Ethics Principles

1. Confidentiality
   - ➤ How are you going to keep the identities of your participants, organizations, and other named entities confidential? Will you use numbers, code, or pseudonyms? How will you disguise the location and types of organizations?
   - ➤ How will you prevent other members of a group or organization from knowing who was a participant and who was not? If you use referrals or nominations, will you identify the nominators? Why?
   - ➤ How will you keep the names of anyone or any organizations mentioned in an interview or journal or focus group confidential?
   - ➤ If you are using groups, how will you keep the information discussed in the group confidential? Will it matter if the group members are able to identify each other?
   - ➤ How will you store the data and when will they be destroyed?
2. Coercion
   - ➤ How will you contact volunteers and obtain their consent?
   - ➤ How will your position or personal relationship with them affect their participation and how will you guard against feelings of coercion?
   - ➤ How will you make sure that the supervisors/teachers/therapists of your participants (if relevant) do not exert any pressure on them to participate?
   - ➤ How will you ensure that the supervisors/teachers/therapists will not know who participated and who did not (if this is a consideration)?
   - ➤ How will you make it clear that participants can withdraw from the study or withdraw all or some of the data they have generated?
3. Consent
   - ➤ Do you tell your participants everything about what is expected of them, including what they must do, what the time commitment is, what the procedures are, and so forth? If not, why not?

(Continued)

Substitute gender-neutral words and phrases for gender-biased words. A common mistake is the inadvertent use of sexist terms that are deeply entrenched in our culture, such as "chairman" instead of "chairperson," "mothering" instead of "parenting," and "mankind" instead of "humankind."

Use designations in parallel fashion to refer to men and women equally. Example: "5 men and 14 women," *not* "5 men and 14 females."

Do not assume that certain professions are gender-related (e.g., "the scientist . . . he") and avoid sexual stereotyping (e.g., "a bright and beautiful female professor").

Table 12.3

Continued

> ➤ Do you tell the participants what the study is about? If not, why not?
> ➤ Do you identify yourself, the name of your faculty supervisor, and your institution on the informed consent form?
> ➤ Do you tell members of any group who may be excluded why their data or their participation is unnecessary?
> ➤ Do you make clear that participants have the right to withdraw any or all of the data they have generated without adverse consequences for any employment, therapy, educational services, etc. to which they are entitled?
> ➤ Do you make clear what the risks and benefits of the research are for the participant?

4. Care
> ➤ Do you describe the risks and benefits of your research fairly?
> ➤ What will you do if someone experiences distress as a result of participating in your research?
> ➤ Do you make it clear that you will be available to answer questions?
> ➤ Have you considered the effects of any personal questions you intend to ask and do you warn your participants that there will be personal materials involved in the research?

5. Communication
> ➤ How will you check out the accuracy of your transcripts and quotes (if applicable)?
> ➤ How will you inform your participants about the outcome of your study?
> ➤ Did you make a copy of the informed consent form available to the participant?

SOURCE: "The Five C's: Principles to Keep in Mind," in Research Ethics Committee, The Fielding Institute, *Fielding Institute Research Ethics Procedures* (1999).

Avoid gender-biased pronouns (e.g., "A consultant may not always be able to see *his* clients"). A few nonsexist alternatives to this pervasive problem are to

> ➤ Add the other gender: *"his or her* clients." This alternative should be used only occasionally because it can become very cumbersome. It is, however, preferable to awkward constructions such as *s/he, him/her,* or *he(she)*.

> ➤ Use the plural form: "Consultants . . . *their* clients."

> ➤ Delete the adjective: "to see clients."

➤ Rephrase the sentence to eliminate the pronoun: "Clients may not always be seen by their consultants."

➤ Replace the masculine or feminine pronouns with *one* or *you*.

Do not identify people by race or ethnic group unless it is relevant. If it is relevant, try to ascertain the currently most acceptable terms and use them.

Avoid language that suggests evaluation or reinforces stereotypes. For example, referring to a group as "culturally deprived" is evaluative, and remarking that the "Afro-American students, *not surprisingly*, won the athletic events" reinforces a stereotype.

Don't make unsupported assumptions about various age groups (e.g., that the elderly are less intellectually able or are remarkable for continuing to work energetically).

NOTE

1. A thoughtful article by McHugh, Koeske, and Frieze (1986) describes how unintentional sexism may creep into the design of a study at the level of method, theory, or conceptualization and offers suggestions for excluding it.

References

American Psychological Association. (1990). Ethical principles of psychologists (amended June 2, 1989). *American Psychologist, 45*, 390-395.

American Psychological Association. (1994). *Publication manual of the American Psychological Association* (4th ed.). Washington, DC: Author.

Argyris, C., Putnam, R., & Smith, D. M. (1985). *Action science.* San Francisco: Jossey-Bass.

Armstrong, D. G. (1994). *The dreams of the blind and their implications for contemporary theories of dreaming.* Unpublished doctoral dissertation, The Fielding Institute, Santa Barbara, CA.

Bailey, P. A. (1992). *A phenomenological study of the psychological transition from being a mother of dependent daughters to being a mother of adult daughters.* Unpublished doctoral dissertation, The Fielding Institute, Santa Barbara, CA.

Bainbridge, W. S. (2000). Web-based research approaches. In J. K. Hadden & D. E. Cowan (Eds.), *Religion on the Internet.* Greenwich, CT: Jai Press.

Baron, R. M., & Kenny, D. A. (1986). The moderator-mediator variable distinction in social psychological research: Conceptual, strategic, and statistical considerations. *Journal of Personality and Social Psychology, 51*, 1173-1182.

Barrett, H. D. (1990). *Adult self-directed learning, personal computer competency and learning style: Models for more effective learning.* Unpublished doctoral dissertation, The Fielding Institute, Santa Barbara, CA.

Becker, C. (1986). Interviewing in human science research. *Methods, 1*, 101-124.

Belenky, M., Clinchy, B., Goldberger, N., & Tarule, J. (1986). *Women's ways of knowing: The development of self, voice and mind.* New York: Basic Books.

Bell, M. (1988). *An introduction to the Bell Object Relations Reality Testing Inventory.* Unpublished manuscript, V. A. Medical Center, Psychology Service, West Haven, CT.

Bevan, W. (1991). Contemporary psychology: A tour inside the onion. *American Psychologist, 46*, 475-483.

Caddell, D. P. (1989). *Moral education in the college environment.* Unpublished master's thesis, California State University, Fullerton.

Campbell, D. T., & Stanley, J. C. (1966). Experimental and quasi-experimental designs for research and teaching. In N. L. Gage (Ed.), *Handbook of research on teaching.* Chicago: Rand McNally.

Cohen, J. (1988). *Statistical power analysis for the behavioral sciences* (2nd ed.). Hillsdale, NJ: Lawrence Erlbaum.

Cohen, J. (1990). Things I have learned so far. *American Psychologist, 45,* 1304-1312.

Colaizzi, P. R. (1973). *Reflections and research in psychology.* Dubuque, IA: Kendall/Hunt.

Connell, D. (1992). *The relationship between Siddah meditation and stress in psychotherapists: A transpersonal perspective.* Unpublished doctoral dissertation, The Fielding Institute, Santa Barbara, CA.

Cook, T. D., & Campbell, D. T. (1979). *Quasi-experimentation: Design and analysis issues for field settings.* Chicago: Rand McNally.

Cresswell, J. W. (1998). *Qualitative inquiry and research design: Choosing among five traditions.* Thousand Oaks, CA: Sage.

Cronbach, L. J. (1975). Beyond the two disciplines of scientific psychology. *American Psychologist, 30,* 116-127.

Davenport, L. (1991). *Adaptation to dyslexia: Acceptance of the diagnosis in relation to coping efforts and educational plans.* Unpublished doctoral dissertation, The Fielding Institute, Santa Barbara, CA.

Demoville, D. B. (1999). *The dynamics of organizational alignment.* Unpublished doctoral dissertation, The Fielding Institute, Santa Barbara, CA.

Denzin, N., & Lincoln, Y. (1998). *Collecting and interpreting qualitative materials.* Thousand Oaks, CA: Sage.

Dillman, D. (1999). *Mail and Internet surveys: The tailored design method.* New York: John Wiley.

Dong, L. (2000). *The impact of ethnic identification and self esteem on Southeast and East Asian juvenile delinquents.* Unpublished doctoral dissertation, The Fielding Institute, Santa Barbara, CA.

Dumas, C. (1989). *Daughters in family-owned business: An applied systems perspective.* Unpublished doctoral dissertation, The Fielding Institute, Santa Barbara, CA.

Einhorn, J. (1993). *Help-seeking interactions in women's friendships: A relational perspective.* Unpublished doctoral dissertation, The Fielding Institute, Santa Barbara, CA.

Elliott, J. M. (1997). *Bridging of differences in dialogic democracy.* Unpublished doctoral dissertation, The Fielding Institute, Santa Barbara, CA.

Erikson, E. (1962). *Young man Luther.* Mangolia, MA: Peter Smith.

Ewing, N. R. (1992). *Psychodevelopmental influences in augmentation mammoplasty.* Unpublished doctoral dissertation, The Fielding Institute, Santa Barbara, CA.

Feyerabend, P. K. (1981a). *Philosophical papers: Vol. 1. Realism, rationalism, and scientific method.* Cambridge, UK: Cambridge University Press.

Feyerabend, P. K. (1981b). *Philosophical papers: Vol. 2. Problems of empiricism.* Cambridge, UK: Cambridge University Press.

Geltand, H., & Walker, C. J. (1990). *Mastering APA style: Student's workbook and training guide.* Washington, DC: American Psychological Association.

Gergen, M. M. (1988). Toward a feminist metatheory and methodology in the social sciences. In M. M. Gergen (Ed.), *Feminist thought and the structure of knowledge.* New York: New York University Press.

Gigerenzer, G. (1991). From tools to theory: A heuristic of discovery in cognitive psychology. *Psychological Review, 98,* 254-267.

Giorgi, A. (1985). *Phenomenology and psychological research.* New York: Harper & Row.

Glaser, B. G., & Strauss, A. L. (1967). *The discovery of grounded theory: Strategies for qualitative research.* Chicago: Aldine/Atherton.

Glass, G. V. (1976). Primary, secondary, and meta-analysis of research. *Educational Researcher, 5*(10), 3-8.

Glover, L. (1994). *The relevance of personal theory in psychotherapy.* Unpublished doctoral dissertation, The Fielding Institute, Santa Barbara, CA.

Goffman, E. (1961). *Asylums.* Garden City, NY: Doubleday.

Goldberg, N. (1991). *Writing down the bones/Wild mind.* New York: Quality Paperback Book Club.

Goodman, G. (1998). *The relationship among affect integration, emotion-engaged coping, empathy, and interpersonal violence in adolescents.* Unpublished doctoral dissertation, The Fielding Institute, Santa Barbara, CA.

Greenwood, D., & Levin, M. (1998). *Introduction to action research: Social research for social change.* Thousand Oaks, CA: Sage.

Guba, E., & Lincoln, Y. S. (1981). *Effective evaluation.* San Francisco: Jossey-Bass.

Hamilton, L. (1990). *Modern data analysis: A first course in applied statistics.* Pacific Grove, CA: Brooks/Cole.

Hardwick, C. (1990). *Object relations and reality testing in adult children of alcoholics: An exploratory and descriptive study.* Unpublished doctoral dissertation, The Fielding Institute, Santa Barbara, CA.

Harlow, D. D., & Linet, M. S. (1989). Agreement between questionnaire data and medical records. *American Journal of Epidemiology, 129,* 233-248.

Harlow, L. L., Mulaik, S. A., & Steiger, J. H. (Eds.). (1997). *What if there were no significance tests?* Hillsdale, NJ: Lawrence Erlbaum.

Hersen, M., & Barber, D. (1992). *Single case experimental designs: Strategies for studying behavioral change* (2nd ed.). New York: Pergamon.

Hewson, D., & Bennett, A. (1987). Childbirth research data: Medical records or women's reports? *American Journal of Epidemiology, 125,* 484-491.

Holmes, T., & Rahe, R. (1967). The Social Readjustment Rating Scale. *Journal of Psychosomatic Research, 11,* 213-218.

Horwitz, R. I. (1986). Comparison of epidemiological data from multiple sources. *Journal of Chronic Disease, 39,* 889-896.

Hoshmand, L. T. (1989). Alternate research paradigms: A review and teaching proposal. *Counseling Psychologist, 17,* 3-79.

Human and Organization Development Program of The Fielding Institute (HOD). (1998). *Inquiry and research knowledge study guide of the Human and Organization Development Program of The Fielding Institute.* Santa Barbara, CA: The Fielding Institute.

Jonas, M. R. (1996). *Footprints of the soul: Journeys from trauma to resilience.* Unpublished doctoral dissertation, The Fielding Institute, Santa Barbara, CA.

Kachigan, S. K. (1986). *Statistical analysis: An interdisciplinary introduction to univariate and multivariate methods.* New York: Radius.

Katz, S. R. (1995). *The experience of chronic vulvar pain: Psychosocial dimensions and the sense of self.* Unpublished doctoral dissertation, The Fielding Institute, Santa Barbara, CA.

Kazdin, A. E. (1997). *Research design in clinical psychology* (2nd ed.). New York: Harper-Collins.

Keen, E. (1975). *A primer in phenomenological psychology.* Lanham, MD: University Press of America.

Kerlinger, F. N. (1977). *Foundations of behavioral research* (3rd ed.). New York: Holt, Rinehart & Winston.

Kerlinger, F. N., & Lee, H. B. (1999). *Behavioral research: A conceptual approach*. New York: Holt, Rinehart & Winston.

Kratochwill, T. R., & Levin, J. R. (Eds.). (1992). *Single-case research design and analysis: New directions for psychology and education*. Hillsdale, NJ: Lawrence Erlbaum.

Knowledge Index. Palo Alto, CA: Dialog Information Systems, Inc.

Kuhn, T. (1962). *The structure of scientific revolutions*. Chicago: University of Chicago Press.

Kvale, S. (1996). *Interviews: An introduction to qualitative research interviewing*. Thousand Oaks, CA: Sage.

La Pelle, N. (1997). *Thriving on performance evaluations in organizations*. Unpublished doctoral dissertation, The Fielding Institute, Santa Barbara, CA.

Lazarus, R. S., & Folkman, S. (1984). *Stress, appraisal and coping*. New York: Springer.

Leon, J. M. (1991). *Family and peer relations of delinquent juvenile gang members and non-gang members*. Unpublished doctoral dissertation, United States International University, San Diego, CA.

Lewin, K. (1948). *Resolving social conflict*. New York: Harper.

Liebow, E. (1967). *Tally's Corner: A study of Negro streetcorner men*. Boston: Little, Brown.

Lincoln, Y. S., & Guba, E. G. (1985). *Naturalistic inquiry*. Beverly Hills, CA: Sage.

Locke, L. F., Spirduso, W. W., & Silverman, S. J. (1997). *Proposals that work: A guide for planning dissertations and grant proposals*. Newbury Park, CA: Sage.

Macdonald, S. (1990). *Empathy, personal maturity, and emotional articulation*. Unpublished doctoral dissertation, The Fielding Institute, Santa Barbara, CA.

Mahoney, M. J. (1990). *Human change processes*. New York: Basic Books.

Mann, T. (1987). *A guide to library research methods*. New York: Oxford University Press.

Marshall, C., & Rossman, G. B. (1999). *Designing qualitative research* (3rd ed.). Thousand Oaks, CA: Sage.

McHugh, M. C., Koeske, R. D., & Frieze, I. H. (1986). Issues to consider in conducting non-sexist psychological research. *American Psychologist, 41*, 879-890.

Miles, M. B., & Huberman, A. M. (1994). *Qualitative data analysis: A sourcebook of new methods*. Thousand Oaks, CA: Sage.

Mishler, E. G. (1991). *Research interviewing: Context and narrative*. Cambridge, MA: Harvard University Press.

Moore, E. R. (1995). *Creating organizational cultures: An ethnographic study*. Unpublished doctoral dissertation, The Fielding Institute, Santa Barbara, CA.

Morgan, E. S. (1995). *An explanation of the meaning of business ethics in a cross-cultural context with Russians and Americans*. Unpublished doctoral dissertation. Santa Barbara, CA: The Fielding Institute.

Morse, J. M. (1994). *Critical issues in qualitative research methods*. Thousand Oaks, CA: Sage.

Morse, J. M. (1998). Designing funded qualitative research. In N. K. Denzin & Y. S. Lincoln (Eds.), *Strategies of qualitative inquiry*. Thousand Oaks, CA: Sage.

Moustakas, C. (1994). *Phenomenological research methods*. Thousand Oaks, CA: Sage.

Nachmias, D., & Frankfort-Nachmias, C. (2000). *Research methods in the social sciences, 6th ed*. New York: St. Martin's.

National Opinion Research Center (NORC). (1998). *General Social Survey*. Chicago: Author.

Neighbors, J. (1991). *Factors influencing psychologists' attitudes towards education and training*. Unpublished doctoral dissertation, United States International University, San Diego, CA.

Neimeyer, R. A. (1993). An appraisal of constructivist psychotherapies. *Journal of Consulting and Clinical Psychology, 61,* 221-234.

Nesbary, D. (1999). *Survey research and the World Wide Web.* Boston: Allyn & Bacon.

New, N. (1989). *Professional identity and gender: Impact on private practice management procedures.* Unpublished doctoral dissertation, United States International University, San Diego, CA.

Newton, R. R., & Rudestam, K. E. (1999). *Your statistical consultant: Answers to your data analysis questions.* Thousand Oaks, CA: Sage.

Newton, S. G. (1991). *The incidence of depression, substance abuse, and eating disorders in the families of anorexic probands.* Unpublished doctoral dissertation, The Fielding Institute, Santa Barbara, CA.

Nicholas, S. K. (1995). *Identity formation in gay and lesbian adolescents.* Unpublished doctoral dissertation, The Fielding Institute, Santa Barbara, CA.

Paape, J. (1992). *Health values and expectancies as predictors of preventive health behavior, health risk-taking behavior and risk-mix.* Unpublished doctoral dissertation, The Fielding Institute, Santa Barbara, CA.

Packer, M. J. (1985). Hermeneutic inquiry in the study of human conduct. *American Psychologist, 40,* 1081-1093.

Paganini-Hill, A., & Ross, P. K. (1982). Reliability of recall of drug usage and other health-related information. *American Journal of Epidemiology, 116,* 114-122.

Patterson, G. R., DeBaryshe, B. D., & Ramsey, E. (1989). A developmental perspective on antisocial behavior. *American Psychologist, 44,* 329-335.

Patton, M. Q. (1990). *Qualitative evaluation and research methods.* Newbury Park, CA: Sage.

Peplau, L. A., & Conrad, E. (1989). Beyond nonsexist research: The perils of feminist methods in psychology. *Psychology of Women Quarterly, 13,* 379-400.

Polkinghorne, D. E. (1983). *Methodology for the human sciences: Systems of inquiry.* Albany: State University of New York Press.

Polkinghorne, D. E. (1989). Phenomenological research methods. In R. S. Valle & S. Halling (Eds.), *Existential-phenomenological perspectives in psychology.* New York: Plenum.

Polkinghorne, D. E. (1991). Two conflicting calls for methodological reform. *Counseling Psychologist, 19,* 103-114.

Popper, K. (1965). *Conjectures and refutations: The growth of scientific knowledge.* New York: Harper & Row.

Quittner, A. L., Glueckauf, R. L., & Jackson, D. N. (1990). Chronic parenting stress: Moderating versus mediating effects of social support. *Journal of Personality and Social Psychology, 5*(6), 1266-1278.

Rasche, C. (1991). *The yearning for a child in midlife women.* Unpublished doctoral dissertation, The Fielding Institute, Santa Barbara, CA.

Rennie, D. L., Phillips, J. R., & Quartaro, G. K. (1988). Grounded theory: A promising approach to conceptualization in psychology. *Canadian Psychology, 29,* 139-150.

Research Ethics Committee, The Fielding Institute. (1999). *Fielding Institute research ethics procedures.* Santa Barbara, CA: Author.

Richards, N. (1991). *School-based assessment of students at risk for drug abuse.* Unpublished doctoral dissertation, United States International University, San Diego, CA.

Rico, G. L. (1983). *Writing the natural way.* Los Angeles: J. P. Tarcher.

Rogers, S. J., Parcel, T. L., & Menaghan, E. G. (1991). The effects of maternal working conditions and mastery on child behavior problems: Studying the intergenerational transmission of social control. *Journal of Health and Social Behavior, 32*(2), 145-164.

Rubin, H. J., & Rubin, I. S. (1995). *Qualitative interviewing: The art of hearing data*. Thousand Oaks, CA: Sage.

Sangster, M. J. (1991). *Judgment and decision making under conditions of uncertainty*. Unpublished doctoral dissertation, The Fielding Institute, Santa Barbara, CA.

Schaefer, J. A., & Moos, R. H. (1998). The context for personal growth: Life crises, individual and social resources, and coping. In R. Tedeschi, C. Park, & L. Calhoun (Eds.), *Post traumatic growth: Theory and research in the aftermath of crisis*. Hillsdale, NJ: Lawrence Erlbaum.

Schutz, W. C. (1966). *FIRO: A three dimensional theory of interpersonal behavior*. Palo Alto, CA: Science and Behavior Books.

Searight, H. R. (1990). The neglect of qualitative evaluation in psychological training: Issues and alternatives. *Journal of Training and Practice in Professional Psychology, 4(2)*, 33-43.

Selye, H. (1956). *The stress of life*. New York: McGraw-Hill.

Shapiro, J. J., & Nicholsen, S. (1986). *Guidelines for writing papers*. Santa Barbara, CA: The Fielding Institute.

Sherman, K. L. (1998). *Negotiating intimacy and autonomy in the marital dyad*. Unpublished doctoral dissertation, The Fielding Institute, Santa Barbara, CA.

Slanger, E. (1991). *A model of physical risk-taking*. Unpublished doctoral dissertation, The Fielding Institute, Santa Barbara, CA.

Smith, M. B. (1991, August). *Human science—Really!* Invited symposium address, American Psychological Association Annual Convention, San Francisco, CA.

Spradley, J. P. (1979). *The ethnographic interview*. New York: Holt, Rinehart & Winston.

Stevick, E. L. (1971). An empirical investigation of the experience of anger. In A. Giorgi, W. F. Fischer, & E. Von Eckartsberg (Eds.), *Duquesne studies in phenomenological psychology* (Vol. 1). Pittsburgh: Duquesne University Press,.

Strauss, A., & Corbin, J. (1998). *Basics of qualitative research: Grounded theory procedures and techniques*. Thousand Oaks, CA: Sage.

Stringer, E. T. (1999). *Action research: A handbook for practitioners* (2nd ed.). Thousand Oaks, CA: Sage.

Susman, G. I., & Evered, R. D. (1978). An assessment of the scientific merits of action research. *Administrative Science Quarterly, 23(4)*, 582-603.

Sutherland, E. (1924). *Principles of criminology*. Philadelphia: W. B. Saunders.

Tabachnik, B. G., & Fidell, L. S. (1996). *Using multivariate statistics*. New York: Harper-Collins.

Tashakkori, A., & Teddlie, C. (1998). *Mixed methodology: Combining qualitative and quantitative approaches*. Thousand Oaks, CA: Sage.

Toulmin, S. (1972). *Human understanding: The collective use and evolution of concepts*. Princeton, NJ: Princeton University Press.

van Kaam, A. (1966). Application of the phenomenological method. In A. van Kaam, *Existential foundations of psychology*. Lanham, MD: University Press of America.

Volkman, N. (1991). *Belonging, a study of home and homelessness: A contribution to a theory of personality*. Unpublished doctoral dissertation. The Fielding Institute, Santa Barbara, CA.

Wardell, W. (1985). *The reunion of the male prison inmate with his family*. Unpublished doctoral dissertation, The Fielding Institute, Santa Barbara, CA.

Wegmann, M. F. (1992). *Information processing deficits of the authoritarian mind*. Unpublished doctoral dissertation, The Fielding Institute, Santa Barbara, CA.

Weiss. R. S. (1994). *Learning from Strangers*. New York: The Free Press.

Weitzman, E. A., & Miles, M. B. (1995). *Computer programs for qualitative data analysis: A software sourcebook.* Thousand Oaks, CA: Sage.

Williams, R. L. (1989). *Finding voice: The transition from individualism to social advocacy.* Unpublished doctoral dissertation, The Fielding Institute, Santa Barbara, CA.

Winograd, T., & Flores, F. (1986). *Understanding computers and cognition: A new foundation for design.* Norwood, NJ: Ablex.

Witt, J.V.P. (1997). *Learning to learn: Action research in community college administration.* Unpublished doctoral dissertation, The Fielding Institute, Santa Barbara, CA.

Name Index

Subject Index

About the Authors

RAE R. NEWTON, Ph.D., is Professor of Sociology at California State University–Fullerton and Senior Statistician at the Child and Adolescent Health Services Research Center in San Diego, California. He received his doctoral degree in sociology from the University of California, Santa Barbara, and postdoctoral training at Indiana University. He is author of *Your Statistical Consultant: Answers to Your Data Analysis Questions* (Sage, 1999, with Kjell Rudestam) and numerous articles in professional journals. His research interests include statistical analysis, particularly structural equation modeling, health services delivery and family violence.

KJELL ERIK RUDESTAM, Ph.D., is an Associate Dean at The Fielding Institute, Santa Barbara, California. He was previously Professor of Psychology at York University, Toronto. He received his doctoral degree in psychology from the University of Oregon. He is author of *Methods of Self-Change, Experiential Groups in Theory and Practice*, and *Treating the Multi-Problem Family* (with Mark Frankel), and *Your Statistical Consultant: Answer to Your Data Analysis Questions* (with Rae Newton), as well as numerous articles in professional journals. His research interests are in the areas of suicide, psychotherapy, and family and organizational systems. He is a licensed clinical psychologist and a Diplomate of the American Board of Examiners in Professional Psychology (Clinical).

297

JODY VEROFF, Ph.D., is a faculty member in the Human and Organizational Development Program at The Fielding Institute in Santa Barbara, California. She completed her doctoral degree in Clinical Psychology at the University of Michigan. She has had a lifelong interest in writing and currently devotes a large proportion of her work to writing critiques of students' essays and doctoral dissertations. Current interests include gender issues in research, multicultural education, and the exploration of the interface between family and organizational systems. Her publications include a book coauthored with Joseph Veroff, *Social Incentives: A Life-Span Developmental Approach.*